P9-DWG-342

Corporate Venturing

Corporate Venturing

Creating
New Businesses
within the Firm

Zenas Block
Stern School of Business
New York University

and

Ian C. MacMillan
The Wharton School
University of Pennsylvania

Harvard Business School Press
Boston, Massachusetts

97 96 95 94 93   5 4 3 2 1

Library of Congress Cataloging-in-Publication Data

Block, Zenas.
    Corporate venturing : creating new businesses within the firm /
Zenas Block and Ian C. MacMillan.
        p. cm.
    Includes bibliographical references and index.
    ISBN 0-87584-321-2 (acid-free paper)
    1. Entrepreneurship. 2. New business enterprises. I. MacMillan,
Ian C., 1940– . II. Title.
HB615.B625 1993
658.1′6—dc20   92-28830
                                                              CIP

Dedicated to the innovators who create new businesses regardless of obstacles, to organization leaders wise and skillful enough to reduce those obstacles, and to the pioneering researchers without whose work this book would not have been possible.

Contents

Preface

The principal purpose of this book is to present concrete management practices that have proved effective for creating new businesses and successfully generating innovation within existing organizations.

It represents a drawing together of knowledge from many sources: our own hands-on experience at every level in starting new businesses, both within and outside of existing organizations; the published research of many others; case research on venturing by our students; our own research; and our work with large, medium, and small companies seeking to become more effectively innovative and entrepreneurial.

Senior managers and venturers who attempt to make organizations more entrepreneurial and encourage corporate venturing will find that the existing literature contains a great deal of valuable information and many contributions to theory. Unfortunately, they will also find that much of what has been written about these topics focuses on getting things started and that there is a major information gap when it comes to the nitty-gritty of managing new ventures and managing an organization's overall venturing activity.

Much of what must actually be done is in direct conflict both with traditional management "principles" and with the standard practices of most companies. Just stopping harmful practices helps, but this is by no means enough. If senior managers and venturers are to implement the necessary alternatives to usual practices, they must also know *what* has to be done, *why,* and *how.* This book will provide them with significant assistance in their efforts to successfully build new and innovative businesses.

ACKNOWLEDGMENTS

We are especially grateful to Tait Elder (for seven years general manager of 3M's New Business Ventures Division and now at the Carlson School of Management, University of Minnesota) for his extraordinarily thorough and helpful analysis, comments, and suggestions on an earlier draft; to Susan Cohan, copy editor, who contributed greatly to the clarity of our book; to Hollister (Ben) Sykes and Ari Ginsberg (Stern School, Graduate Division, New York University) for their comments and to Howard Stevenson (Harvard Business School) for his participation in the early planning of this book. We also wish to express our appreciation to Carol Franco, senior editor at Harvard Business School Press, for her continued help, support, encouragement, and patience.

We appreciate the help of now former NYU graduate assistants, Bipin Batra and Karim Khouri, as well as the clerical, administrative, and typing assistance of Patricia Miller and Loretta Poole at NYU and Patricia Adams at Wharton.

Introduction

Today's marketplace is characterized by fast-paced and unremitting competition on a global scale. To survive in this environment, organizations need a level of innovation, speed, and flexibility that was unheard of even a decade ago. The challenge for the United States is to create and revitalize organizations so they can successfully and continuously innovate and generate new businesses.

Although many large companies have lumbered around like elephants in this environment, small ones have proved the power of innovation. In the past decade, there has been an explosion of new-business formations by independent entrepreneurs. New incorporations have reached a rate of 600,000 per year. In spite of a reported failure rate of 50% within five years, these startups account for almost all the new jobs in the economy, while large corporate work forces have plateaued or declined. Between 1980 and 1990, *Fortune*

1

500 companies eliminated 3.4 million jobs, while companies with less than 500 employees created more than 13 million.

In a world in which innovators are kings, interest in internal corporate ventures has grown tremendously. Many large organizations are anything but entrepreneurial, though. They have foundered, seeking "critical mass" or survival through acquisition—or they have been sold or merged into other companies.

Because of all this M&A activity, some say that the term *corporate venture* is an oxymoron. But innovation at such companies as Merck, 3M, Motorola, Rubbermaid, Johnson & Johnson, Corning, General Electric, Raychem, Compaq, Wal-Mart, and many others has shown that large size need not be antithetical to venturing. Yet the fact that so few large companies are effective innovators indicates the difficulty of achieving this success.

Why do some organizations do so much better than others at creating new ventures through product and market innovations? Attempts to explain this difference and provide approaches for others to follow spawned a new literature on corporate renewal, innovation, and entrepreneurship, sometimes referred to as "intrapreneurship." *In Search of Excellence,* by Peters and Waterman, was followed by Rosabeth Kanter's *The Change Masters* and more recently her *When Giants Learn to Dance.* Although these contributions had a great impact on the attitudes and approaches of U.S. managers toward innovation, new ventures, and management in general, their primary emphasis has been on highlighting the culture and values that distinguish successful and innovative organizations. Drucker's *Innovation and Entrepreneurship,* which argues the need for a disciplined approach to innovation, offers organizations rules and guidelines both for adopting such an approach and for finding opportunities. Pinchot's *Intrapreneurship* provides examples of new products that resulted from the enterprise and persistence of individuals in large companies and challenges corporate employees to take the initiative.

Some have interpreted this literature to mean that any

company seeking to become more innovative and entrepreneurial should attempt to duplicate the cultures of existing organizations that have already achieved these goals. This has led to a proliferation of value statements, resounding slogans, and programs of cultural change among large organizations—accompanied, however, by little substantive change in management practices. These organizations continue to operate with rigid planning; interdepartmental functional handoffs; multiple approval levels; and inappropriate controls, compensation, and performance evaluation methods.

The "innovation-by-imitation" approach overlooks the importance of the individual character of each company. An innovative culture cannot simply be transferred indiscriminately from one company to another any more than a heart can be transplanted indiscriminately from one body into another. Although there is little, if any, disagreement that a company's culture is a major factor in encouraging or discouraging innovation and entrepreneurship, and that a supportive culture is highly desirable, it is neither a prerequisite to, nor absolutely essential for, the success of ventures. The fact is that every organization has its own history, population, industry, and competition and must create a unique culture relevant to those elements. It's highly unrealistic to expect, say, a food manufacturer to duplicate 3M's culture, which resulted from decades of commitment in a particular setting.

Developing a unique entrepreneurial culture from within does not raise dramatic expectations the way a culture transplant would, but it does have a far greater likelihood of success. In this book, we propose a fitness program that managers can use to strengthen innovation within their organizations. It allows corporations to become leaner, healthier, and more entrepreneurial. Like any transformation, cultural change, if achievable, takes a long time, usually several years (five years is not unrealistic); moreover, it is often impossible without a change in top management. Most corporations underestimate the complexity and duration of this change process.

Yet organizations simply cannot afford to wait for the

slow, evolutionary process of cultural transformation to run its course before they start innovating and creating new businesses. Instead, they can immediately initiate those actions, practices, and policies that many companies have found effective for developing new products, technologies, and businesses. In so doing, they will find that these measures also contribute to the development of an entrepreneurial culture.

To develop an organization that continually identifies and selects opportunities and then transforms them into new and profitable businesses, three elements are crucial:

1. Leadership that defines and communicates a unifying vision, together with a strategy for achieving it
2. For long-term effectiveness, an organizational culture that encourages and supports initiative and innovative behavior
3. The skills and management practices required for managing both individual ventures and the organization's overall venturing activity

In this book, we show how companies can develop and strengthen all three elements, with particular emphasis on the skills, knowledge, and management methods needed to manage individual ventures as well as an entrepreneurial corporation.

BASIC PREMISES

The following six premises form the cornerstone of this book:

1. Entrepreneurship is a process, not a single act.
2. Entrepreneurs are made, not born. They vary considerably in their capabilities, which can be improved significantly through experience and training.
3. Existing organizations provide an environment that

has a major impact—positive or negative—on the creative and entrepreneurial drive of their members.

4. Entrepreneurs are *not* risk seekers; they are risk managers.

5. The entrepreneurial process can and must be managed as a component of the management of organizations.

6. Most large organizations, driven by the need to protect and optimize the use of existing resources, discourage the pursuit of opportunity.

The following subsections examine each of these premises more closely.

Entrepreneurship Is a Process

If entrepreneurship is viewed as a process rather than as a mysterious potpourri of actions that can only be executed by a born entrepreneur, it becomes clear why it is so commonly the case that product champions who start a new venture are rarely around afterward, compensation and incentive plans are hard to design, customary planning methods are ineffective, the policies and procedures that work so well for the parent organization seem to cripple the venture project, and traditional project-financing methods fail to meet the venture's needs.

What, precisely, does the entrepreneurial process consist of?

Its stages are universal and cannot be avoided, whether executed by an independent entrepreneur or a team in a corporation.

An opportunity must be identified.

The opportunity must be evaluated.

A solution must be found or invented to fulfill the opportunity.

Resources must be acquired: money, people, plant, and equipment.

Those resources must be managed to start up, to survive, and to expand.

In the case of the independent entrepreneur, the business is professionalized and may be harvested through whole or partial sale.

In the case of a corporate new venture, it is institutionalized as part of the parent organization.

Applying this universal process to venturing in an established company requires adaptation to a corporate environment, and the design and management of the venturing process. Its specific stages, not necessarily occurring in the sequence shown, are:

1. *Lay the groundwork for venturing:* Conditions conducive to the generation of entrepreneurial ideas are created, and a process for managing entrepreneurial activity is designed.
2. *Choose ventures:* Opportunities (i.e., ideas or needs) are identified, evaluated to determine whether they're feasible and worth the effort, and selected. Managers are selected to implement the venturing program.
3. *Plan, organize, and start the venture:* The venture's location within the organization is determined, a business plan is developed, use of the needed resources (people, money, plant, and equipment) is obtained, and operations are begun.
4. *Monitor and control the venture:* The overall venturing process is monitored and controlled, as are the day-to-day operations of the venture itself and the level of risk associated with it.
5. *Champion the venture:* As the new entity is expanded, institutionalized, and established as an ongoing activity of the organization, its management learns to survive and manage the internal corporate politics of venturing.
6. *Learn from experience:* By collecting and examining information on the venturing experience, the organization learns to manage both individual ventures and the overall venturing process more effectively.

These six stages constitute the venturing process model, which is discussed in greater detail in the following section.

Given the premise that entrepreneurship is a process consisting of several stages, it becomes abundantly clear that only very rarely can a single person successfully lead an organization through all the stages of the process. Steve Jobs definitely qualifies as an entrepreneur, even though he led his company only up to the point of institutionalization. Although he recognized the need for new management skills, he was unable to accept the disciplines required and was forced to leave. Ray Kroc also qualifies as an entrepreneur, even though he did not invent the McDonald's operation; he discovered it in California. Contrary to popular belief, entrepreneurs are not multitalented wizards who can accomplish everything personally. Indeed, we believe that the really great entrepreneurs are precisely those who realize they must supplement their own talents, desires, and skills and act accordingly. There is simply no basis, then, for believing that the first choice for venture management will remain the right choice as the venture moves through later stages.

Entrepreneurs Are Made, Not Born

Of course, people are born with varying talents. There are great, good, fair, and poor physicists, grocers, tennis players, and entrepreneurs. But no one has yet been able to predict who will or will not be a successful entrepreneur. Even a previous track record is not a reliable guide. The entrepreneurial drive to pursue opportunity is a combination of many factors, chief among them motivation and attitude. These attributes are, in turn, affected by childhood influences, role models, and later environments, not the least of which is the environment of the workplace. Although, providing they work hard, those with more talent will clearly do better than those with less, entrepreneurial ability *can* be directly influenced by education, training, and experience, which result in the accumulation of knowledge and skills required to carry out all or part of the entrepreneurial process.

7

In the words of a colleague, "No matter how many tennis lessons I take, I'll never be as good as John McEnroe, but I'll sure as hell play better tennis."

Successful entrepreneurs do have some characteristics in common, including a high energy level, great persistence, resourcefulness, and the desire and ability to be self-directed, together with a reasonably high need for autonomy—a need that is greater in independent entrepreneurs than in corporate entrepreneurs. These characteristics, however, do not distinguish entrepreneurs from other groups of high achievers, nor are they enough to ensure success.

One aspect of managing the entrepreneurial process involves being able to match the evolving needs of the process with people who can effectively meet those needs, while keeping in mind that initial personnel choices are very unlikely to be permanent.

The Corporate Environment Is Critical to Entrepreneurial Success

The organizational culture affects the extent to which entrepreneurial talent will surface, how people work with one another, and the content and execution of policies and procedures. How the management of the venturing process treats unsuccessful entrepreneurial experience—as an opportunity to gain insight or an exercise in finger pointing—is probably a key to the creation or destruction of an entrepreneurial environment. Corporations with a record of successful innovation and entrepreneurial activity demand learning rather than allocate blame.

Entrepreneurs Are Risk Managers

It is quite understandable why so many organizations, in seeking to become more entrepreneurial, want their people to take greater risks. This attitude is sometimes carried to such an extreme that the amount of risk taken is considered a badge of honor, a true indicator of an entrepreneur's character. This is an unwise and probably short-lived reaction to the risk aversion prevailing in those companies that are driven either by the need to protect existing resources or by the belief that they must avoid risk because they are in a highly regulated industry.

Successful entrepreneurs keep their eye on the ball and do not value risk for its own sake. Instead, they work diligently to reduce the risks they must take and ultimately take the greatest risk of all—the risk of failure. As one entrepreneur astutely observed, "You take the risk, I'll take the reward."

One interesting example of the interpretation of entrepreneurship as an activity that inherently involves taking big risks is offered in Harold Geneen's *Managing,* where he writes that entrepreneurship is impossible in a corporate setting because it means you have to be ready to bet the company, something no responsible CEO can be expected to do. Yet Geneen did rather well as an entrepreneur after his retirement from ITT and did not bet any companies! The point is, a risk-seeking and risk-taking character does not indicate entrepreneurial competence (although it may indicate a fondness for gambling).

The Entrepreneurial Process Can and Must Be Managed

The idea that the entrepreneurial process can and must be managed is rather fundamental. Although it is obvious that a new venture has to be managed, managing the overall entrepreneurial process is quite a different task, requiring professional managerial skills. Managing the process means creating and operating the mechanisms that cause the generation and evaluation of opportunities as well as every other step in the venturing activity. Throughout the book, in keeping with this premise, we distinguish between tasks pertaining to the management of the parent corporation and tasks pertaining to the management of the venture itself. We also present alternative organizational possibilities for handling the function of managing the venturing process.

Optimizing the Use of Resources Discourages the Pursuit of Opportunity

As we compare management practices that are effective for stable organizations with those that are needed for start-ups, it becomes evident that "business as usual" (i.e., optimizing the use of corporate resources, adhering to established policies and procedures, requiring that all proposals be subjected to a bureaucratic review process) tends to stifle entrepreneurial creativity and discourage the pursuit of opportunity.

Each stage of the entrepreneurial process in fact requires its own unique combination of management skills and strategic focus. In keeping with this dichotomy between the needs of a startup and those of an established business, we have organized this book around a venturing process model that integrates the elements of primary concern to the parent company with those of primary concern to individual ventures.

VENTURING PROCESS MODEL

As noted above, successful new-business creation involves two distinctly different leadership and management roles—that of the parent sponsoring organization (senior management) and that of the people running the venture itself (venture management). The relationship between these roles is illustrated in the venturing process model (Table I-1), which shows the six major stages of the venturing process and provides a broad overview of the responsibilities that pertain to senior management and venture management at each stage. You will notice that this model also forms the backbone of our book, by outlining its structure and flow and indicating the chapter in which each major topic is discussed.

10

Table I-1: Venturing Process Model

Setting the Stage	
Senior management decides whether venturing is strategically desirable and necessary for the organization, creates conditions that will encourage a flow of venture ideas, and designs and frames the process for managing the venturing activity. (*Chapters 1–3*)	

Choosing Ventures	
Senior management selects venture management and may also establish the compensation basis at this point. (*Chapter 5*)	**Venture champions** identify, evaluate, and select opportunities and build venture proposals for presentation to senior management. (*Chapter 4*)

Planning, Organizing, and Starting the Venture	
Senior management determines where each venture should be located within the organization and how it should interface with other units. (*Chapter 6*)	**Venture management** completes the development of a business plan for the approval of senior management and, upon approval of the plan, organizes and launches the venture. (*Chapters 7 and 8*)

Monitoring and Controlling the Venture	
Senior management monitors and controls corporate risk level. (*Chapter 9*)	**Venture management** manages and controls the venture. (*Chapter 9*)

Championing the Venture	
	Venture management, while continuing to champion the venture, must hone its survival skills and learn how to manage the inevitable challenges of corporate politics. (*Chapters 10 and 11*)

Learning from Experience	
Senior management uses systematic methods of information gathering and analysis to learn how to manage the internal venturing process more effectively. (*Chapter 12*)	**Venture management** uses systematic methods of information gathering and analysis to learn how to manage ventures more effectively. (*Chapter 12*)

Although we would remind you that venturing is a dynamic process that rarely proceeds in precisely the sequence shown in the table, every step in this process does eventually occur—deliberately or accidentally—and needs detailed examination and management. The model is intended to serve as a useful framework for presenting and coordinating a wide range of information and recommendations.

Simply stated, the objective of this book is to provide information, guidance, and decision alternatives that will enable venture managers and senior managers to reconcile the needs of a new venture with those of its parent organization, in such a way as to prevent damage to either and contribute to the continuing success of both.

1

Corporate Venturing: What Is It? Why Do It? What Is Its Track Record?

Every ten years or so there is a surge of interest in internally generated new businesses—i.e., corporate ventures. Is this merely a recurring fad, or has it had a real impact on organizational performance?

The track record is mixed—a combination of dramatic failures, successes, and mediocre results. Although many companies have been discouraged, others have demonstrated the power of venturing by using it as a strategy for propelling themselves into dynamic profitability and growth. This record leaves little doubt about *whether* organizations can venture successfully. The real challenges involve *how* to do so.

We start this chapter by defining ventures and providing examples of a variety of ventures. We then consider why companies start venturing, examine research findings that challenge many common beliefs about venturing's track record, and consider why some companies stop venturing. Fi-

13

nally, we explore the proposition that venturing in some form may in fact be essential for all organizations.

WHAT IS A CORPORATE VENTURE?

We consider a project a venture when it:

- Involves an activity *new* to the organization
- Is initiated or conducted *internally*
- Involves significantly *higher risk* of failure or large losses than the organization's base business
- Is characterized by *greater uncertainty* than the base business
- Will be *managed separately* at some time during its life
- Is undertaken for the purpose of increasing sales, profit, productivity, or quality

Although a venture may originate externally and may be augmented with a foothold acquisition, the venturing activity is organizationally part of the parent company. Internal corporate ventures (ICVs) may include major new products, development of new markets, commercialization of new technology, and major innovative projects. They can involve a marked diversification or be closely related to the company's other businesses. The key differentiating qualities are risk, uncertainty, newness, and significance.

The dividing line between a new venture and an extension of normal business activity is not always clear, but it is important to determine this. From an operational standpoint, deciding that the business is in fact a new venture helps an organization define the kind of management the project will need. That decision is critical to the project's success.

Creating a new business is different from modifying an old one to meet new challenges, because new ventures require a fundamentally different approach to management—one consisting of integrated entrepreneurial management and leadership. This contrasts sharply with the traditional approach to management, in which activities are separated into functional departments and a new project passes through an interminable process of interdepartmental handoffs and sign-offs as it wends its slow, weary, and excessively expensive way to commercialization.

Examples of Corporate Ventures

In this subsection, we briefly describe a variety of corporate endeavors, whose products range from children's clothing to crawfish bait, and examine why each of these seemingly disparate activities qualifies as a new venture.

Recreational Vehicle Refrigerators. The evolution of a recreational vehicle (RV) refrigerator is a good example of the difference between product and market changes that extend normal business activities and those that result in new ventures.

The early electric refrigerator was simply a compartment that kept foods cold. Then along came the ice maker. Although this enhancement undoubtedly posed some technical challenges at the time, the markets—home and institutional—did not change, nor did the environment in which the machine was required to operate.

Even with the next steps in the refrigerator's evolution—the addition of a frozen-food storage compartment, followed by the automatic defroster—the product still served the same markets and operated in the same environment. Product or project managers may have been involved, but the challenges were not significant enough for the commercialization of any of these new models to be regarded as separate ventures.

The development of refrigerators for recreational vehicles was a different case. There was a need for machines that would operate reliably in a completely different environment. Although the product was still a refrigerator, it had to be sold to a totally different set of customers (RV owners or

15

manufacturers of RVs). Service requirements were different, too. Developing such a product called for venture management, which involved treating the endeavor as a new business about which many things were new and uncertain and much had to be learned. Continuous interaction and integration between manufacturing, engineering, marketing, and other functions were required. The combination of uncertainty, the need to learn in each of the individual functional areas, and the need to integrate the activities of the various functional areas in order to enter a new market moved this project into the new-venture domain.

CBS Cable. CBS started a cultural cable TV venture in 1982. Although it was organized as a separate entity, it reported directly to the CEO, William Paley. This appeared to be a familiar product in a familiar market but was actually a closely related new-product/new-market combination. Although CBS certainly had expertise in the television business, it had no experience in the cable business. It faced two uncertainties: whether there would be sufficient acceptance of a cultural channel and whether enough advertising could be sold. As it turned out, neither occurred, and the fledgling operation was shut down. It was uncertain, high-risk, and new—clearly a venture.

Kids "Я" Us. When Toys "Я" Us founded a children's clothing business, Kids "Я" Us, it used its in-depth knowledge of the market and retailing to create a new-product/existing-market combination. Although the product line was new to Toys "Я" Us, the children's market was very familiar. Kids "Я" Us was launched as a major business and has since provided significant growth to the parent corporation. It clearly qualifies as a venture because of the magnitude of the risk and the newness of the product line to Toys "Я" Us, requiring acquisition and integration of the people, knowledge, and skills needed to select styles and manufacturers; to buy, display, and sell products; to process information; and to establish inventory control systems in a highly competitive field.

USA Today. Gannett's *USA Today* is an example of a new-product/new-market/new-technology application in Gannett's familiar newspaper industry. It is a classic example of a new business started by an existing company. Begun in 1982, *USA Today* has become a national newspaper. The venture involved the use of new printing technology, the creation of a new national newspaper market, and an innovative approach to reporting, coupled with enormous financial risks. As of the end of 1991, more than $800 million had been invested, and the paper had lost $18 million in 1991. Except for the news-gathering function itself, risks and uncertainties surrounded every aspect of this undertaking: production, national circulation, logistics, technology, costs, marketability, and sale of advertising.

ZapMail. Federal Express's ZapMail was launched in 1983. The concept, which involved delivering high-quality hard copy within two hours, was made possible by the development of the facsimile machine and communications satellites. Federal Express saw the venture as both an opportunity and a defensive strategic step.

In this case, the newness of the transmittal technology, the growing competition of direct ownership of fax machines by the target market, and the enormous investment required to launch the business created the risks and uncertainties that define a venture. Federal Express lost a total of more than $600 million before shutting the venture down in 1986.

Du Pont's Crawfish Bait. An interesting example of a diversifying internal corporate venture is Du Pont's crawfish bait business. Du Pont? Crawfish bait? Yes, indeed! The venture originated at a Du Pont polymer plant in Louisiana. One of the plant's employees loved crawfish, which he caught by setting out baited traps in the bayous. The problem was that the bait had to be replaced every two days because it disintegrates. It occurred to the crawfish lover that perhaps a Du Pont polymer could be used to hold the bait together longer. He co-opted one of the plant's chemists, who provided him with samples, and the collaboration resulted in the development of a bait that did not disintegrate for five days. Although the product was created with a skunk-works approach, the polymer division decided to market it, using Du Pont's agricultural product distribution and sales arm for the purpose. The crawfish bait venture is now a multimillion-dollar business for Du Pont. Although the financial risk was low, this project certainly involved a new market and entrepreneurial management!

Learning: The Distinguishing Feature of Ventures

In each of the cases described in the preceding subsection, there is a common thread—the need to learn a great deal and apply it fast. The most useful guide to classifying a new organizational activity is to answer this question: What does the activity *primarily* involve? Does it involve learning, or does it simply involve administering what is already known? Does the business's very survival depend on its ability to adapt to what is learned?

Of course, all businesses must continually learn. But when learning is absolutely essential to both structuring and running the business, when it is needed to develop a "formula" for the business while building it, then the business is a venture and entrepreneurial management is called for.

Given this focus on learning, an enterprise classified as an internal corporate venture by one company might not be so classified by another company. It depends on the amount of learning needed as well as the perceived level of risk and consequences *for that particular organization*. The judgment often depends on the outlook of the decision maker. If the project involves a new product, requiring new technology in a new market, the answer is relatively clear. When in doubt, our advice is to treat the project like an ICV. The learning processes built into ICV management, as described in this book, are more likely to produce success than traditional management practices.

To illustrate the importance of deciding whether a new

activity should be classified as a venture—and the importance of managing it as a venture—consider the case of a software company that we'll call PCY. The company's principal product line was software used in large wide area networks that link PCs to mainframes, both nationally and internationally. PCY had been successful with its initial product and had established excellent relationships with many major corporations in the United States and abroad.

With the growth of wide area networks, PCY developed a product to efficiently update databases and programs for the hundreds, and sometimes thousands, of PCs in such networks. At first, PCY did not handle this new-product introduction as a new venture. Although its managers recognized that the individuals who normally bought PCY products would not be the ones making the buying decision regarding the new product, they felt confident that the existing relationships with their customers would be helpful in reaching the new target buyers. The company's sales management convinced senior management that the product should be handled by PCY's present salesforce.

After a year of effort, not a single sale had been made. Because most of its customers were multinational giants, PCY found that its existing contacts often did not know who would make the buying decision for an update program such as the one PCY was offering. Responsibility for the network buying decisions was centralized, whereas responsibility for updating was scattered across the subsidiaries.

At that point, PCY decided to treat its new-product introduction as a new venture. A unit was established under the direction of a very entrepreneurial leader and provided with separate sales, marketing, and technical support. The unit was treated as a profit center, with considerable input from the CEO. The integration of prospect solicitation, follow-up calls, identification of customizing requirements, application of technical support, demonstrations, pricing, and terms occurred simply and rapidly. Sales began within 60 days, and the business was highly profitable within one year, with the prospect of full recovery of investment in the product within a two-year period. Those involved agree that this change in orientation from a "new product" to a "new business" was a decisive factor in PCY's success.

WHY DO COMPANIES VENTURE?

Companies venture primarily to grow and to respond to competitive pressures. A 1987 survey by Block and Subbanarasimha (1989) of 43 U.S. and 149 Japanese companies found that for both the U.S. and Japanese companies, the most common reasons for venturing were "to meet strategic goals" and "maturity of the base business." Table 1-1 highlights the reasons for venturing that were considered "very important" or "critically important" by the companies studied.

An organization's very survival depends on constant growth and defense against competition. From a defensive

Table 1-1: Reasons for Venturing

Reasons for Venturing	U.S. Companies (%)	Japanese Companies (%)
Maturity of the base business	70	57
To meet strategic goals	76	73
To provide challenges to managers	46	15[a]
To develop future managers	30	17[a]
To survive	35	28
To provide employment	3	24[a]

Source: Adapted from Z. Block and P. N. Subbanarasimha, "Corporate Venturing: Practices and Performance in the U.S. and Japan," working paper (Center for Entrepreneurial Studies, Stern School of Business, New York University, 1989).

Note: The data represent the percentage of companies that rated each reason as 4 ("very important") or 5 ("critically important") on a 1 to 5 scale.

[a] Indicates a statistically significant difference between the figures for U.S. and Japanese companies.

Figure 1-1: Growth Paths

Markets Products	Old	New
Old	Greater Penetration Increase Share	Develop New Markets
New	Develop New Products	Diversification

Source: Adapted from H. Igor Ansoff, *Corporate Strategy* (New York: McGraw-Hill, 1965), p. 99.

standpoint, long-run competitiveness cannot be maintained without innovation and the generation of new ventures. As shown in Figure 1-1, growth can be achieved by *increasing market penetration* within existing markets with existing products; by *introducing new products* to existing markets; by *entering new markets* with existing products; or by *introducing new products* to *new markets*.

The more mature a market, the more difficult and expensive it gets for a company to grow by increasing its market share (penetration). Defending share also gets more expensive. Thus, it becomes imperative for the company to innovate and develop new products and new markets. If familiar markets and products are in decline, the company may be forced to sell out or to buy or develop new businesses in order to survive or grow.

Productivity, quality, and service must be improved simultaneously if an organization is to remain competitive. In an era of dynamic technological change, the organization must also remain technologically competitive, either through internal research and development or through alliances. But technology-driven R&D often produces new knowledge that has no practical utility unless a new business is created to make use of it.

Now that we've considered some of the goals that companies commonly hope to achieve through venturing, let's look at the record and see whether companies that have tried venturing have found it to be an effective strategy for achieving those goals.

WHAT IS VENTURING'S TRACK RECORD?

Judging from media reports, you might think that venturing *doesn't* work. For example, an August 17, 1990 headline in *The Wall Street Journal* reads: "KODAK EFFORT AT 'INTRAPRENEURSHIP' FAILS." The subheading reads: "The practices that make corporations successful—training procedures, personnel policies, hierarchical management structures—are anathema to risk-taking, free-wheeling entrepreneurs." The story goes on to report that of the fourteen ventures created by Kodak, six have been shut down, three have been sold, four have been merged into the company, and only one still operates independently. *The Wall Street Journal,* while conceding IBM's success with the PC and Xerox's success with half a dozen companies, still concludes that " 'intrapreneurship' has lost its cachet."

To paraphrase Mark Twain, reports of the death of intrapreneurship have been greatly exaggerated. Although "intrapreneurship" may have lost its "cachet" (along with "MBO," "matrix management," and other buzzwords), innovation and the generation of new ventures have not ceased. Indeed, Kodak's venturing performance as reported by *The Wall Street Journal* compares favorably with that of the venture capital industry, at least in terms of the number of ventures and their fate. (We don't know the actual performance of these ventures in terms of profit, loss, or investment.)

22

The reality is that venturing has proved successful for many organizations over a broad industry spectrum ranging from specialty retailing to high-technology products and a host of service businesses. Examples include Johnson & Johnson, Merck, Motorola, GTE, Hewlett-Packard, Intel, IBM, General Electric, Citicorp, Allied Corporation, Rubbermaid, Procter & Gamble, Du Pont, and many others ("The Innovators" 1988; "Innovation" 1990). The following are among the more notable corporate-venturing success stories:

- 3M has successfully required that 25% of its business come from products not in existence five years earlier. With 60,000 products and hundreds of operating entities, 3M has diversified quite widely from its original product—sandpaper that worked underwater!
- The Raychem Corporation is a highly innovative high-technology company that has achieved sales of over $1 billion annually through continuous development of new products and new markets. The CEO and founder, Paul Cook, says, "To be an innovative company you have to ask for innovation. . . . It's that simple—and that hard" ("Interview with Paul Cook" 1990, 98).
- Woolworth (yes, Woolworth!) has started, and achieved success with, dozens of new ventures in specialty retailing, including Footlocker, and in the process has transformed the company (Gray 1989).

But individual success stories, however numerous, do not constitute proof. So let's turn our attention from anecdotal evidence to hard data. To determine the track record of internal corporate venturing, two specific elements must be examined: (1) the performance of individual ventures (i.e., the percentage of "successful" ventures) and (2) the profitability of organizational venturing efforts as a whole. Studying the performance of individual ventures can give us some clues to the general probability of an individual venture's success and enable us to develop fact-based expectations. Study-

23

ing the results of many companies' total venturing efforts can show us the overall impact of venturing on companies and enable us to make some judgments about the value of venturing as a growth strategy. We can then move beyond the statistics to identify those organizations that have and have not been successful, which would permit us to probe for an understanding of the factors that may account for success or failure.

Appendix A summarizes eight significant studies of corporate venturing. Each summary includes the subject of research, the results obtained, and the conclusions reached by the authors. These studies involve a total of more than 2,000 ventures in 150 U.S. companies and 149 Japanese companies. What does this research tell us about venturing's track record? In particular, what does it tell us about how well corporate venturing works as a fundamental component of a growth strategy?

A review of this research calls into question, and even directly challenges, some common assumptions about the track record of internal corporate venturing. It suggests the following conclusions:

- Results vary enormously from one company to another, with performance ranging from outstanding to disastrous even within the same industry.
- Although venturing is risky, many companies do well at it, and internal startups may be less risky than acquisitions as a means of diversification. (See Table A-1 in Appendix A.)
- Contrary to popular belief, it is not always necessary to wait five to eight years to see profitable results from new ventures. In fact, it is common for ventures to achieve profitability within two to three years. On average, according to a recent report, the percentage of ventures that reach profitability within a six-year period is much higher than is generally believed (nearly 50% in U.S. companies).
- In spite of that high average, only about one company in seven finds that its total venturing activity yields an

ROI better than that of its base business within a six-year period.

- Companies that produced a higher ROI from venturing than from their base business had an average venture age of 2.8 years, which further challenges the widespread belief that new ventures inevitably take 5 to 8 years to become profitable. (Although it is true that some ventures can require decades to achieve profitability—for example, those that open totally new market possibilities—overcommitment to doomed ventures in the name of patience is risky.)
- Controlling potential damage from large-scale ventures that are headed for failure is probably more important than either the percentage of profitable ventures or any other single factor in achieving high ROI performance from an organization's total venturing activity.
- Separate venturing divisions or new-venture divisions appear to have had a short life in virtually all companies. This does not reflect the performance of ventures themselves; rather, it reflects the hazards of choosing that particular form of organization.
- The best reasons reported for venturing are strategic necessity and maturity of the existing businesses; the worst are developing management and providing challenges. Although managerial development and challenges are likely by-products of venturing, they are not in themselves valid reasons for venturing.
- The data seriously challenge the fashionable and almost religious belief that all companies should "stick to their knitting" and that diversification per se is a poor strategy. The truth is that such admonitions are not universally applicable. Many companies have demonstrated a capacity to successfully diversify to new fields and new industries through venturing—and many have not. See Porter data in Appendix A.
- Some failures are inevitable: probably half the ventures initiated in most companies will not pan out.
- Many companies that have made a systematic effort

25

to learn how to conduct an effective internal venturing program have found it to be a viable, effective strategy for creating new businesses.

A high percentage of companies reported a net profit from their total venturing effort, but as indicated in the preceding summary, only a small percentage reported higher profitability from venturing than the ROI of the base business. We suggest two possible explanations for the difference:

1. The six-year time span used in the Block and Subbanarasimha (1989) study may be too short for many ventures—particularly R&D-based high-tech ones— to achieve a satisfactory ROI (although the study found no difference between the results of high- and low-tech companies).
2. A few big losers can wipe out the gains of many winners. Anecdotal evidence suggesting that this may be true is confirmed both by discussions with corporate managers and by the experience of venture capital firms. It takes either a few very big winners or many smaller profitable ventures to offset the losses running into the hundreds of millions from such ventures as Exxon oil shale (with a $4 billion loss), ZapMail (with a $600 million loss), CBS Cable, and RCA's Selectavision.

Do Ventures Funded by Venture Capitalists Outperform Corporate Ventures?

Why do venture capitalists do so much better than their corporate counterparts? They probably don't if the same criteria are used to evaluate both groups. Although media reports of corporate venturing performance might suggest that venture capitalists have a far better track record than corporations in selecting and supporting new ventures, this may, in fact, be an "optical illusion."

The performance of venture capital funds is simply not measured in the same way as the performance of a new venture or an established corporation. Venture capitalists make money by selling their interest in an investment to either the public or a buyer. In effect, they capitalize expected, not actual, earnings. Corporations and corporate ventures make money by earning a profit over the short and long run—an actual profit, not a multiple of expected earnings. Since venture capitalists are really at the mercy of the stock market, the performance of that industry is fairly spotty. An evaluation of the performance of ventures funded by venture capitalists must also take into account the unrealized market value of unsold shares. When the market drops, those unsold equities decline in value, thus impacting venture capitalists' overall performance.

Nevertheless, corporate managers can learn a great deal from venture capitalists about selecting, staffing, and controlling ventures and about giving entrepreneurs the freedom necessary to run their businesses, while ensuring that supplementary skills, contacts, and capital are provided as the businesses grow. On average, in terms of the percentage of successes and failures, venture capitalists probably do no better than corporations. It is "generally accepted" that about one investment in ten turns out to be a blockbuster, two or three yield mediocre returns, and the balance are no good, either losers or among the living dead.

WHY DO COMPANIES STOP VENTURING?

Despite the benefits of internal corporate venturing outlined above, some companies do abandon such efforts. To determine why, it is critical to examine the actual work of creating new businesses and distinguish between organizational entities (such as venture companies, new-venture divisions, and venture divisions) and activities involving the development of new products, new markets, and combinations thereof.

Much of the publicity surrounding intrapreneurship has centered on the establishment of separate organizational units within companies—such as Allied Corporation's New Ventures operation, which existed for five years; Colgate's Venture Company, which rose and fell in three short years; and Kodak's New Opportunity Development. The track record of new-venture *divisions* (Fast 1978) should not be confused with that of new ventures.

Sykes and Block (1989) suggest that the demise of new-venture divisions is due in part to the fact that such divisions are highly visible and involve a concentration of expense, making them an inviting target when the company is squeezed and goes into a consolidation mode. Venture divisions can have a longer life and be more useful by serving as opportunity finders and evaluators rather than as centers for venture operations. Fast (1979) reports that diversification tends to be the driving force behind the establishment of new-venture divisions and that as that drive diminishes, the new-venture divisions are often reduced to a micro (analytical) operation or eliminated. He also points out that the high expectations usually associated with the creation of a new-venture division increase the likelihood of dissatisfaction.

In addition to eliminating venturing divisions or departments, organizations do reduce innovation and venturing efforts as well. The reasons include a new CEO; a decline in the company's performance accompanied by a perceived need to reduce costs; competing capital investment opportunities; bad experience with venturing; shattered expectations; and the conclusion that acquisition is preferable as a growth strategy. Nor are such retrenchments limited to large companies. *The Wall Street Journal* of December 12, 1990 reports that 250 manufacturers in the $10 million to $200 million sales category would be spending their money on plant modernization to enhance productivity rather than on innovation. Half the companies stated that they had no plans to introduce new products in the next two years.

Organizations that put all their venturing eggs into a new-venture-division basket are likely to stop venturing when they disband the venturing division, only to resume, as a matter of necessity, after the passage of time.

SHOULD ALL COMPANIES VENTURE?

We suspect that ultimately, all companies *should* venture—at least, if the timing and level of investment are right. Venturing is an absolute necessity if business and strategic goals require innovation and the transformation of innovations into new businesses, related or otherwise. Furthermore, venturing is probably called for if desired growth cannot be achieved with a current less risky activity, and it is also a must if opportunities in an industry are not to be ceded to the competition.

Companies that are achieving all their goals and have ample opportunity to continue doing so by expanding their efforts to new geographic areas or extending their product lines might best choose a venturing strategy focused on enhancing quality, service, and productivity by means of technical development and process improvement.

Companies that are not prepared to commit to internal venturing as an absolute necessity to ensure either the achievement of their strategic goals or their survival probably should not undertake a venturing effort until they make such a commitment.

It is clear that all organizations must innovate and venture in order to survive competitively, but not every organization must at all times be prepared to mount a program to start new businesses internally. Other options include creating spin-offs and venturing with corporate venture capital. The following subsections provide a brief overview of these alternatives.

Creating Spin-Offs

When an innovation occurs, especially one involving the development of new technology, a company may perceive a

29

new business opportunity. But suppose the opportunity would entail bringing new products to new markets, particularly unrelated markets, and the company is not ready to support venturing activity in any form. Does this mean the opportunity should be ignored? Not necessarily. In such cases, the company can choose the spin-off option, which has proved very effective in Japan (Ito 1990). (Toyota was a spin-off!)

Using this option, the existing company invests (and not necessarily as a controlling investor) in a new company organized for and dedicated to the development of the new business. This approach is based on the existing company's recognition that it cannot be a supportive host for the new business and that the new business will do much better as a separate organization. It is also based on the unstated premise that the existing company's culture cannot or should not be changed in order to create a supportive base for the new business.

Venturing with Corporate Venture Capital

Over a hundred major U.S. corporations have tried using corporate venture capital programs as a form of venturing and as a way of promoting new-business development. Such programs involve either creating a pool of funds specifically earmarked for venture capital investment or funding deals on an ad hoc basis. Although a few corporate venture funds have thrived, many others have sputtered and finally discontinued operations.

Few comprehensive studies of corporate venture capital efforts have been undertaken to date, and those that have been done are more case-oriented rather than focusing broadly on the corporate venture capital community. However, it is safe to conclude that any organization hoping to conduct a successful corporate venture capital program must be fully prepared to deal both with the considerations that apply to other internal corporate ventures and with the considerations that are unique to the investment of corporate venture capital. For a more detailed consideration of the use of corporate venture capital, refer to Appendix B.

CONCLUSION

Internal corporate venturing involves using a learning-intensive project approach to create new businesses in order to commercialize innovation and technological advances. In essence, it presents the unique challenge of conducting an entrepreneurial activity within the framework of an existing corporation.

Companies venture mainly to ensure growth and survival in the face of ever-increasing competition. According to a number of studies, venturing is a surprisingly effective means of achieving these goals—at least, for companies that create venturing programs for the right reasons; structure, manage, and monitor the programs carefully; and continually learn from their venturing experience.

Although organizations may temporarily abandon their venturing efforts for a variety of reasons (which fairly often involve disenchantment with the use of a new-venture division as a vehicle for venturing), they eventually tend to resume venturing in response to competitive pressures.

Although no organization should attempt venturing until it has made a well-thought-out commitment to the venturing process, it must recognize that despite the difficulty of undertaking a successful venturing program, innovation and expansion in some form are vital to the financial well-being of nearly every organization.

Guidelines

1. Don't venture unless venturing is an integral part of your organization's strategy and is seen as essential

to survival and the achievement of corporate objectives. If this is not the case, reconsider your options.
2. Recognize that venturing in some form and at some level is essential to your organization's long-term survival in a competitive world.

REFERENCES

Block, Z., and Subbanarasimha, P. N. 1989. "Corporate Venturing: Practices and Performance in the U.S. and Japan." Working paper. Center for Entrepreneurial Studies, Stern School of Business, New York University.

Fast, N. 1979. "Key Managerial Factors in New Venture Departments," *Industrial Marketing Management* 8:221–235.

———. 1981. "Pitfalls of Corporate Venturing." *Research Management* (March): 21–24.

Fast, Norman. 1978. "The Rise and Fall of Corporate New Venture Divisions." Ann Arbor, MI: UMI Research Press.

Gray, Jackson. 1989. Presentation to a New York University fall-semester class in corporate venturing.

"Innovation." 1990. *Business Week* Bonus Issue (June 15).

"Interview with Paul Cook." 1990. *Harvard Business Review* (March–April): 97–106.

Ito, Kiyohiko. 1990. "Spinoffs: A Flexible Strategic Alternative." Working paper. Stern School of Business, New York University.

Labich, Kenneth. "The Innovators." 1988. *Fortune* (June 6): 50–64.

Sykes, H. B., and Block, Z. 1989. "Corporate Venturing Obstacles: Sources and Solutions." *Journal of Business Venturing* 4, no. 3: 159–167.

2

Getting Started

Senior managers can be an organization's greatest promoters of innovation and new ventures or its greatest obstacles to such an effort. Senior managers who fail to recognize the role they must play or learn effective strategies for creating new ventures will inevitably find themselves at the helm of a venture creation program that fails to live up to its potential. Venture managers will experience a great deal of frustration as they try to develop new ventures in a climate that is inhospitable to their growth.

When a new entrepreneurial venture is created outside an existing organization, a wide variety of environmental factors determine the fledgling business's survival. Inside an organization, in contrast, senior management is the most critical environmental factor. But because entrepreneurial activity is often at variance with the existing corporate culture, the actions or neglect of senior managers may suffocate a new business rather than nurture it.

How can managers strike a balance between support and control? How can they build new businesses without compromising the strengths of the parent company? Senior managers must be able not only to identify the characteristics and skills of successful venture managers but also to create a corporate environment conducive to entrepreneurial ideas and actions. If such an environment is lacking, even the best venture managers will be forced to deal with unnecessary obstacles and frustration. If such an environment is present, it will create a culture of innovation that excites the organization and draws new ideas from every member.

Perhaps an even more fundamental question is whether it is important for senior managers to be involved in the new-business development program at all. If entrepreneurial activities occur outside the parent corporation's standard operating procedures and culture, what role is there for senior managers? Research has shown unequivocally that unless the firm's leaders are willing to rise to a number of critical challenges, the entire venturing program will more than likely be worthless (Hill and Hlavacek 1972; Maidique 1980; Fast and Pratt 1981). Although some U.S. companies have been remarkably successful at generating new ventures, the fact that few have been able to develop corporate venturing programs that have produced successful new-business growth on a *sustained* basis would appear to indicate that senior management's efforts are indeed falling short.

In this chapter, we examine the aforementioned critical challenges, together with strategies that senior managers can use to meet these challenges and thereby contribute to the successful creation and operation of new ventures. These challenges include:

1. Creating a venturesome climate and a pervasive commitment to venturing

2. Selecting the business development strategy—i.e., the strategy that drives the venturing effort
3. Defining and using venture selection criteria
4. Managing disappointment

Before we discuss these challenges, though, we want to take a moment to point out that the conclusions presented in this chapter reflect observations and findings from numerous studies of the thorny problem of new-business development. Many of these conclusions are based on a detailed study by MacMillan of five successful and four unsuccessful divisions of companies wrestling with this problem. It is important to note that these successes and failures were at the *divisional* level rather than the corporate level. The successful units included a division of an equipment manufacturer, a financial services division that grew to a multibillion-dollar diversified business in 15 years, an information services company that has increased revenues twentyfold since 1975, a manufacturer of engineering materials that added $2 billion in sales from new business in a decade, and a highly diversified minicon-glomerate that has spawned 30 new businesses in 20 years. The unsuccessful units included an insurance division, a division of a telecommunications company, a publishing division, and a division of an industrial products manufacturer.

MacMillan's study concentrated on management's role in internal new-business development rather than on such topics as new-product development, invention, or innovation. Although those latter topics are all related to and intertwined with the issue of new-business development, they do not specifically focus on the heart of the matter—i.e., the problem of how to create *profitable* new businesses within an existing organization.

Research has shown that the differences between successful and unsuccessful corporate venturing programs can be attributed first and foremost to senior management behavior, which leads us to believe that if a firm is to succeed in creating and sustaining a profitable venturing program, senior managers must bear the responsibility for managing the four strategic challenges discussed in the following sections.

CHALLENGE 1: CREATING A VENTURESOME CLIMATE

Perhaps the most critical challenge for senior management is creating a pervasive commitment to new-business development. In the words of the senior manager of the information services company: "If you can't create the culture, the right climate, the commitment to grow continuously through new business development, then nothing else matters—none of the methods and systems and checklists and procedures that everyone is looking for will work. Concentrate on nurturing enthusiasm, and the rest can be provided easily" (MacMillan 1987, 441). But enthusiasm alone is not enough, and an organization can accomplish a great deal while it is creating an entrepreneurial culture.

Fostering an organizationwide commitment to new-business development means more than merely paying lip service to innovation. In fact, a superficial commitment is almost worse than no commitment at all. This was one area in which the unsuccessful divisions in MacMillan's study failed without exception. The halfhearted approach is so inevitably counterproductive that we're tempted to propose the following "rules of the road to certain failure":

1. Announce to the company that from now on, it is going to "become entrepreneurial."
2. Create a separate venture department charged with the job of developing new businesses. Hold no one else responsible.
3. Bring in a horde of consultants and self-professed experts to harangue management and employees at all levels to aggressively seek new-business ideas.
4. Hold several one-day senior management retreats to discuss the need to become more entrepreneurial.

5. Make no further changes in management practices or the behavior of senior managers.

Don't be led down this road! Senior managers who confined their efforts to this type of cheerleading behavior created initial enthusiasm, followed by confusion, then disillusionment and bitterness or cynicism.

In contrast, leaders of the successful venturing divisions somehow managed to infuse their entire organization with a pervasive commitment to innovation. How did these managers create fire rather than just smoke? Their effort was largely driven by a personal, *demonstrated* commitment at the very top. They recognized that creating a venturesome climate would require *sustained* time and attention on their part.

The following ten strategies for creating a venturesome climate summarize what senior management must do in order to steer an organization down the road to success:

1. Insist that the entire division pursue new-business development.
2. Don't assume the firm must offer specific, extrinsic rewards for new-business activities.
3. Demonstrate significant and visible personal commitment.
4. Sustain the commitment over a long period of time.
5. Assign very good people to the new business.
6. Assign the necessary resources to the new business.
7. Develop an in-depth knowledge of customers and markets.
8. Build organizational confidence.
9. Empower the creators of the new business.
10. Build momentum.

In the following subsections, we'll consider how senior managers can use each of these strategies to foster an entrepreneurial and innovative organizational mind-set.

Insist That the Entire Division Pursue
New-Business Development

In their study of new-product development in Japan, Ta-keuchi and Nonaka (1986) observed that the successful companies they studied had succeeded in creating a pervasive, challenging pressure to produce new products. In a similar vein, the managers of the successful venturing divisions studied by MacMillan were adamant that *every* manager in their division had to be able to demonstrate that a significant percentage of revenues in any particular year came from business created in the past three years. Although all the senior managers had new-business development functions or departments within their operation, they nonetheless insisted that new-business development be a concern of *every* manager reporting to them. These subordinates were evaluated annually on their performance in new-business development—and this aspect of the job was a significant element in their overall performance evaluation.

Creating such a climate of pervasive pressure in which *everyone* is focused on new-business development can go a long way toward defusing the political problems that often arise between a powerful, entrenched, established operation and a new-venture division.

Don't Assume the Firm Must Offer Specific, Extrinsic
Rewards for New-Business Activities

If the entire organization is seeking and developing new-business opportunities, then creating new businesses becomes part of the job, not a special assignment calling for unique reward systems that sow discontent among those managing ongoing operations. A recent study by Block and Ornati (1987) found no evidence that special reward systems encouraged new-business development. Von Hippel (1977) found that many successful new-venture managers regarded the venture as yet another project in their career—a project that would serve as a test of their managerial skills and could be considered a recognition of, and a compliment to, their competence.

This approach was reflected in the reward systems used by the managers of the successful venturing divisions. As the manager of the financial services firm observed: "Nobody who starts a business gets special incentives here—the real incentive is that if you start a business that is really successful, and you *keep* it successful, you can have a whole division grow under you—it's a fast-rising platform to promotion" (MacMillan 1987, 442). Other managers felt the same way— that the reward for new-business development lies in the excitement, the challenge, the fun, and above all, the personal recognition and the opportunity to start another new business.

But as discussed in Chapter 5, there are significant, often industry-dependent, exceptions to this principle. One successful organization that did not have a venturesome culture found that creating a potential for significant financial rewards was useful in building such a culture. Financial rewards were regarded as evidence of senior management's commitment to the venturing activity. The opportunity to start more ventures is a frequently sought reward as well. In some firms, particularly on Wall Street, the existing corporate culture calls for incentives and rewards directly related to performance, whether for new ventures or for established operations.

Demonstrate Significant and Visible Personal Commitment

If senior managers are to succeed in creating a venturesome climate, they must be both strongly and publicly committed to innovation (Quinn and Mueller 1963). The leaders of the failed venturing divisions studied by MacMillan allowed their time and energy to be diverted by other problems (often for urgent, perfectly legitimate reasons, since crises litter the typical senior manager's calendar). In contrast, the leaders of the successful divisions systematically and single-mindedly promoted new-business development.

The manager of the financial services firm deliberately put new-business development at the top of the agenda for *every* major meeting with his subordinates, using the following approach to clarify organizational priorities for them:

> If someone tells me there is a fire in the main computer room, then I tell him that is clearly a problem, and we must get to it, but *first* we need to discuss the important business which is new business development! If I don't keep new business on the top of my agenda, if I let it slip to the bottom, then it will slip to the bottom of everyone else's agenda and then you can forget about new business. (MacMillan 1987, 443)

This senior manager's subordinates who were responsible for new-business development had to report to him once a month on their progress in this area. At that time, they were put through the wringer and left his office knowing they would be back again in 30 days to report further progress. Such a system generates intense pressure for the creation of new businesses.

The leader of the information services company goes one step further in promoting the process of new-business development:

> It's not even enough to do it only at formal meetings—you have to keep at it all the time—in the halls, in the elevators, even in the washrooms, I keep asking people how the new businesses are going and finding the time to listen and maybe give advice, but they hear from me enough to know that I am thinking about it and taking it seriously and they believe me when I say that it's important to me because it *is*. (MacMillan 1987, 443)

Sustain the Commitment over a Long Period of Time

Although everyone realizes that it takes time to forge a major change in organizational culture, few realize what it demands of the senior manager. As Roberts (1980) points out, *sustained* persistence is what's essential.

Not one of the senior managers of the successful venturing divisions studied by MacMillan felt that he or she had accomplished the turnaround in attitude in less than three years. The manager of the information services division inherited a staff of senior managers who averaged 25 years' tenure with the company. Upon assuming his executive position, he spent much of his time meeting *one-on-one:* first with his direct reports to develop new-business ideas, then with the next level down. This process took the manager 5 years—which meant *5 years* of the kind of strong personal commitment and direct personal attention discussed in the preceding subsection.

When the managers of the unsuccessful divisions embarked on their ill-fated new-business development efforts, they neither appreciated the huge personal commitment that would be required nor realized for how long the commitment would have to be sustained. None could focus his or her attention for more than a year, and all eventually allowed themselves to get sucked into the maelstrom of enticing, attention-distracting crises that daily beset senior managers.

Assign Very Good People to the New Business

Aside from the commitment of their personal time, there is no better way for senior managers to demonstrate the seriousness of their intent than by the quality of people they assign to each new-business development effort. Any reluctance to put top-notch people on the project may be interpreted as clear evidence that senior management is unwilling to devote the organization's best resources to the venture—

41

which is a damning indictment of management's true priorities.

Commit the Necessary Resources to the New Business

In their early stages, new ventures are like fragile seedlings, which need nurturing. If senior management is not prepared to protect these seedlings from the solidly rooted forest giants, they will wither and die, for they cannot stand against the entrenched power of major established products. New businesses may also need far more resources than their early results might appear to justify on a pro rata basis. Senior managers, who have the power to provide the required protection, must demonstrate their commitment to new-business development by ensuring that ventures receive resources commensurate with their status as emerging, growing concerns.

Develop an In-Depth Knowledge of Customers and Markets

A clear understanding of the customers' needs can yield a wealth of ideas for new ventures. A remarkable attribute of all the managers of the successful divisions studied by MacMillan was the passion with which they pursued in-depth personal knowledge of the markets, and particularly the customers they served, as well as the time they spent keeping themselves up-to-date.

Such familiarity can allow a senior manager to hear out a new-business proposal and then, instead of ordering a market research study or some other similarly time-consuming investigation, respond decisively with, "This is what concerns me" or "Let's go do it!" This intimate knowledge of customers is especially critical when the senior manager must evaluate a business idea involving a product category that is not yet in existence and for which normal market research would therefore be useless.

One senior manager felt that the only way to uncover real opportunities was to truly know the customers and their problems. New-product ideas can emerge weekly, if not daily, from an in-depth understanding of those problems. Another executive was scornful of managers who remain aloof from their customers:

> Show me a firm that says it can't grow because it's in a mature industry and I'll show you a firm that was asleep at the wheel—a firm in which the senior manager has allowed himself to be surrounded by a staff of bureaucratic nay-sayers who don't want to do anything new—let alone develop new businesses. You either know your customers and *their* markets and how they are developing, so that you grow and develop along with them or you end up in a "mature industry." (MacMillan 1987, 444)

Build Organizational Confidence

The strategies outlined in the preceding subsections can create intense internal pressure for innovation. But this pressure will only lead to frustration if the organization's people lack the confidence to rise to the challenge. MacMillan found that another fundamental difference between the managers of unsuccessful and successful divisions was the extent to which senior management was prepared to devote time and effort to building confidence among subordinates. The managers of the unsuccessful divisions were inclined to expect too much, too fast—they sought rapid diversification via grand corporate ventures into unknown markets. In contrast, the managers of the successful divisions pursued a strategy of confidence building—*showing* their subordinates that they were fully capable of developing new businesses.

In the information services company, which grew tenfold in revenues and fiftyfold in profits in 18 years, senior management focused first on rethinking the *existing* businesses. In the words of one top manager, "Most companies don't really know their customers and markets well. They can't see that there are often years of new business development opportunities to be found simply by mining existing territory" (MacMillan 1987, 445).

By working with middle management and systematically examining alternative ways of offering, delivering, packaging, pricing, segmenting, or otherwise reconfiguring the existing array of products and services, senior management built middle managers' confidence in their *own* ability to discover and implement new-business opportunities. Over time, the momentum generated by this confidence-building effort has carried the division from simple, print-based, domestic products into increasingly diversified, on-line electronic services in widely diversified international markets.

Empower the Creators of the New Business

Once their confidence has been developed, venture managers must be able to act on that confidence. It is imperative that senior management empower venture management with the freedom to take the initiative without having to get permission to implement well-conceived ideas. Managers of the successful divisions all felt strongly that it is vital for their subordinates to feel free to *act* on ideas and repeatedly insisted that they did not *need* to know everything that was going on.

On the other hand, all the firms with unsuccessful venturing divisions were obsessed with the need for tight control and clung to their slow, rigid, multilevel approval process and periodic progress reviews, which smothered anything at odds with existing policies and procedures. Thus, their divisions remained mired in their own bureaucracies.

Notice the contrast: In the unsuccessful divisions, managers demanded performance from subordinates who had little confidence that they could deliver on those demands. In the successful divisions, managers *demonstrated* to subordinates their belief that the subordinates could do the job and then gave them the freedom to take the initiative. The former approach alternately precipitated alarm and frustration, whereas the latter approach generated enthusiasm, confidence, and perceptible momentum.

Build Momentum

The long-term perspective that is such an important part of top management commitment and confidence building should also characterize the venture creation process. Managers should focus on generating momentum rather than on achieving quick returns. Starting and implementing several modest new initiatives simultaneously is preferable to pouring all available resources into a single megaproject. This steady building of momentum helps subordinates develop the confidence that comes both from success and from their growing recognition that they really can do it themselves.

We found that an important component of building both confidence and momentum was for an organization to begin fairly close to its current competence base—to start off with evolutionary rather than revolutionary ventures, as discussed in the following section. In keeping with the findings of earlier research (Von Hippel 1977; Fast 1979; Roberts 1980; Maidique and Zirger 1985), none of the successful divisions studied by MacMillan started off too far from an existing competence base. The managers of these divisions didn't throw all their energies into pursuing ventures in areas where they knew neither the product nor the market. Rather, the divisions began either by aggressively expanding into "adjoining" markets with existing products or services or by creating new offerings for existing customers.

However, the pervasive, constant pressure generated by this activity ensured that over time, the divisions did diversify, and significantly so. In the course of this progressive diversification, new competencies were gained, and these, in turn, became the seeds for even more new businesses.

CHALLENGE 2: SELECTING THE BUSINESS DEVELOPMENT STRATEGY—REVOLUTIONARY OR EVOLUTIONARY

The next major challenge for senior management is selecting a business development strategy, which defines the trajectory of new-business growth. Are you going to send an astronaut to the moon or add new routes to your existing flight paths? The organization can either pursue a revolutionary strategy by using new technology to develop new products *and* enter new markets, or it can pursue an evolutionary strategy by aggressively extending existing product and market know-how into new product *or* market areas.

In this section, we outline the markedly different revolutionary and evolutionary approaches to new-business development and then examine the advantages and disadvantages of each strategy.

Revolutionary New-Business Development Strategy

A revolutionary strategy focuses on creating new businesses radically different from an organization's existing business base. Such a strategy makes sense only if the new businesses are driven by technology that the organization is developing.

Here are five guidelines for creating new businesses using technology as the driver:

1. Focus on a core technology.
2. Commercialize evolving technology early and aggressively.

3. Compress the time required for prototype development.
4. Identify and select the pace-forcing technology.
5. Press for technological pace matching.

These guidelines, which draw significantly on the concepts of Itami (1987) and MacMillan and McGrath (1992), are discussed briefly in the following subsections.

Focus on a Core Technology.   Core technologies are those carefully chosen, key technologies in which a company elects to excel. Selectivity is crucial simply because even in the unlikely event that the company could manage to excel in many technologies simultaneously, doing so would be prohibitively expensive. For example, Asahi Glass has focused on liquid-crystal display (LCD) technology and is now a world leader in LCD technology and the technology of LCD-based products, and GE Plastics has concentrated on molecular-level polymer engineering.

By achieving and retaining leadership in a core technology, an organization can continually adapt to changing customer needs, search for new markets, and develop successive generations of products—i.e., create and maintain momentum in the commercialization of innovations.

Commercialize Evolving Technology Early and Aggressively.   Fully developing a new product before exposing it to the market creates a huge potential for mistakes and expensive failures. An organization can minimize these risks by getting the product out to market as early as possible. For example, Sanyo knew that the commercial advantage of solar-cell technology lay in heat-exchange efficiency. But it marketed the technology long before high efficiency was achieved by entering markets in which efficiency wasn't important—watches and calculators. As a result, Sanyo compiled a wealth of production and market information, which will come in very handy when a high level of efficiency is achieved. Another example is Sony, which took its first modest step into the U.S. TV market with a 6-inch television set. In short, any market can best be learned by entering it.

Early commercialization is even more important in light of the shrinking product cycles typical of today's business environment. Rapid changes in technology, market uncertainty, and competitive pressures have forced organizations to accelerate commercialization. Furthermore, marketing a product early tends to create an entry barrier to competing products simply because of the cost involved in switching from an existing product.

The task for senior management is to encourage, support, and require multifunctional teams very early, in order to reduce the time it will take the project to progress from engineering to production to marketing. Formalized handoff procedures from one function to the next must be eliminated if the organization is to achieve early and successful commercialization.

An aggressive approach to commercialization provides an effective response to the following major problems associated with the revolutionary business development strategy:

- *Market uncertainty:* The market may not want the product, or a competing technology may preempt the market, as illustrated by many examples—e.g., the RCA videodisks that didn't record and were therefore swept away by videotapes; the Polaroid instant movie cameras that were rendered obsolete by electronic camcorders.
- *Know-how development:* Before a product can be produced, sold, or distributed, an enormous amount of know-how must be developed, including:
  —Production know-how—the company must learn how to make the product.
  —Marketing know-how—the salesforce must learn how to sell the product.
  —Distributor and supplier know-how—these groups

must learn how to deliver, distribute, and service the product.

—User know-how—customers must learn how to use the product.

Early commercialization, as in Sanyo's case, generates production, marketing, and supplier knowledge that can help the company successfully commercialize the mature product once it becomes available.

- *Cash burn:* If a firm waits until its technology is perfected before marketing a new product, it can lay out money for years before getting any revenues. With early commercialization, the firm can use initial, modest market wins to generate a cash flow that can be used both to provide an increased level of funding for each successive round of technology and to fund future market moves.

Compress the Time Required for Prototype Development. Senior managers need to maintain pressure for rapid prototype development and manage design cycle time. Although the research group should develop a working prototype, a multifunctional team should be created as quickly as possible to address the tasks of simplifying the product and/or expanding its functionality. This team should attempt to *use* the new technology to reconfigure the industry.

Senior management can play an important role in identifying and eliminating bottlenecks, such as a shortage of test equipment in the engineering stage. Senior management should also use a teamwork approach and provide for an overlap of functions, so that learning will take place by joint action rather than by formal communication.

Identify and Select the Pace-Forcing Technology. When any major new product is created, a number of different technologies must be developed in parallel. Selecting which of these technologies will force the pace is critical. For example, Matsushita's introduction of the 8-millimeter video required the simultaneous development of tape, tape deck, recording heads, playback heads, parts, and assembly. Matsushita chose tape technology as the driver, hoping that by using the company's metal vacuum deposition technology, it could leapfrog conventional metal powder deposition technology. This choice then forced all the related technologies to keep up (which is another important consideration for senior management, as we'll see in the following subsection)—and advances in those related technologies were fed back to improve Matsushita's existing product line.

Press for Technological Pace Matching. Management must also make sure that other needed technologies keep pace with the development of the core technology and that the salesforce, the production department, suppliers, and distributors are constantly kept abreast of the applications of these evolving technologies. Toray made a costly mistake when it developed a nylon process technology different from Du Pont's but failed to develop necessary related technologies. Because Toray needed finishing process equipment and know-how (involving such operations as spinning, dyeing, and finishing) as well as access to U.S. and other markets, it was forced to make an almost crippling financial commitment to license from Du Pont. Toray realized that without advances in the related areas, all its production know-how was worthless.

Evolutionary New-Business Development Strategy

Evolutionary new business development involves extending existing know-how into new products/services and/ or new markets. Because the company is not starting from scratch, aggressive extension of know-how offers a greater likelihood of success than the revolutionary approach of entering areas in which both the market and the product/service are unknown. Over time, though, the company can still become highly diversified if it is aggressive enough.

In the course of marketing new products/services and

Figure 2-1: Example of Evolutionary New-Business Development through the Aggressive Extension of Know-How

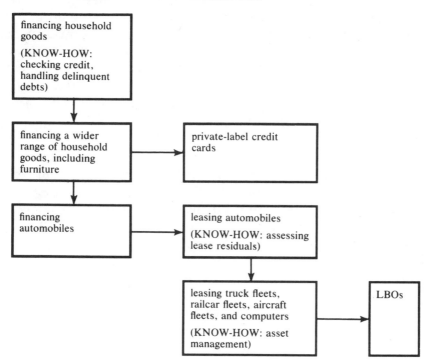

entering new markets, a firm develops new know-how. The key to success with the evolutionary approach lies in the firm's being aware of the specific know-how that it is redeploying as it embarks on each new venture. An interesting example of extending know-how is presented in Figure 2-1, which shows how in just 15 years the financial services company studied by MacMillan has grown into a highly diversified organization with $60 billion in assets.

The company started as an internal supplier of financing to domestic durables purchasers, thereby developing know-how in checking credit and handling delinquent debts. It then used this know-how to move aggressively into financing other domestic durables, such as furniture, and eventually, automobiles.

51

All these steps involved extending existing product know-how (leasing and sale/leaseback) to new markets. However, the firm then moved into a new product, leasing, in the automobile market. In addition to its existing know-how in checking credit and handling delinquent debts, the firm had to develop know-how at estimating the residual value of a car when the lease expires, which is the key to leasing success. Its next step was to aggressively extend this new know-how (assessing lease residuals) to ever more diverse new markets—trucks, railcars, aircraft, and even computers. In the process, the firm developed know-how in asset management, which it used to aggressively build a leveraged buyout (LBO) business. In the meantime, the firm has become so effective in the household-financing business that it has moved into private-label credit cards.

Advantages and Disadvantages of Both Strategies

The major disadvantage of the revolutionary strategy is that the organization has little or no know-how on which to base its entry into the market—it knows neither how to produce the product nor how to sell it to customers and distributors nor how to service it. Entering the market against established competition is immensely expensive under such conditions, *unless* the organization has elected to use new technology as the driver, as Du Pont has repeatedly done (Cohen 1988). Additional disadvantages of the revolutionary strategy include the following:

- The new technology may not be "user-friendly" for either the firm, its new customers, or its new distributors.
- Customers or distributors are often highly resistant to using a new technology in its early stages.
- Although a firm can win big with the revolutionary strategy, such wins are infrequent.
- Large-scale entry with the wrong product at the wrong

52

time can produce large-scale disappointment, which may have a negative impact on the firm's other venturing efforts.

The major advantages of a revolutionary strategy are that:

- New technology can permit breakthroughs that transform the industry, making huge wins possible.
- The know-how of existing competitors is of no use in helping them quickly counter such a new technology.
- The company is likely to achieve a strong proprietary position.

The advantages and disadvantages of the evolutionary new-business development strategy are essentially the reverse of the advantages and disadvantages of the revolutionary strategy. The advantages are as follows:

- Some or all of the company's existing know-how can be applied to the new venture.
- The fact that the technology is already familiar to the company, its customers, and its distributors tends to minimize both user-friendliness problems and resistance to the product on the part of customers and distributors.
- The probability of success is higher, even though the wins are often more modest than with a new-technology-driven market entry.
- By sticking close to its existing know-how base, the company reduces the risk of a large-scale failure that might adversely affect its overall venturing program.

Conversely, the disadvantages of the evolutionary new-business development strategy are as follows:

- Huge wins, of the industry-transforming kind, are much less likely.

53

- Some or all of the know-how of existing competitors will be useful to them in attempting to counter the firm's new offering.
- The firm is unlikely to gain a strong proprietary position.

Although it might seem logical to try combining the revolutionary and evolutionary strategies in order to mitigate the disadvantages of each, a combination strategy is often too costly and may spread the organization too thin in terms of its resources and talents. A viable alternative, however, is for different organizational units to pursue different strategies.

CHALLENGE 3: DEFINING AND USING VENTURE SELECTION CRITERIA

As we said in the Introduction, the concept of entrepreneurship as an endeavor characterized by undisciplined, spontaneous, rash, and risk-seeking behavior is a myth. On the other hand, rigid, lock-step adherence to a fixed set of rules can be the kiss of death for entrepreneurship. New ventures do need discipline, but it's a different type of discipline than what established organizations need. Senior management bears the responsibility for requiring discipline that is *appropriate* to the unique conditions of venturing. Choosing which ventures the organization will support is one of the most important areas in which discipline must be exercised.

We start this section by examining the types of criteria that organizations often define as a guide to venture selection. We then consider how organizations use these criteria to help them choose ventures that are consistent with corporate strategy, feasible, and worthwhile.

Defining Venture Selection Criteria

Venture selection criteria are the standards by which senior management judges new-venture ideas and chooses those it will support. Both general and specific criteria must be defined, and they must be clear enough to enable senior managers to select ventures that will prove successful and profitable. General criteria flow from the goals chosen for the venturing activity as a whole and from the strategic goals of the parent company. (For example, Motorola's strategy of being first and dominant in portable communication devices inevitably provided guidance for its position in the emerging cellular phone business.) More specific criteria may be defined as well, involving such considerations as evidence of consumer or customer want or need, specified competitive advantage and insulation against competition, indications of the company's capability to satisfy the perceived need, and various financial criteria.

Firms often establish screening criteria with respect to the following critical aspects of an internal corporate venture. Note that these criteria are very broad and only serve to define the general "territory." For a more detailed examination of the criteria used for evaluating specific business proposals, see Chapter 4.

- *Strategic fit:* The company may define the types of markets, products, and technology on which it wishes to focus. Conversely, it may define how much diversity from present markets, products, and technology is acceptable.
- *Potential size:* Limits may be established on the size of ventures the company will support. Some firms will not consider ventures having only a relatively small potential; others ignore potential size. Limits may also be established regarding potential size as it relates to time (i.e., how quickly a venture must be expected to reach a given size).
- *Market position:* Some companies require a number 1 or number 2 position or a specified minimum market share.
- *Investment limitations:* Limits may be imposed on how much the company is willing to invest to reach each stage of venture development as well as on the

total amount it is willing to invest before profitability is achieved.

- *Financial performance requirements:* Criteria may be established regarding ROI, gross margins, sales growth rate margins, and potential sales.
- *Time horizon:* The company may specify the time period within which a venture is expected to become profitable. This can range from under three years to ten years or more, depending on whether the target market exists or requires development. A venture's expected business life can also be a consideration.
- *Risk levels:* The company may define the level of financial and regulatory risk it is willing to take.
- *Social responsibility and corporate values:* Criteria may be established to ensure that ventures are consistent with the company's mission and value system and with how the company sees its role in society.
- *Feasibility:* The company may define certain fundamental determinants of a venture's feasibility, such as the likelihood of gaining a strong proprietary position; availability of the systems, management, and leadership required to adequately control the venture; and how much of the firm's existing know-how can be applied to the venture.
- *Impact:* Criteria may also be established regarding a potential venture's impact on the company's reputation or on its existing customers.

Although we are not suggesting that an organization must establish detailed criteria for each issue mentioned in the preceding list, it should define enough criteria to enable managers and potential innovators to determine that a proposed venture is consistent with the firm's overall strategy, likely to produce worthwhile results, and feasible for the firm to undertake.

Now that we've seen the rather wide array of venture selection criteria that companies can define, let's consider which criteria are most commonly used in screening ventures

Table 2-1: Criteria for Selecting Ventures

Selection Criteria	United States (39 Companies)	Japan (126 Companies)
Strategic fit	4.1	3.9
Competitive advantage	4.0	3.8
Potential ROI	3.9	3.6[a]
Existence of a market	3.9	4.4[a]
Potential sales	3.9	3.9
Risk/reward ratio	3.8	3.6
Presence of a product champion	3.6	4.0
Synergy	3.5	3.7
Amount of money risked	3.3	3.6
Closeness to the present market	3.3	3.3
Presence of an executive protector	3.3	3.4
Opportunity to create a new market	3.1	3.8[a]
Closeness to present products	3.1	3.2
Closeness to present technology	2.9	3.5[a]
Patentability	2.3	2.9[a]

Source: Adapted from Z. Block and P. N. Subbanarasimha, "Corporate Venturing: Practices and Performance in the U.S. and Japan," working paper (Center for Entrepreneurial Studies, Stern School of Business, New York University, 1989).

Note: Criteria were rated on a scale of 1 ("unimportant") to 5 ("critically important"). The numbers presented here are the average ratings.

[a] Indicates a statistically significant difference between the figures for the U.S. and Japanese companies.

and how these criteria relate to venture performance. Block and Subbanarasimha (1989) examined this issue in a study involving a number of U.S. and Japanese companies. The principal selection criteria used by these companies are shown in Table 2-1, which lists the criteria in order of declining importance to the U.S. sample. Block and Subbanara-simha's findings regarding the correlation between selection criteria and venture performance are as follows:

- Better-performing companies, those with a higher ROI and profit contribution from total venturing activity as well as a higher percentage of profitable ventures, gave the highest ratings to risk/reward ratio and potential sales as criteria for selecting ventures.
- Poorer-performing companies gave the highest ratings to the presence of a venture champion as a criterion for selecting ventures. (Note: A venture champion may be necessary to get a venture supported, but the presence of such a champion is not a sufficient reason for starting a venture.)
- The study found no correlation between performance and the "closeness to present products" or "closeness to present technology" criteria. This may be due to the tremendous variation in performance among companies with diversifying ventures. (See the discussion of the Porter study in Appendix A.)
- The high rating for strategic fit as a criterion for individual venture selection is consistent with the principal reason for venturing noted in Chapter 1 (i.e., "to meet strategic goals").

Thus far in this subsection, we've considered a variety of venture selection criteria and how some of the most commonly used criteria relate to venture performance. At this point, you may be wondering just how senior management can synthesize all this information into a set of company-specific guidelines that can be used to effectively evaluate venture ideas. What follows is a sample statement of venture selection criteria that we have developed for a fictitious technology-based food ingredient and food-processing-machinery business with current sales of $150 million and a 16% ROI.

- We are interested in developing proprietary products, equipment, systems, and businesses for the food-

processing and food service industry—baking, dairy, confectionery, frozen foods, fast foods.
- The potential size of ventures we select must exceed $5 million in annual sales within a three-year period. Ventures should offer gross margins of not less than 35%. No venture that promises less than 40% annual pretax return on investment within a five-year period will be considered.
- Products shall be nutritionally sound and contribute to improved product quality and profitability for our customers.
- The product/business shall be capable of obtaining leading market share based on clear competitive advantages that can be retained or renewed over a time period that is long enough to enable the product/business to achieve market leadership.
- Ventures should require an initial investment level of less than $500,000 to reach break-even.

In the following subsection, we turn our attention to the issue of what senior management should do with venture selection criteria once they have been defined—i.e., how the criteria can most effectively be applied in practice.

Using Venture Selection Criteria

MacMillan's study found significant differences between how senior managers in companies with successful and unsuccessful venturing divisions used venture selection criteria to manage the process of generating venture ideas, evaluating those ideas, and then selecting or rejecting them.

One difference between the unsuccessful and successful venturing divisions involved the screening process used by senior management to select ventures for support. The companies with unsuccessful venturing programs generally required that fully developed business plans be submitted to management committees, which, after much deliberation, handed down a decision, generally negative, with little explanation. To a venture's proponents, the process was akin to dealing with the Delphic oracle: the basic selection criteria emerged only over time and after the rejection of many seemingly viable ideas.

Managers in the companies with successful venturing programs generally took a much different approach. They developed a limited number of key criteria, as discussed in the preceding subsection, to be used for the initial screening of proposals. They then disseminated those criteria, both *widely* and *continuously,* within the organization. Because the criteria gave the firm's members a clear sense of direction, by specifying the types of venture ideas in which the firm was interested, the criteria tended to stimulate the generation of ideas.

Dissemination of the criteria also prompted a considerable amount of *self*-screening, in which ideas were either rejected or repackaged by subordinates themselves, thus saving hundreds of hours of unnecessary plan preparation and subsequent disappointment. As a manager in the engineering materials company put it: "The problem is not with too few ideas—the problem is with choosing from many ideas. The best people to discard ideas that just don't fit are the people who are thinking about proposing them" (MacMillan 1987, 447). This voluntary reduction in the number of unsuitable ideas submitted allowed senior management to focus serious and sustained attention on more feasible ideas right from the start.

Another significant difference between the companies with unsuccessful and successful venturing divisions involved how managers handled the rejection of ideas. In the companies with unsuccessful programs, senior managers uniformly used selection committees (often composed of high-level staff bureaucrats) who turned down each idea as a committee. In general, senior managers in the companies with successful programs turned down ideas personally and took the time to explain why. As the senior manager of the financial services firm put it:

It is not easy to tell someone why you aren't going ahead with an idea that they think is great. Sometimes it *is* great, but it just doesn't fit. If it doesn't fit, I owe it to the guy who thought of it to tell him why we aren't going ahead. I'm not about to get into an argument about it, but I am going to tell him, eye to eye. Hiding behind a committee is a cop-out. (MacMillan 1987, 447)

One final advantage of developing and widely disseminating a statement of venture selection criteria is that the criteria provide unambiguous standards for the rejection of unsuitable ideas. Hence, although many ideas will be rejected for failing to meet the stated criteria, such objective turndowns tend to be far more acceptable to the ideas' proposers.

CHALLENGE 4: MANAGING DISAPPOINTMENT

Even if a firm is able to reduce the risks associated with a startup through astute selection of new-business ideas and meticulous attention to venture design, failures will still occur. Because new businesses inherently involve uncertainty and lack of knowledge, they simply fail more often than established businesses. Thus, the last and most sensitive area in which senior managers face a major challenge involves managing the failures that inevitably accompany any serious drive toward new-business development.

The MacMillan study found four fundamental differences in the way failure was handled by managers in companies with successful and unsuccessful venturing divisions. In companies with successful divisions, the managers had learned to:

1. Distinguish between bad decisions and bad luck
2. Focus on learning
3. Redirect the venture
4. Shoot the wounded (have the courage to quit)

In the following subsections, we consider how each of these strategies can help senior management either salvage a positive outcome from initially negative results or, failing that, at least prevent initially negative results from escalating into a major loss for the company.

Distinguish between Bad Decisions and Bad Luck

In the companies with successful venturing programs, managers were very careful to distinguish between plain bad luck and bad management. As the senior manager of the equipment-manufacturing company put it:

> Some managers came to me and told me that their venture had failed and that they had lost me several million dollars. When I reviewed the decisions they made, I realized that in their circumstances *I* would have made the same decisions. They had done everything about right, but their luck ran badly and they were blindsided by an unexpected technology. So I called the whole company around and I said to them: "Here's a couple of guys who took a big swing and missed, but for all the right reasons, and I want you to notice that though we lost a few million I'm promoting them." If I hadn't done that, people would have just stopped taking risks. On the other hand you have to make sure that everyone understands that we can't condone sloppy management, no matter what. (MacMillan 1987, 449)

Focus on Learning

Another key characteristic exhibited by managers in companies with successful venturing programs was a determination to learn from failures, even to capitalize on them (Maidique and Zirger 1985; Block and MacMillan 1985). The equipment-manufacturing company analyzed a major setback in a domestic venture and turned it into a promising international business. The engineering materials company analyzed a disappointment in one market and identified a whole new opportunity in another market—an opportunity it subsequently pursued with great success. This determination to salvage learning from the wreckage of failure closely parallels the finding of a fascinating longitudinal study of several innovative organizations by Maidique and Zirger (1985), who observed that spectacular new-product successes often emerged as an outgrowth of what companies learned from major failures.

Redirect the Venture

In companies with unsuccessful venturing programs, the managers tended to assess a venture's progress by holding periodic committee reviews and making a "go/no-go" type of decision on the venture at each review.

In companies with successful venturing programs, on the other hand, the mind-set of senior managers was completely different. They generally measured progress according to predetermined milestones (Block and MacMillan 1985). At each milestone, the managers decided *how to change direction* rather than whether or not to proceed. Several major successes at 3M occurred only because senior management recognized unexpected new applications for work performed in connection with ventures whose original product entries had failed.

As the leader of the information services company observed: "New business development is like mountain climbing. When you reach an obstacle you can either stop and weep or you can strike out in another direction. If you don't keep trying new directions, you never get up the mountain" (MacMillan 1987, 450).

63

Shoot the Wounded (Have the Courage to Quit)

An especially painful duty of the senior manager is to shut down ventures that are just not working out. The pattern in the companies with unsuccessful venturing programs was that once projects were well under way, they were allowed to flounder on, consuming valuable effort and resources long after they should have been terminated.

Although senior managers in companies with successful venturing programs also hated to terminate failing projects, they had no hesitation about doing so, and all of them delivered the news personally. Here's how the financial services company manager explained the dangers of mishandling project terminations: "If you don't shut them down personally and tell them that you're shutting down and why, they'll think that *they* failed. It's important to make them realize that it's the business that failed, not *them*. . . . If you don't, you lose them, and who likes to lose good people?" (MacMillan 1987, 450).

CONCLUSION

Senior managers play a critical role in enabling new ventures to grow and develop while maintaining a necessary balance with the organization's ongoing businesses. On the one hand, the scale, scope, and degree of aggressiveness of the venturing program must be tailored to the firm's capabilities in order to avoid crises that can cause unnecessary damage to both. On the other hand, creating a venturesome climate will have a positive impact on the opportunity-seeking spirit of the existing organization.

This chapter identified several key areas in which senior management involvement is essential to a successful venturing program—creating a venturesome culture, selecting a business development strategy, defining and using venture selection criteria, and managing disappointment. If senior management fails to meet these challenges, individual new ventures may succeed, but it is unlikely that the company will be able to sustain a profitable venturing program for any length of time. At best, it will experience sporadic success.

By meeting these challenges, senior management will have made a solid start toward an effective venturing program. But there is more that corporate leaders must do in order to build a strong, entrepreneurial culture that will continually generate successful new businesses. Not only must they understand and support innovation, but they must design the venturing process itself, which is the subject of Chapter 3.

Guidelines

Creating a Venturesome Climate

1. Require innovation and new-business development in every business unit and function.
2. Build organizational confidence by showing subordinates that they are capable of developing new businesses, by demonstrating visible and continuing personal commitment, and by empowering and nurturing new-business creators and units.
3. Start close to the organization's current competence base and extend from there.

Selecting the Business Development Strategy— Revolutionary or Evolutionary

1. Focus on a core technology and/or industry in which the company is determined to excel.
2. Commercialize early and aggressively.
3. Use a revolutionary strategy only if the new business is driven by technology that the company is developing.
4. Use an evolutionary strategy for extending existing know-how into new products and new markets.

Defining and Using Venture Selection Criteria

1. Develop and disseminate a limited number of key criteria that will serve to clarify corporate objectives and that can be used for initial screening. Encourage self-screening of new-business ideas.
2. Turn down unacceptable new-business ideas by personally advising the proposer of the decision and explaining its rationale.

Managing Disappointment

1. Focus on learning, not blame.
2. Focus on redirection, not venture continuation or termination, at each milestone.
3. Have the courage to shoot fatally wounded ventures personally and in a timely fashion.
4. Distinguish between venture failure and managerial failure, between bad luck and bad decisions.

REFERENCES

Block, Z., and MacMillan, I. C. 1985. "Milestones for Successful Venture Planning." *Harvard Business Review* (September–October): 184–196.

Block, Z., and Ornati, O. 1987. "Compensating Corporate Venture Managers." *Journal of Business Venturing* 2, no. 2 (Spring): 41–52.

Block, Z., and Subbanarasimha, P. N. 1989. "Corporate Venturing: Practices and Performance in the U.S. and Japan." Working paper. Center for Entrepreneurial Studies, Stern School of Business, New York University.

Brandt, S. 1986. *Entrepreneuring in Established Companies.* Homewood, IL: Dow Jones–Irwin.

Cohen, A. 1988. "Innovation at Du Pont—A Real-Time Perspective." *Research Technology Management* (November–December): 47–52.

Elder, T., and Shimanski, J. M. 1988. "Redirection Decisions in Successful Corporate Ventures." *Frontiers of Entrepreneurship Research* (Babson College): 510–526.

Fast, N. D. 1979. "The Future of Industrial New Venture Departments." *Industrial Marketing Management* 8: 264–273.

Fast, N. D., and Pratt, S. E. 1981. "Individual Entrepreneurship and the Large Corporation." *Frontiers of Entrepreneurship Research* (Babson College): 443–450.

Hill, R. M., and Hlavacek, J. D. 1972. "The Venture Team: A New Concept in Marketing and Organization." *Journal of Marketing* 36 (July): 44–50.

Itami, Hiroyuki. 1987. *Mobilizing Invisible Assets*. Cambridge, MA: Harvard University Press.

Kanter, R. M. 1983. *The Change Masters*. New York: Simon & Schuster.

———. 1989. *When Giants Learn to Dance*. New York: Simon & Schuster.

MacMillan, I. C. 1987. "New Business Development Challenges for Transformational Leadership." *Human Resource Management* 26, no. 4: 439–454. 439–454.

MacMillan, I. C., and McGrath, R. G. 1992. "Technology Strategy." *Journal of High Technology Management Research*, forthcoming.

Maidique, M. A. 1980. "Entrepreneurs, Champions and Technological Innovation." *Sloan Management Review* (Winter): 136–152.

Maidique, M. A., and Hayes, R. H. 1984. "The Art of High-Technology Management." *Sloan Management Review* (Winter): 17–31.

Maidique, M. A., and Zirger, B. J. 1985. "The New Product Learning Cycle." *Research Policy* 14: 299–313.

Peters, T. J., and Waterman, R. H., Jr. 1982. *In Search of Excellence*. New York: Harper & Row.

Quinn, J. B., and Mueller, J. A. 1963. "Transferring Research Results to Operations." *Harvard Business Review* (January–February): 49–66.

Roberts, E. B. 1968. "A Basic Study of Innovators: How to Keep and Capitalize on Their Talents." *Research Management* 11, no. 4: 249–266.

———. 1980. "New Ventures for Corporate Growth." *Harvard Business Review* (July–August): 134–142.

Takeuchi, H., and Nonaka, I. 1986. "The New New Product Development Game." *Harvard Business Review* (January–February): 137–145.

Tichy, N. M., and Devanna, M. A. 1986. *The Transformational Leader*. New York: John Wiley & Sons.

von Hippel, E. 1977. "Successful and Failing Internal Corporate Ventures: An Empirical Analysis." *Industrial Marketing Management* 6: 163–174.

3

Framing and Managing the Venturing Process: Senior Management Decisions

If senior managers are to generate a steady flow of innovation, they must do more than provide an encouraging environment. They must actively develop and manage a process that produces ventures having a high probability of success. Doing so requires an understanding of the available decision options and who must make these decisions.

In this context, it is important to distinguish between decisions that are the responsibility of senior management and those that are the responsibility of each venture's management (Burgelman 1984), because managing the venturing function is not the same as managing a venture. Senior management of the parent corporation or unit should manage the venturing function or process, not the venture itself. Management of the venture should be left to venture managers. This does not mean, however, that senior management should be detached or disinterested. On the contrary, it means that senior management should provide support and input, evaluate performance, and demand results, but not direct day-to-day operations. In this chapter, which deals with process and venture design, we concentrate on issues and decisions involving senior managers (i.e., those to whom venture managers report), not venture managers.

Senior managers need to make decisions about venturing activities on two levels. The first involves the organization and management of the overall venturing process (Burgelman 1983). At this level, senior management is concerned with the process elements on a firmwide (or business unit) scale. The second level involves the design and monitoring (*not* the operation) of individual ventures. The effectiveness of these decisions is a major determinant of the organization's ultimate venturing performance.

In this chapter, we build on the venturing process model shown in the Introduction (see Table I-1), which outlines the responsibilities of senior management and venture management at each stage of the venturing process. Senior management's responsibilities include taking action in the following five areas:

1. Formulating the corporate venturing strategy
2. Generating new-business ideas
3. Analyzing and selecting new-business ideas
4. Designing the venture
5. Launching and monitoring the venture

Before discussing each of these areas, we want to emphasize that our objective is to provide guidelines for creating a *process* that will enable an organization to generate a continuing stream of innovations and new businesses and optimize its chances of using venturing as an effective long-term growth strategy, not to provide guidelines for merely achieving an occasional venturing success. Although an organization can actually start by taking action in any of the preceding five areas, and sooner or later, with or without conscious planning, every one of these areas will require action on the part of senior management, this does not mean the organization should rely on serendipity to structure its venturing effort. Building a coherent and internally consistent venturing process through thoughtful management is far more likely to pay off in terms of the avoidance of major errors, cumulative learning, and more effective performance.

And finally, we wish to emphasize that although process design and management can increase an organization's odds of success, individual creativity is an absolute essential for which no process can be substituted.

FORMULATING THE CORPORATE VENTURING STRATEGY

In developing its venturing strategy, a firm should examine its fundamental reasons for venturing, set the overall direction of its venturing effort, and decide on the size and number of ventures it is willing to support.

Deciding to Venture: What Will Drive the Engine?

Research shows that employing venturing as an organization's source of growth and renewal is preferably a strategic decision (Burgelman 1984; Block 1982; and Hanan 1976). Figure 3-1 illustrates the relationship between venturing and strategic goals.

Many key people in the firm, including the CEO but not just the CEO, must be convinced of the strategic necessity of venturing. Furthermore, they must become convinced of this need well before events in the marketplace bludgeon the firm into a belated awareness of missed opportunities and competitive disadvantages.

NYNEX and IBM provide examples of how venturing can be used to achieve strategic objectives. NYNEX has a growth objective that exceeds the projected growth of its traditional telephone businesses. To achieve that objective, it

Figure 3-1: Venturing as a Strategic Growth Option

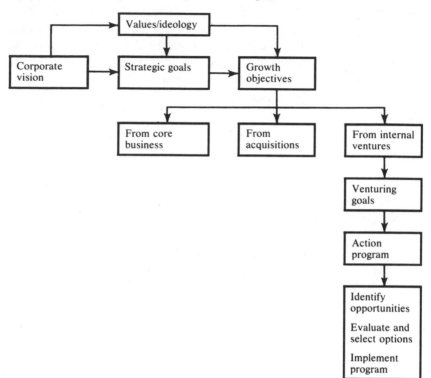

must enter new businesses, which is being done with cellular telephones and with telephone stores in the United States and abroad.

In the case of IBM, the company's entry into the personal computer business achieved two strategic objectives— providing growth as well as serving a defensive function. A current example of a venture that exemplifies a long-term commitment to venturing as a necessary component of strategy fulfillment is Prodigy, the joint venture between IBM and Sears whose purpose is to supply information and other services to PC owners via videotext. By September 1990, more than $600 million had reportedly been invested with no profit to that date. What accounts for this commitment is the clear inevitability of the growth of PCs and the services that will be needed (i.e., the potential risk/reward ratio), strategic fit, and the deep pockets of the partners. CBS, an earlier backer of the Prodigy venture, "bailed out in 1986 after seeing how far off the payback would be" (Rothfelder and Lewyn 1990). From a strategic standpoint, Sears must be in the electronic selling business in the future, and IBM must be in the computer software and service business. As of July 1992, when contacted, a spokesperson for Prodigy reported that 2 million members were expected by year end and that recent data on investment and profitability were not publicly available.

Venturing is often initiated as a consequence of strategic necessity when a business's goals cannot be achieved without new-product/new-market entries or when the maturing of existing businesses requires internal venturing or acquisitions as a defense or to achieve growth. In practice, however, that necessity often goes unrecognized, and companies begin by simply seizing an opportunity or responding to a threat, as was the case, for example, with IBM's PC entry. Some ventures originate as a by-product of an internal competence—e.g., Aetna's entry into mutual funds or Boeing's computer service business or Du Pont's energy consulting activity. Firms with large research and development operations frequently find themselves with new technologies that require commercialization, sometimes outside the scope of existing business activity. A venture may be undertaken in order to obtain a window on a new industry or technology, as Exxon did with its exploration of wind energy in the 1970s. More recently, companies have introduced venturing in order to stimulate innovation and initiatives, as Colgate did with its Venture Company and Kodak with its New Opportunity Development.

There's nothing wrong with a mixed strategy in which a firm both actively seeks opportunities and responds to unexpected opportunities. Smaller organizations or units within large corporations can be far more flexible in their reaction time than the giants, starting smaller and increasing resource allocation as the probability of success increases.

73

And there are some companies in which venturing is such a deeply embedded activity, recognized as so fundamental to organizational life and growth, that the companies themselves are considered venturing entities. Such is the case with 3M and Hewlett-Packard, and was for a long time the case with Texas Instruments; it is also the case with many other firms in industries that are constantly changing. The more turbulent a business or environment, the greater the need for innovation and the greater the likelihood that venturing will be essential for survival.

Setting the Direction of the Venturing Effort: Goals and Limits

Setting the direction of the venturing effort can be done in a wide range of ways. At one extreme, a firm may clearly define what is expected to result from its venturing activity; specify its goals, both quantitatively and qualitatively; and then design plans to meet those goals. At the other extreme, the firm may simply react to opportunities, without stating any goals or objectives, other than possibly the fields or industries in which it is interested in venturing.

A strong case can be made for establishing venture goals. Goals—which specify industries of interest and market position sought and express economic performance objectives in terms of sales, total profit, and margins—provide direction to the organization's effort. Goals create pressure for action, establish linkage with strategic objectives, and can serve as a basis for evaluating performance. We are referring here to goals for the total venturing effort within either a business unit or the total organization, not to specific goals for an individual venture, which are a separate matter.

Providing direction to the venturing effort through the formation of goals that clearly reflect the organization's reasons for venturing can also prevent venturing from moving in a direction that conflicts with corporate objectives. The potential for such a conflict is aptly illustrated by the case of a multibillion-dollar company's venturing activity, whose manager identified its mission as "stimulat[ing] innovation." In contrast, the parent corporation's chief operating officer stated in an interview that his criterion for venturing success was the development of a new business with minimum sales of $100 million per year within five years! Furthermore, the formation of goals establishes a clear rationale for assessing individual venture proposals—one that can be used both by those submitting venture proposals and by decision makers.

A case can also be made for stating what is *not* of interest to the firm, in order to sharpen the focus on the firm's strategic goals with respect to the industries and markets chosen. For example, a food ingredient manufacturing company decided that it lacked the know-how, experience, and leadership required to successfully market food products to consumers but that it was highly skilled and effective in developing, manufacturing, and marketing products for other food producers. Its statement of strategic objectives therefore made it clear that the firm would not undertake internal ventures in consumer food products.

Organizations should avoid being overly narrow in establishing a direction and goals for their venturing efforts. Excessive caution could result in the rejection of a blockbuster proposal that might arise out of a technological discovery, an innovation, or the emergence of a totally new and as yet nonexistent market that doesn't fit within the scope of the formulated direction and goals. It could also result in the rejection of extraordinarily creative, imaginative, and "wild" ideas having great potential.

An early example of such goal-limiting myopia involved the invention of a method for producing a water ice confection on a stick. The inventor approached a firm in the bakery supply business and was rejected because the product and market were not related to the firm's existing business. The inventor then approached a competing firm, which saw the potential for a new business and commercialized the invention with great and enduring success as the Popsicle.

Although, as noted, firms should avoid being overly narrow in establishing the venturing effort's direction and goals, neither should they be unrealistically optimistic. It makes little sense to establish goals that are clearly impossible to achieve, since any organizational unit created for the purpose of achieving such goals will inevitably fail and will then be disbanded.

Deciding on the Size and Number of Ventures

The firm's strategy may be to seek and implement either a relatively small number of very large-scale ventures or, conversely, a larger number of smaller ventures (i.e., a portfolio strategy).

In choosing its strategy, a company just beginning to venture should consider the value of a learning period, in which smaller ventures are desirable. The company must also consider the possible failure rate (50% is a good assumption, although 80% is possible) and what it can afford to lose in terms of time and money by pursuing the chosen strategy. Ideally, firms that have never ventured should start small, with two or three ventures, limited investment, and a reasonable possibility of reaching cash break-even within a short period of time (three years or less). As experience is gained and more is learned about venturing, the level of activity can be increased and the objectives enlarged. Big companies looking for single-digit growth rates will require giant ventures to produce it. A $15-billion company seeking a 5% growth rate from new ventures needs a strategy that will produce sales growth of $750 million per year! This contrasts with a $200-million firm seeking a 10% growth rate, for which sales growth of $20 million per year would be the target.

In simplest terms, the choices are as follows:

- Will the company aggressively seek ventures in specific areas, or will it respond opportunistically to whatever possibilities arise?

- Will the company sponsor a few ventures or many? How few? How many?
- Will a minimum size potential be required?

GENERATING NEW-BUSINESS IDEAS

An organization seeking to stimulate a flow of viable new-business ideas would be well advised to start by examining its venture bases (Hanan 1976)—i.e., its special competencies, the answers to the following questions: What is this company or unit particularly good at? What does it know a lot about? What skills, intellectual capital, technology, market position and market information, distribution channels, and organizational skills does the company have that can form the basis for a new business?

In a well-managed venturing process, operating and staff people are challenged to define the competencies that provide competitive advantage and that can serve as take-off points for a new venture. This requires leadership, evidence of commitment to venturing as part of the firm's strategy, and training to enable personnel to identify opportunity. It is also important that this approach be combined with external sources of opportunity, as described in Chapter 4. No matter how great the firm's internal competency, unless that competency fits an existing or potential market, the idea generation exercise will be an answer in search of a question rather than a valid need in search of a solution.

ANALYZING AND SELECTING
NEW-BUSINESS IDEAS

If an organization succeeds in generating a flow of new-business ideas, many of those ideas will probably not be accepted. The process of analyzing and selecting ideas must be managed so that idea proposers don't become demoralized by rejection and senior managers don't feel compelled to accept ideas merely to avoid demoralization. Several approaches to the analysis and selection process have proved effective in stimulating the generation of ideas rather than turning proposers off.

One approach involves judiciously controlling the complexity of the required approval process. Nothing is more demoralizing to an entrepreneurial and creative individual than an obstacle course consisting of multiple approval levels or ponderous committee deliberations before an idea can even be explored for feasibility. As described in detail in Chapter 7, an idea evolves into a business by going through successively more complex and expensive stages. The organization's process for approval or rejection should therefore be appropriate to the venture's current stage. For example, if an idea is in an early stage and approval is needed simply for testing a concept, no more than a one-stop review should be required. At the other extreme, if enough work has been done on an idea to warrant the preparation of a business plan and approval is needed for launching the venture, and if the commitment sought is large enough, then it may be reasonable to require a more formal approval process (e.g., presentation to and discussion with a board or other authorizing body).

Other useful approaches to the analysis and selection process have been tried by 3M and Kodak. At 3M, idea proposers are encouraged to look anywhere in the firm for support. Kodak, through its New Opportunity Development facilitators, actually helped proponents of new ventures to develop and modify their proposals in an effort to get support. Proposals were not rejected; instead, they were simply not accepted, and the proponents could continue modifying them and trying to obtain support. Ultimately, it was the proponents themselves who decided to drop ideas if they received no support.

Venture selection criteria (discussed extensively in Chapter 2) are another effective tool for managing the analysis and selection of new-business ideas. By advising its employees of the key criteria that ventures must meet in order to qualify for organizational support, a company can take much of the guesswork out of the idea generation process and ensure a flow of more viable ideas right from the outset. Venture selection criteria can also aid in providing a rational basis for the rejection process, by providing an objective standard against which new-business ideas can be compared.

Assessing Venture Needs and Corporate Fit Requirements

One result of evaluating an opportunity and a venture proposal is that senior management becomes aware of the critical factors required for the new enterprise's success. The next and perhaps most significant step in promoting that success is to ensure that the parent organization can in fact meet the needs of the venture that the parent is responsible for meeting. This requires carefully analyzing the venture's needs versus the parent organization's existing ability to meet those needs and determining what must be done to fill any gaps. This analysis will be used in making decisions about the venture's design and organization.

In performing such an analysis, the following specific questions must be answered:

- What risks are involved? Can the firm afford to take them?
- What resources, skills, and knowledge are required? Can the firm supply them?
- What values, culture, practices, and procedures are necessary to support the proposed venture? Can the firm adapt?
- What are the timing requirements for launching the venture and seizing market share? Can the firm satisfy those requirements?

These issues are examined briefly in the following subsections.

Risks. In assessing the risks that are involved in a proposed venture and deciding whether those risks are affordable, senior management must consider both financial and nonfinancial risks.

Financial risks. The venture will need an infusion of cash until the first commercial sale is made, positive cash flow results, profitability is achieved, and the venture's goals are reached. There will be an impact on the parent organization's profit at each of these stages. The venture's affordability is determined by the parent's current and projected cash flow, balance sheet strength, competing demands for cash, and projected profitability.

Nonfinancial risks. Venture-generated risks include strangeness of the new business and inability to evaluate performance, impact on company positioning and reputation, conflict with existing customers, impact on morale within the company, excessive demands for management time, and diversion of resources from existing businesses. The effect of Murphy's law, which applies to all new ventures, must be kept in mind as well.

The parent organization's ability to afford these risks is affected by the tenure and security of corporate management, the political climate within the parent, and attitudes regarding risk embedded in the company's culture.

Before leaving the topic of risk, we wish to offer two general observations about the risks involved in undertaking any new venture. First, senior management should recognize and accept the fact that running a new venture is very different from running a railroad. The company will not be dealing with trains traversing existing tracks according to established, tested schedules. Rather, it will typically be dealing with comparatively high levels of uncertainty and risk, and every management practice must be oriented toward managing uncertainty, not toward managing a predictable operation. The management practices suggested throughout this book are designed precisely for the purpose of managing uncertainty.

Second, senior management should recognize and accept the fact that failures are inevitable. Some ventures will never become profitable, will make too little for the investment required, or will fail to meet (often exaggerated) expectations; some will ultimately be closed down. This probability therefore dictates a portfolio policy for venturing, contrary to the findings of Biggadyke (1979). The failure of individual ventures cannot be used as a basis for evaluating an entire venturing program any more than the loss on a single stock investment could be used to evaluate the performance of a portfolio manager who produced an overall gain.

While we're on the topic of failure, it's worth mentioning New Coke (a product "failure" that ultimately resulted in Coca-Cola's regaining leading market share!) and pointing out that there are plenty of New Coke examples around. The only true failures, then, are those from which nothing has been learned.

Resources, Skills, and Knowledge.   The requirements for resources, skills, and knowledge include the availability of entrepreneurial management, knowledge of the industry and market, functional skills (financial, marketing, R&D, service, etc.) appropriate for the specific business, facilities, regulatory knowledge, and perhaps most critical, the ability to evaluate performance.

Values, Culture, Practices, and Procedures.   Senior management must identify the values, culture, practices, and procedures needed to support the proposed venture. Differences in formality, communication openness, how mistakes are treated, attitudes toward customers, and internal competitiveness can generate serious problems. Conflicts arising from autocratic versus participative management styles and compensation philosophy and practices are particularly irksome. There may be disparities between parent and venture culture as well as between the parent's practices and procedures and those needed to support the venture. Will the parent be able to adapt to those needs—especially those involving compen-

81

sation, incentives, control procedures, and capital request formalities?

Timing Requirements. The timing requirements for launching the venture and seizing market share are determined by the venture's proprietary protection, the time window available for establishing market position, competitive action, and the availability of key people. These factors may require very rapid decisions regarding head count, capital expenditures, changes in strategy, salaries, and incentives. If the parent organization has ground rules that prevent rapid response, such as lengthy capital approval procedures or head-count limits that cannot be exceeded without approval (i.e., the bureaucratic and procedural machinery designed for an established business), the venture can be crippled. In one firm, a new venture delayed building a plant in the East for an entire year because the project required use of the corporate manufacturing staff department, which was too busy to undertake the project immediately. During the waiting period, more than the cost of the plant was wasted in excess freight charges.

DESIGNING THE VENTURE

Comparing venture needs and parent company characteristics, as described in the preceding section, will highlight the discrepancies and gaps between the venture's needs and the parent's ability to fulfill them. In designing the venture, senior managers must then attempt to overcome these discrepancies and gaps in order to ensure that the venture's needs can be met without jeopardizing the parent's strengths.

Designing the venture requires decisions regarding five major issues:

1. Composition of the venture management team and how team members are to be compensated

2. What form the venture will take—from project team to wholly owned subsidiary or spin-off
3. Structure and organizational positioning of the venturing function
4. Milestones that will be used to trigger successive financing steps
5. The venture's strategy and business plan

Before discussing these issues, though, we would caution you that designing the venture should not be regarded merely as a finite stage of an organization's venturing effort. Rather, it should be regarded as an ongoing process. As a new venture develops and grows, its needs will inevitably change, as will the ability of the venture team and the parent to fulfill those needs. Thus, the design will require continual changes, which are the responsibility of senior management.

Composition of the Venture Management Team

The issues of selecting, evaluating, and compensating the venture management team are discussed fully in Chapter 5. At this point, we merely wish to make one key observation about venture management. Namely, ventures call for entrepreneurial managers, not caretakers. Founders of successful new ventures typically display attitudes, motivations, behavior, and work habits that differ markedly from those of traditional corporate managers. Persistence, energy, flexibility, resourcefulness, charisma, team-building skills, and knowledge of the market are essential. As ventures evolve, professional managerial capabilities become increasingly necessary. Founders either recognize the need for these capabilities and develop them, or they resist changing their style. Outstanding business starters should not be regarded as failures simply because they aren't willing or able to become professional managers. Their talents should be used again—for starting more new businesses.

What Form the Venture Will Take

Whether the venture will take the form of a project team, a wholly owned subsidiary, or a spin-off is a format decision that must be made early in the venture creation process. The key question is: Shall the company operate the venture alone, or does it need a partnership of some kind with an outside organization? The answer will depend on the affordability of the risks involved and the availability of know-how.

Alliance possibilities run the gamut from having a minority partner to being a minority partner to simply licensing to an outside organization. Temporary alliances may be considered as well. The nature of any alliance will depend on the particular problem to be solved. Firms have formed partnerships in order to be able to attract needed entrepreneurial leadership and free themselves from the restrictions of existing compensation and incentive systems. IBM and Sears' Prodigy videotext venture involves sharing needed know-how and financial risk. Roberts (1980) and Roberts and Berry (1985) have reported the effectiveness of "new style joint ventures," in which a large firm joins with a much smaller firm in order to gain access to markets or technology and proposes alternate strategies linked to the degree to which product, market, and technology are familiar to the parent corporation.

Structure and Positioning of the Venturing Function

Organizational positioning of specific ventures is discussed in detail in Chapter 6, but here we address the question of the structure and positioning of the venturing function itself within the firm. The possible alternatives are:

- A corporate venturing division or unit directly responsible for venturing in the firm—either as part of the corporate business development or corporate planning function or reporting directly to the CEO or COO. Fast (1978 and 1979) has described such venturing units and provided case histories of their rise and fall. An inherent problem with such units is the ease with which they can be eliminated with a change in CEO, a reversal of corporate fortunes, or share market price pressure to increase short-term profitability (Sykes and Block 1989).

- A corporate staff unit responsible for facilitating, stimulating, and supporting new-venture activities that are managed elsewhere—for example, by an operating unit or as a separate individual venture reporting to another organizational entity.
- A line or staff function similar to those just described but operating within a business unit—e.g., a division, subsidiary, or department (Du Pont has $4-billion departments)—rather than at the corporate level.
- No special structural arrangement with no separate unit responsible for any aspect of venturing. Business unit management initiates and operates ventures as an ongoing part of each unit's responsibilities.
- Combinations of the preceding approaches.

The choice of structure depends on the following factors:

- The organization's know-how and experience in venturing
- The magnitude and urgency of the intended venturing effort
- The size of the firm or unit
- The degree of the parent organization's commitment to venturing (i.e., the strength of its conviction that venturing is essential to the fulfillment of its strategic goals)
- The organization's culture
- The nature and number of the ventures to be sought

At one extreme would be the ideal state, in which the firm has a strong and widespread commitment to venturing, a favorable corporate culture, and considerable venturing experience and know-how, and the ventures undertaken range in diversity from very related to relatively unrelated. In this environment, one would expect to see each operating unit, if large enough, having its own venturing subunit to support and guide ventures—to nurture them until they can fly alone. The corporation would also have a unit that initiates and operates unrelated ventures until they can be spun off or operated as new business units of the firm. All forms of venturing would be in use.

At the other extreme would be a company with little experience in venturing and a strong sense of urgency to start the venturing process. In such a case, a corporate unit may be needed to spearhead the effort—i.e., to gain experience by operating a few ventures, which should preferably be related to ongoing businesses. This effort should be undertaken in collaboration with operating units and with the understanding that each venture will be turned over to the relevant operating unit once it has been established. The corporate venturing unit thus serves as a stimulus, catalyst, and teacher. As operating units gain familiarity with the venturing process and become convinced both of the value of venturing and of their own ability to manage ventures, the central unit should begin to function in an advisory role, encouraging the efforts of operating units and attempting to create self-sufficient venturing capability in them, which will ultimately eliminate the need for a corporate unit.

Many large companies engaged in venturing have used every one of the previously mentioned forms at various stages of the firm's development. At one time, Du Pont had a centralized new-business development operation, which has since been decentralized to its very large departments. Du Pont is still searching for more effective methods of venturing that will enable the company to cope with the new realities of very rapid technological change. GE has had every form imaginable—from internal ventures generated within operating units to central business development units. Similarly, IBM and Exxon have employed every possible variation. Experience appears to indicate that the closer an organization

can get to the operating unit as the sponsor, the more successful the outcome is likely to be. Firms that must diversify are
an exception, though, since in their case, it seems preferable
for the venturing activity to be conducted by a central unit
that can handle acquisitions along with internal development.

Milestones That Will Be Used to Trigger Successive Financing Steps

The corporation should establish a series of milestones,
each of which can be used to trigger the release of additional
financing to get the venture to the next milestone. Milestone
planning is explained in detail in Chapter 7, and at this point,
we simply want to emphasize the need for establishing financing milestones at the outset of a venture. Much can be
learned from venture capitalists in this regard. Rather than
indicating a lump-sum amount that it is prepared to spend,
the company specifies how much will be spent for concept
testing, for feasibility study, for product development, for
market testing, etc. Businesses in development require additional financing for subsequent stages, which they don't get
unless the preceding milestones have been achieved (i.e., unless the earlier results justify it).

The Venture's Strategy and Business Plan

Approving the business plan and participating in establishing the venture's strategy are decisions that must be made
by senior management. Neither of these decisions is operational, but they determine the context within which the venture's operations are conducted and dramatically affect the
outcome of those operations. In effect, they define the boundaries of a "playpen" within which venture management is
free to operate. Depending on the size of the parent company
as well as the significance of the venture to the company,
these decisions might be made by the parent board, by a

87

venture board that includes parent members, or by a senior manager or senior management group of either the parent company or a venturing division.

Approving the business plan and participating in formulation of the venture's strategy require professional management by the parent organization. Making these key design decisions is a constructive and supportive alternative to operational interference and overcontrol of the entrepreneurial venture team and is perhaps the most important preventive step the firm can take to establish controls designed to protect it from major unexpected losses.

As noted earlier, a number of these design decisions will obviously have to be remade as the venture develops—e.g., project teams can evolve into new operating units, startup managers may not develop into expansion and growth managers, original alliances and formats may not suit later needs. Thus, senior management has a continuing responsibility both for determining when changes in the venture's strategy and business plan are needed and for making such changes. This does not mean that venture management cannot participate in the design or even originate it, but the approval responsibility rests with senior management.

LAUNCHING AND MONITORING THE VENTURE

Once the new venture is designed and launched, senior management must avoid two dangers: (1) paying no attention to the venture or (2) paying too much attention. At this point, senior management's principal tasks are to protect and support the venture and track its performance, both to help assure its success and to control the cost of failure if that should be the outcome (and for some ventures, it will be). By focusing on the control elements we describe in Chapter 9, senior management can direct its efforts toward correcting or modifying the venture's design and strategy rather than toward micromanaging operations, which will paralyze the venture team's flexibility and effectiveness.

CONCLUSION

The two main tasks of senior management with respect to venturing are to create and manage the context in which it occurs and to ensure that ventures are structured in such a way as to maximize their chances for success.

By addressing these tasks effectively through strategy making, generating a flow of ideas, choosing ventures that are consistent with the organization's strategy, analyzing the needs of the chosen ventures and the firm's ability to meet them, and designing ventures in such a way that those needs can be met, senior managers can craft a venture creation process that produces a continuing stream of successful ventures.

Guidelines

Formulating the Corporate Venturing Strategy

1. Determine what will drive the venturing program. Does the organization see venturing as fundamental to future competitiveness? As a strategic necessity to ensure survival and growth? Will it actively seek ventures or simply respond to opportunities that arise?
2. Decide how detailed and quantified goals should be and then formulate them.
3. Specify the venture's expected relatedness to the firm's existing businesses.
4. Specify the portfolio characteristics sought: number and size of ventures, minimum size of opportunities to be pursued, limitations regarding industries and markets to be entered.
5. Design the venture selection process—how ideas will be processed, how decisions will be communicated, and who will be responsible for decision making.

Generating New-Business Ideas

1. Challenge units to define the internal competencies that are venturable.
2. Provide guidance designed to stimulate ideas that are consistent with the firm's strategy, worth the effort, and feasible for the firm to exploit.

Analyzing and Selecting New-Business Ideas

Establish a process for assessing venture needs and corporate fit requirements in the following areas:
—The affordability of financial and nonfinancial risks
—Resources, skills, and knowledge
—Values, culture, practices, and procedures
—Timing requirements

Designing the Venture

1. Select the format, management and compensation plan, organizational positioning, and financing milestones that meet the needs of the individual venture and fit the capabilities of the parent corporation.
2. Assume that the venture's initial design will require changes and be prepared to make them.

REFERENCES

Biggadyke, R. 1979. "The Risky Business of Corporate Diversification." *Harvard Business Review* (May–June): 103–111.

Block, Z. 1982. "Can Corporate Venturing Succeed?" *Journal of Business Strategy* 3, no. 2: 21–33.

Block, Z., and Subbanarasimha, P. N. 1989. "Corporate Venturing: Practices and Performance in the U.S. and Japan." Working paper. Center for Entrepreneurial Studies, Stern School of Business, New York University.

Burgelman, R. A. 1983. "A Process Model of Internal Corporate Venturing in a Diversified Major Firm." *Administrative Science Quarterly* 28: 223–244.

———. 1984. "Managing the Corporate Venturing Process." *Sloan Management Review* 25, no. 2 (Winter): 33–48.

Fast, N. D. 1978. "The Rise and Fall of New Venture Divisions." Ann Arbor, MI: UMI Research Press.

————. 1979. "The Future of Industrial New Venture Departments." *Industrial Marketing Management* 8: 264–273.

Hanan, Mack. 1976. *Venture Management,* 25–63. New York: McGraw-Hill.

Roberts, E. B. 1980. "New Ventures for Corporate Growth." *Harvard Business Review* (July–August): 134–142.

Roberts, E. B., and Berry, C. A. 1985. "Entering New Businesses: Selecting Strategies for Success." *Sloan Management Review* 26, no. 3 (Spring): 3–17.

Rothfelder, J., and Lewyn, M. 1990. "How Long Will Prodigy Be a Problem Child?" *Business Week* (September 10): 75.

Sykes, H. B., and Block, Z. 1989. "Corporate Venturing Obstacles: Sources and Solutions." *Journal of Business Venturing* 4, no. 3: 159–167.

4

Identifying, Evaluating, and Selecting Opportunity: Building the Venture Proposal

An organization's culture has an enormous influence on the generation of innovative ideas, but as noted in the Introduction, achieving cultural change can be a very slow process. However, there are actions an organization can take in the meantime to increase the flow of new ideas and simultaneously contribute to the development of an innovation-promoting climate. In particular, this chapter discusses the steps a firm can take to identify the opportunities open to it, evaluate them, and select those opportunities most likely to result in successful ventures.

IDENTIFYING OPPORTUNITY

Not all ideas are opportunities, and many opportunities are not right for all firms. As we discussed in the preceding chapter, when a company conducts the process of searching for opportunity and generating ideas by providing overall direction and focus designed to improve the fit between the company's vision, strategy, and goals and the ideas generated, it increases both the number of acceptable ideas and the efficiency of the selection process.

In order to identify opportunity, an organization must generate a flow of high-quality ideas; it must also become skilled at examining various types of information that can provide knowledgeable senior managers with clues to venture possibilities.

Creating a Flow of Ideas

It is important for a firm to generate more ideas than it can possibly exploit, since the quality of its choices is considerably improved when it is able to choose, with minimal expenditure, from among a hopperful of viable new-venture possibilities. Two critical contributors to generating a flow of ideas are the organization's people and the training they receive.

People. People vary greatly in their creative capability. The company's recruiting process should be examined to make sure it is seeking creative people with pertinent capabilities. A good indicator of creativity is evidence of it in a job candidate's history. It should be emphasized that creativity is not simply imagination or speculative skill. Highly creative people will have been *productively* creative at something, sometime, somewhere.

Examine the company's performance evaluation and compensation system. Is creative behavior rewarded, ignored, or even punished? Is evidence of innovation routinely considered during the performance evaluation process? Are managers evaluated for stimulating innovation in their unit? (We have seen performance evaluation forms that allocate a maximum of 5 points out of 100 for "creativity" and others that simply ignore innovation and creativity altogether.) If innovative and creative accomplishments are neither recognized nor rewarded (and the reward need not necessarily be financial), some creative people will quit; others will play by the rules of the company game and do only what is expected and rewarded, suppressing their creative impulses or finding an outlet for them outside the business.

Training. Some people cannot be discouraged from innovating, and others will not innovate no matter what is done to encourage them. But it is the very large group in between these extremes that training can help most—by providing them with information, enhancing their skills, and helping them develop an opportunity-seeking attitude. There is little on the face of the earth that cannot be improved. Many people simply complain about what's wrong; others, with an attitude of creative discontent, see problems and seek solutions.

Many programs are available to help people discover and use their creative capacity and enable them to develop a "can-do" attitude. In fact, the material we present in the balance of this chapter can serve as the nucleus around which to build a program for providing training and practice in opportunity identification.

Sources of Opportunity

Opportunities can be found within the firm itself, in the industries and markets it serves, and in the external environment. It is up to the firm to become familiar with these sources of opportunity and learn to identify venturable possibilities.

Necessity is still the mother of many inventions, and most viable opportunities, regardless of their specific source, spring from problems, needs, and change—e.g., a tamper-proof lock developed in response to a rise in the crime rate or new cancer treatment drugs developed from monoclonal antibodies as an outcome of major changes in biotechnology.

Therefore, broadening the company's awareness of problems, needs, and change is a positive first step.

Internal Sources. Internal sources of opportunity may be found in every aspect of a business. Examples include the need for, or the possibility of, reducing rejects in a manufacturing process, improving overall quality, supplying better service to customers, or replacing a raw material. MacMillan and George (1985) suggest that if a firm is totally new to the venturing game, this internal area is a good starting point for learning how to manage venture projects.

Another approach to internal sources, discussed briefly in Chapter 3, is to identify the organization's areas of special competence that could be venturable—the process earlier noted as venture basing. These areas can become the basis for creating a new business or improving the firm's competitive position. The question is: What skills does the organization have that are outstanding and unequivocally excellent? Here are some examples:

- Japanese automakers absolutely had to manufacture more reliable cars if they were to penetrate foreign markets in which their service network was inadequate. They could have attempted to develop an adequate network but instead elected to build cars that did not require as much service. Their outstanding competence was the ability to manufacture high-quality products at low cost. However, since the reliability of their products was no greater than that of the least reliable component, they proceeded to teach their suppliers how to manufacture extremely reliable components. The success of this approach immediately became evident in the reliability of the cars these companies produced.
- General Electric, unable to obtain suitable materials from the plastics industry, was forced to create its own special plastics for use in its electrical products. In so

doing, the company developed special competence at producing engineered plastics and decided to aggressively enter the engineered plastics market. This is now one of GE's major businesses, producing an operating profit of $1 billion in 1991.

- Sears combined its many locations and consumer franchise with the financial service skills of its Dean Witter unit to launch the Discover card, now a profitable new business for Sears.
- GTE and other telephone companies have launched businesses utilizing their excellence in maintenance and service, as has GE in servicing power plants.
- Anheuser-Busch has proliferated businesses closely related to beer, such as the maintenance and repair of refrigerated cars; it has also founded theme parks that are totally unrelated to beer but that do a brisk business selling beer and snacks that go with beer.
- Allied Corp., 3M, Inco, Motorola, Kodak, and other high-tech firms have a long record of new-venture attempts based on internally developed technologies.

The great advantage of basing new ventures on internal sources of opportunity is the company's familiarity with the resource that has been identified, which increases the odds for success if it can use that resource to meet a need. The great disadvantage of this approach is that there may not be any really worthwhile opportunity to which that resource can be applied. "Stick with what you know best" may be eminently sound advice, but it won't do much good if nobody wants the resulting product or service.

Although the odds of achieving success with technological innovations are small, such innovations have produced the really big hits, resulting in the creation of whole new industries. This was the case with semiconductors and biotechnology, and will surely be the case with superconductivity. Businesses created in this way tend to continue for many years, an example being Du Pont and nylon.

97

Industry and Market Changes.   Changes in a given industry or market are a major source of new opportunities (Drucker 1985) and are probably the most fruitful source of opportunities having a high probability of success. As von Hippel (1978) suggests, in a study of industrial product ventures, customer ideas are a great source of new-venture possibilities, since customers are likely to be quite knowledgeable about the needs of their market and changes in their industry.

Mergers are one type of industry change that can produce new-venture opportunities. A frequent consequence of a merger between two firms is that less attention may be paid to product lines that were originally important to one of the individual firms but have now become relatively less important in the context of a much larger organization. These neglected product lines become vulnerable to competitive attack by a new entrant.

Here are some examples of ventures generated by industry or market change. (Note the absence of ventures by corporations which remain rooted in the past!)

- As pension fund administrators became a larger factor in the stock market, the need for solid research increased. The highly successful firm of Donaldson, Lufkin & Jenrette was formed in response to this opportunity.
- The increase in the size of department stores was accompanied by a trend toward stocking only the better-moving items and reducing the inventory of specialty items, such as blue jeans and other product lines. The resulting unavailability of certain types of products was partly responsible for the birth of specialty retail stores, the fastest-growing business sector of the 1980s. Examples include specialty toy chains, specialty athletic shoe chains, and the Gap stores, which originally specialized in jeans and then, in response to the changing demographics of the 1990s, adjusted their product line to achieve renewed growth.
- Wal-Mart is perhaps the most dramatic, and certainly

the most successful, instance of a business formed in response to industry and market developments. At the time of Wal-Mart's creation, discount stores tended to be clustered in larger cities, and high-quality national brands were sold at high retail in smaller cities. Clerks in department stores were becoming increasingly less cordial. "We're out of it, but we'll order it for you" became a familiar response to product requests. Sam Walton saw this gap and filled it with the fastest-growing retail chain in history, which kept prices low, provided better service, maintained high inventories of stock, and utilized leading-edge information systems.

- In the baking industry, the problem of increased distribution costs (which, in turn, was attributable to increases in labor, fuel, and other costs) created gigantic changes. An entire section of this industry—bakers who delivered to the home—was unable to survive and disappeared. In an effort to offset rising distribution costs, manufacturing bakeries switched to less costly ingredients, and the resulting decline in quality created a demand for higher-quality products. Supermarkets then proceeded to create in-store bakeries to meet that demand.

  One relatively small manufacturing baker sensed the growing dissatisfaction with product quality and introduced the highest-quality products that could be made on an industrial scale. The company, Entenmann's, swept into the market, with its products becoming a multiregional brand. Entenmann's was acquired by General Foods and, ultimately, by Philip Morris when the latter acquired General Foods. This was clearly a case of an industry change producing a market gap, which was soon recognized as an opportunity and exploited.

The needs and wants of the existing market are the most reliable sources of good opportunities in the short run. But it is the ability to foresee and meet future needs that is the source of long-term opportunity and competitive advantage.

The External Environment. Threats and opportunities produced by the external environment can be excellent sources of venturable ideas. Changing demographics, lifestyles, perceptions and values, government regulations, and tax laws as well as social problems such as crime and drug abuse all create problems and the need for solutions.

Opportunities that buck environmental forces will have a very difficult obstacle to overcome. In fact, opportunities that are not supported by at least one environmental trend are likely to be short-lived. Conversely, opportunities that are linked to environmental forces will rise, like ships with a rising tide.

Consider the explosive growth of fitness centers; low-calorie, low-fat, low-cholesterol foods; and the flood of services and products related to lifestyle changes and perceptions regarding health and exercise. Paradoxically, this trend has been paralleled by the success of ultrarich Lady Godiva chocolates and premium ice creams, which runs directly counter to environmental factors! One explanation offered for this curious phenomenon is that the calories consumed are a reward for the exercise and dieting that presumably preceded. Another is that for part of the population, indulgence is and will always be present.

Drucker (1985) proposes a disciplined and organized approach to identifying opportunity. He argues that the process of opportunity identification can be systematized and that opportunities can be found by monitoring seven basic sources: demographic changes, new knowledge, incongruities (gaps between reality and expectations), industry or market structure, unexpected successes or failures, process needs, and changes in perception.

An incongruity can be illustrated by the success of the steel industry's minimills, which defied the principles of economy of scale and have led to significant changes in the steel industry. Another incongruity involved the practice of building larger and larger vessels for transoceanic shipping in order to reduce costs—which were not reduced. Capital costs were actually higher, and both pilferage and idle time in the dock were greater. This incongruity led to the concept of containerized ships and containerized shipping, which drastically reduced loading time and labor costs and provided increased protection for the products shipped.

An example of an unexpected failure was the Edsel automobile. Prior to that failure, automotive marketing segments had been conceived of in terms of income demographics. Its experience with the Edsel led Ford Motor Company to reexamine its marketing approach and move to the concept of lifestyle marketing segments, a key factor in its great Mustang success.

Federal Express was surprised to see an increase in its shipments of high-priced, low-weight computer components. Upon investigation, FedEx learned that this unexpected success was attributable to companies' using its service to keep their inventory levels down, which opened up new and previously overlooked market possibilities.

To discover the unexpected, as some of the aforementioned companies have done, it helps to have expectations. For every function in a firm for which there is an expectation, a history of performance, or a standard (e.g., sales to a market segment, sales per territory, yields from a process), the appearance of unexpected variation can trigger investigation and the identification of new opportunities.

Process needs refer to interruptions or bottlenecks in a process. The Polaroid Land Camera filled a process need—eliminating the delay between capturing a previous moment and finding out whether the moment had been captured. According to legend, it was Land's daughter who asked him, "Why do we have to wait?" The question led Land to invent the Land Camera and Polaroid film.

Another example of a process need is the delay at highway toll stations. According to a recent report, a system involving a scanner that reads an identifying signal on moving vehicles will be tried. The data will be stored and a bill automatically sent to car owners at the end of each month. No more waiting for change or for stationary vehicles to get moving.

We tested Drucker's recommendations for a systematic search process with students in an executive MBA course in corporate venturing and found that his system helped many students identify opportunities in their company or industry. More important, though, we found that the reason the assignment resulted in the generation of so many ideas was not necessarily because of the effectiveness of Drucker's systematic approach but merely because students were required to complete the exercise! Participants in the assignment were quite excited to realize that they could actually develop interesting and possibly viable opportunities simply by working at it.

To summarize the process of identifying opportunity, we would observe that many factors can trigger a flow of ideas, with change and problems being the best sources. Information and a resulting awareness of developments both within the company and industry and in the world at large are essential to the process. Training, education, exposure to information available at trade shows and conventions, publications such as trade and professional journals, and information sharing are powerful stimulants.

EVALUATING AND SELECTING OPPORTUNITY

The process of evaluating and selecting opportunity marks the point at which a firm decides to enter a new business, right? Wrong! Determining whether an opportunity is possibly right for a company is not the same as deciding to enter a business, nor is evaluating an opportunity the same as evaluating a business plan. (In fact, requiring submission of a serious business plan before a business idea or proposal has been presented and interest expressed results in needless wheel spinning and usually great works of fiction.) Entering a business is appropriate only after it has been determined that the opportunity itself is both valid and right for the company and the company has a business strategy and plan to which it is prepared to commit.

Hence, this step in the evolutionary process of venture development is *not* the point at which the decision to start a business is made. Rather, for the proposer of an idea, it is the point at which a business proposal is developed for further exploration. For the decision maker, it is the point at which a preliminary judgment is made as to whether the proposal merits proceeding to the next step—i.e., concept testing or, if the concept test has already taken place, feasibility study. The *only* issue to be resolved at this time is: "Are we interested in pursuing this idea further?" and not "Shall we start this business?"

The business proposal, which should be as short as possible, will range from a single page to as many as five pages, depending entirely on the nature of the venture being considered. The proposal should tentatively answer the following simple questions:

- Is the opportunity consistent with the firm's strategy?
- Is it worth the effort?
- Is it feasible? (Can the firm do it?)

These questions, which have been touched on in earlier chapters, are examined more fully in the following subsections.

Is the Opportunity Consistent with the Firm's Strategy?

In order to generate ideas that will fit the organization's strategy, the firm's mission and strategic objectives should be known and understood and have commitment throughout the firm. Even if they are, however, it may not always be possible to make a definitive decision regarding strategic fit at an early stage of evaluation if size and profit potential are part of the strategic objectives. But if, on its face, the very nature of an opportunity is inconsistent with the firm's strategy, then it should be passed up. To be clear, we are not suggesting that the venture must fit the firm's current capabilities but rather its strategic objectives. In order to survive and grow, many companies absolutely must diversify to some extent—penetrate new industries, gain new knowledge, and enter new markets—and if strategic fit were interpreted to mean perfect fit with today's competency and knowledge, such companies would be doomed to inevitable decline.

Although we have just recommended passing up venture opportunities that are inconsistent with a company's strategic objectives, what about opportunities that seem too good to pass up? A case in point would be the business proposition that looks extremely attractive but involves entering a totally new industry that the firm has rejected as a strategic objective. If an organization uncovers such an opportunity, a spin-off may be desirable. With the spin-off approach, the venture may begin with full funding and majority ownership by the parent corporation, and in time, as the spin-off develops successfully, the parent's ownership may be greatly reduced. This is not uncommon in Japan (Ito 1990), where the parent firm may end up as a minority investor. In fact, 17.5% of the largest Japanese companies are spin-offs—having once been a division of a parent organization. Examples include Toyota Motor Corporation (which was spun off from Toyoda Auto Loom Works) and Yamaha Motors (which was spun off from Yamaha Musical Instruments).

In order for the company to determine strategic consistency, it must examine the business concept in detail. The initial concept should indicate the product/service to be provided, the market segment targets, examples of customers to be targeted, a guesstimate of market size, and the venture's potential value to the firm. Although its value may be purely economic, a venture can offer less tangible benefits as well. It could, for example, serve a defensive function, enhance the company's reputation, or provide a learning opportunity, by giving the company a window on a business or perhaps even enabling it to simply study a business in order to determine whether and how to enter on a larger scale.

The following subsections examine these key questions, which the firm must answer about any new-business concept:

- What factors produce this opportunity?
- What are the character, size, and nature of the market?
- What factors are required for the proposed venture's success?

What Factors Produce This Opportunity?   Identifying the factors responsible for an opportunity enables an organization to make some meaningful judgments about how long those factors are likely to last. For example, a drop in interest rates might provide an opportunity for a new venture related to the building industry. In evaluating such an opportunity, a firm would have to consider how long those lower rates could be expected to continue, which would greatly affect whether to make the entry and how quickly to enter and exit. In contrast, environmental legislation is here to stay, and as a source of opportunity, that factor can be regarded as fairly durable.

An example of an opportunity based on a new technology, rapid market growth, and ready availability of venture capital was the development of the Winchester hard disk industry. An analysis of that industry by Stevenson and Sahlman (1985) demonstrated that the rush to enter resulted in overcapacity, which, combined with changes in technology and a drop in computer sales growth, resulted in severe profit decline and several failures—a scenario that they concluded was somewhat predictable. A rapidly growing market is not, per se, a durable opportunity-producing factor, especially in a fast-moving technological environment.

Although rigorous probing for the factors producing an opportunity is a necessary part of the evaluation process, this does not mean a venture should automatically be rejected if one or more of the underlying factors prove to be temporary, but it will affect such issues as speed, scale, and aggressiveness of entry; investment level; and return requirements.

An important result of this probe is that it will enable the firm to articulate the most critical assumptions on which the proposed business is based. These assumptions will have major implications for the planning process (discussed in Chapter 7) as well as for later decisions about the venture's direction and fate.

What Are the Character, Size, and Nature of the Market? At what stage of its life cycle is the market—not yet in existence, just emerging, static, growing, exploding, declining? Who are the players? What is known about present and potential competitors? What is the current and potential size of the market? What about pricing practices? Quality levels? Margins? What will this venture contribute in terms of value to the customer and with what competitive insulation?

The venture capital industry is a useful source of information about opportunity evaluation. In a study of 47 venture capital firms to identify the characteristics associated with successful ventures, Timmons et al. (1987) learned the following:

- Rather than merely identifying a broad market in general terms, successful ventures tend to identify the true market in very specific terms, including a well-defined notion of the actual customer population, to whom the value-added by the proposed new product or service is clear.
- A market size between $10 million and $100 million is more likely to yield success than a very small or very large market. (This is one finding whose applicability to corporate ventures by large firms is questionable, although it is quite appropriate for smaller firms with limited available capital. For some corporations, even markets having a potential size of $100 million are uninteresting. This finding may reflect the financing abil-

ity of firms backed by venture capital during their early life and may be irrelevant in the case of potentially major new markets, which require massive investment and a longer time frame for harvest than the normal venture capitalist horizon of five to seven years.)

- Market growth rates between 30% and 60% are more favorable than rates outside that range.
- Competitive insulation through patent protection or unique technologies involving products or services that cannot otherwise be provided with equal quality or satisfaction is a major success factor.
- Successful ventures tend to achieve a market share of at least 20%.

What Factors Are Required for the Proposed Venture's Success? Examining success factors is particularly relevant when a company is considering an opportunity that is not directly related to the base business's technology and markets. Although the firm is likely to be very aware of the differences in success factors in the case of proposed new ventures that involve a totally unrelated line of business, there is a great danger of success factors' being insufficiently considered in the case of businesses that appear to be closely related.

For example, packaged food products sold to consumers and those sold to food service establishments look like very closely related product lines—at first glance. Yet the economic structure is quite different, and for many of these products, the technology, distribution channels, product shelf life requirements, and conditions of preparation are different as well. Marketing methods differ and require different selling skills and knowledge. In this example, some of the factors required for success include knowledge of the conditions under which the product will be used, together with the ability to design and modify products in order to fit the conditions of use; familiarity with the different segments of the food

107

service industry and their unique purchasing practices (e.g., government agencies, large hotel/motel chains, fast-food franchises, individual restaurants versus distributors); technical service capability for products processed in food establishments; and reputation in the industry.

To identify the factors necessary for a proposed new venture's success, the company has to ask the following specific question about every function: How must this function differ in the new business as opposed to our present businesses in order for the venture to succeed? Here are some obvious examples:

- A manufacturer of consumer goods moving into industrial markets: Direct selling must be done by people who understand their customers' business and can develop strong relationships with them.
- A manufacturer moving into retailing: The firm must understand such issues as managing inventories; providing security to protect against theft; recruiting and training salespeople who are congenial, knowledgeable, and helpful to customers; and selecting business locations.
- A manufacturer, retailer, or distributor entering a new industry: The firm must develop knowledge of customer needs and wants, major competitors, supplier sources, technology, usage patterns, and problems.

When analyzing required success factors, the company must also understand the relative importance of the various functions involved (such as marketing, manufacturing, finance, human resources, and R&D). For example, in the retail business, merchandising (what to buy, how to price, how to promote) and information systems are critical; in commodity businesses, buying and trading reign. If a company is considering, say, a venture in which the marketing function is primary, it can be disastrous to initiate the venture under the direction of a manager whose skills lie mainly in the area of technology management.

An organization seeking clues to the factors required for the success of a proposed new business would be well advised to study leading companies in the target industry and identify what accounts for their outstanding track record.

Is the Opportunity Worth the Effort?

To determine feasibility and potential value, a firm must analyze each opportunity's economic potential, asking itself, in effect, what the upside gain and downside loss could be.

For guidelines, we turn once again to the venture capital industry, in which the economic characteristics of successful ventures reportedly include the following:

- A break-even time of less than 36 months
- Stable gross margins of 20% to 50%
- After-tax profit potential of 10% to 15%
- Multiple rather than one-shot investments
- For industrial customers, payback in 18 months or less
- Low asset intensity
- Differentiation on the basis of product rather than price (Timmons et al. 1987)

A few of these attributes are obviously inapplicable to many corporate ventures. A required break-even time of 36 months is not feasible in the case of ventures that are based on new technology, that have a high potential, or that involve new or emerging markets. Low asset intensity is undesirable if the corporation's economic power is to be used to erect entry barriers to competition. New industries are not created with low asset intensity (e.g., semiconductors, biotechnology), nor can new entrants to a field, such as the automotive industry, be competitive without heavy investment in manufacturing facilities.

Nevertheless, the venture capital guidelines stated here are applicable to medium-sized corporations that cannot take

Figure 4-1: Evaluating an Opportunity

Does it contribute to strategy fulfillment?
    If yes, then
What factors produce it? Will they continue?
    If yes, then
Is the market potential sufficient?
    If yes, then
What success factors are required? Can we supply them?
    If yes, then
Do we have a sustainable competitive advantage?
    If yes, then
What are the economics? Is it worth it?

---

large investment risks as well as to big corporations that want to learn about venturing by starting small.

Some additional factors that venturing corporations should consider include:

- Impact on overall corporate performance during the venture's early period—profits, ROI, cash flow
- Impact of entry on the firm's existing customers and business
- Potential impact on total sales, profit, positioning, and the value of company stock
- Impact on firm's overall competitive advantage

Figure 4-1 illustrates the process for evaluating opportunity.

Is the Opportunity Feasible for the Firm?   In evaluating a potential opportunity, the company must also consider whether it is in a position to supply the factors required for the venture's success. The ideal opportunity is one for which the firm already possesses precisely the mix of special competencies needed to provide the success factors and the strategic fit is clear. But if the company lacks the means to provide the required success factors, it can also assemble the necessary competencies through alliances, joint ventures, and so forth.

One universally required success factor is knowledge and experience in the proposed industry (except for cases in which the industry itself is entirely new). Unless the firm has or can employ knowledgeable people or can acquire a foothold firm to provide that knowledge and experience, the opportunity should be dropped or delayed until the firm can learn something about the business through a small-scale entry or an acquisition.

CONCLUSION

To start the process of identifying opportunities, a company creates a flow of innovative ideas, which it can do by recruiting creative people and then stimulating their creativity by providing goals, information, training, and reward systems. Opportunities can be evaluated using practical analytical methods designed to answer the following fundamental questions:

- Will the proposed new business advance the firm's strategy?
- Is it worth the effort that will be required?
- Can the firm do it?

As the organization identifies, evaluates, and selects opportunities, it lays the groundwork for future stages in the venturing process, because the work done at this stage provides information that will prove invaluable for creating and evaluating the venture business plan (discussed in Chapter 7) and making later decisions about managing the venture.

Guidelines

1. Recruit, train, and retain creative people.
2. Clarify the organization's goals.
3. Evaluate the factors responsible for creating a proposed opportunity. Will they last long enough?
4. Learn what factors are required in order to achieve success with the proposed opportunity. Can your company supply those factors?
5. In evaluating an opportunity, you must answer three questions: Does the proposed undertaking advance organizational strategy? Is it worth the risk and effort? Is it feasible for the company?

REFERENCES

Drucker, Peter. 1985. *Innovation and Entrepreneurship.* New York: Harper & Row.

Hanan, Mack. 1976. *Venture Management.* New York: McGraw-Hill.

Ito, Kiyohiko. 1990. "Spinoffs: A Flexible Strategic Alternative." Working paper. Stern School of Business, New York University.

MacMillan, I. C., and George, R. 1985. "Corporate Venturing: Challenges for Senior Managers." *Journal of Business Strategy* 5, no. 3: 34–43.

Stevenson, H. H., and Sahlman, W. A. 1985. "Capital Market Myopia." *Journal of Business Venturing* 1, no. 1: 7–30.

Timmons, J. A.; Muzyka, D. F.; Stevenson, H. H.; and Bygrave, W. D. 1987. "Opportunity Recognition: The Core of Entrepreneurship." *Frontiers of Entrepreneurship Research* (Babson College): 109–121.

von Hippel, E. 1978. "Successful Industrial Products from Customer Ideas." *Journal of Marketing* (January): 39ff.

5

Selecting, Evaluating, and Compensating Venture Management

Organizations committed to creating a venturing program must find and develop people with entrepreneurial talent and skills, learn to evaluate their performance as venture managers realistically, and provide fair compensation and rewards that promote the initiation and long-term success of ventures. Furthermore, these steps must be taken with an awareness of changing management needs during a venture's life cycle.

A corporate environment produces unique human resource management challenges, which can be major obstacles to venturing unless they are effectively handled. This chapter discusses the selection, evaluation, and compensation/incentive practices followed by many corporations and examines the relationship between these practices and venture performance. It also offers selection, evaluation, and compensation/incentive strategies designed to fit the specific needs of both the parent company and venture managers.

113

CHOOSING VENTURE MANAGEMENT

The composition of the venture team is the most important decision that will be made for any new venture. It is at least as critical as the choice of which business to enter, if not more so. In the venture capital community, one often hears such comments as "Bet on the jockey, not on the horse" or "I'd rather back an outstanding entrepreneur with a mediocre business idea than an outstanding business idea with a mediocre entrepreneur." But the selection and motivation of these venture managers is one of the most difficult issues confronting senior corporate managers, particularly human resource executives.

For an entrepreneur operating outside a corporation, selection and motivation are relatively simple issues. The independent entrepreneur simply finds a source of capital and makes a deal. If his or her projections are not fulfilled, a venture capital firm will usually negotiate provisions for greater control of the enterprise or even replacement of the entrepreneur. Compensation arrangements include salary and performance incentives, especially stock ownership and options for members of the venture team. Share values are determined by the marketplace, or in the absence of an existing market, investment bankers may be used to price the stock.

The corporate venturing situation is quite different. A corporation enters a new business in order to ensure its long-term survival and improve corporate performance. Unlike the venture capital firm, the parent of a corporate venture does not normally look for gain through downstream sale of its interest in the venturing unit. From the standpoint of the parent firm, a new venture's performance has a direct impact on the parent's cash flow and profit—and the effect is usually negative for the first few years, if not longer. Thus, the potential economic parameters of a corporate venture are quite different from those of an independent startup. Furthermore, the internal corporate venture manager is an employee of the firm, often recruited rather than self-selected. He or she does not have a choice of alternative funding sources, is unwilling

114

or unable to leave the firm, and may be unwilling to take major personal economic risk.

Despite the fact that internal corporate ventures operate within the parameters of an existing organizational structure and can avail themselves of organizational resources, the choice of venture management is no less critical for corporate startups than for independent ones.

In the following subsections, we consider the roles to be filled on the venture team, how management needs can be expected to evolve over the course of the venture's life cycle, how the company can find potential venture managers and grow new ones, and product champions as potential venture managers.

Roles That Must Be Filled on the Venture Team

In putting together the venture team, senior management must ensure that certain key roles are filled. The following list, drawn largely from studies of technological ventures by Maidique (1980), outlines the most significant of these roles:

- *Technical innovator:* the person who has made the major technical innovation
- *Business innovator (or venture manager):* the internal entrepreneur responsible for the overall progress of the project
- *Product champion:* any individual who makes a decisive contribution to the project by promoting its progress through the critical early stages, particularly up to the point of implementation
- *Chief executive of the innovative organization:* the individual who is in charge of the venture (although not necessarily of the parent firm) and controls the allocation of resources (e.g., a sub-CEO, a division manager, or a venture division manager)
- *Executive champion:* the high-level person in the parent company who acts as buffer, protector, and mod-

ifier of rules and policies and who helps the venture obtain the needed resources

To ensure the venture's success, senior management must see that *all* these roles are filled. For instance, failure to provide an executive champion to run interference for the venture creates additional burdens for the innovators, who should spend their time building the new business instead of overcoming internal obstacles.

In addition to filling the "generic" roles just listed, senior management must also ensure that the venture team contains individuals with the required specific functional competencies. A common practice, to be avoided, is to name a team of competent functional specialists with no clear entrepreneurial leader. A marketing person, plus a finance person, plus a manufacturing person, etc., do not add up to one entrepreneur. No matter how capable individual team members might be, the team must be led and the activities of its members integrated.

Venture Life Cycle and Changing Management Needs

Greiner (1972) has described the changes a maturing business undergoes as it passes through the various stages in its life cycle. (How a venture's life-cycle stage affects its management requirements is discussed in detail in Chapter 10, "A Survival Guide for Venture Managers.") Although we will not detail the skills and management characteristics required at every stage of a venture's development, we will mention a few key considerations.

Even with the help of an executive champion, the corporate venture manager must at every stage of a venture possess the ability to function within a larger corporate framework. This is essential to gain the support and collaboration needed while acting in the best interests of both the corporation and the venture. Beyond this basic fact of life, the leadership of a new venture faces constantly shifting demands. In the following paragraphs, we outline some of the demands facing the venture manager at the inception of a new business, the most critical period of its life cycle.

In the preventure stage, before the venture idea has become an actual business, the outstanding characteristics needed by the person leading the effort are persistence, resourcefulness, high energy, and charisma—together with the ability to communicate clearly and effectively and to sell internally. It is at this preventure stage that the ability to manage the expectations of three primary constituencies—superiors, members of the venture, and members of the organization at large—is crucial. Although unreasonably optimistic expectations will come back to haunt the venture and its manager downstream, excessively conservative expectations can kill all support at the outset. Will the venture leader attract supporters and allies in the firm? Can he or she win and retain the support of an executive champion?

When senior management is considering the choice of a leader for this initial stage, it should examine each candidate's longer-term objectives. Some candidates will want to develop as the manager of the new business over the long term; others will see the task as a step toward promotion to higher levels in the parent firm; still others will want the opportunity to start more new ventures; and some will want to return to their previous position and activity once the venture has achieved the status of an established business. Business starters who want to continue starting new businesses should be able to look forward to that as a reward for successful start-ups (Pinchot 1985).

Senior management must understand and make clear to prospective venture managers that it will not be regarded as a sign of failure if a venture's initial manager is not interested in or is not right for the venture's later stages. In fact, if the experience of the venture capital community is any indicator, the best venture starters are in all probability not going to be the best professional managers.

However, this is not to imply that new-business starters should be ruled out as long-term managers. These individuals can continue to lead their ventures if they recognize their limitations and augment their skills by building a complementary management team. Leaders who are adept at identifying weaknesses, especially their own, and who act to supplement themselves can build highly effective teams and thereby increase their managerial and leadership capabilities.

Sources of Venture Managers

In selecting venture managers, should the organization accept volunteers or seek recruits? The answer is closely related to the firm's risk/reward system and its culture.

It is difficult to get volunteers to expose themselves to significant career risk without the possibility of corresponding gain. Some companies reduce or protect against the risks, whereas others provide high rewards to compensate for them. To encourage volunteers, many firms offer safety nets by guaranteeing return to the former job if either the manager or the venture fails. Sometimes such offers include whatever raises the manager might have gotten had he or she remained at the previous position.

Although these enticements may generate more volunteers, it would appear that an adequate supply of venture managers can be found without them. Even though, as reported by Kanter (1989), ATT Technologies did not offer a guarantee of return to original jobs, it had no difficulty attracting volunteers.

Once an organization has attracted volunteers, how can they be screened? The Foresight Group, a consulting and training organization based in Sweden that assists firms in generating intrapreneurship and training intrapreneurs, works only with volunteers within a firm who have a business idea. When proposals and prospective intrapreneurs are screened, the first question asked of applicants is, "What have you done so far in your life?" The Foresight Group looks for people who have actually accomplished something—virtually anything that indicates initiative, action orientation, and the will and energy to complete a task.

An organization can also find qualified venture managers through internal recruitment. A manager of a Du Pont venture group stated in an interview that in his experience, recruiting can work very well.

Certainly, there is no reason not to choose a volunteer if one is available who meets the venture's requirements, but regardless of whether the venture manager is a volunteer or a recruit, enthusiasm, desire, and competence are essential.

Growing Future Venture Managers

A company that is seriously committed to promoting venturing must do more than passively round up whatever likely looking volunteers or recruits it happens to have available. It must make an active effort to increase the supply of managers with the skills and attitudes necessary to successfully lead new ventures.

One way to spot such potential is to seek individuals in the firm who have shown initiative: the engineer who shepherded a new process through to successful commercial use, the salesperson who developed a new territory, the product manager who managed a new-product launch, the human resource person who developed or initiated new and more effective training methods, the researcher who moved a product into production—all activities requiring leadership and an ability to develop collaboration, cooperation, and support.

A second approach is to give people assignments requiring entrepreneurial behavior—i.e., to create a process that produces a pool of possible venture managers and team members. A researcher who shows signs of commercial interest could be teamed with people from marketing and sales to develop new accounts; market researchers could be put on a new-product commercialization team; or plant managers could be assigned to the startup of a new physical facility.

119

One research director identified staff members with what he called "an instinct for the jugular vein" and offered them opportunities by challenging them to serve on commercialization teams for new-product or new-process introductions, which produced a number of future venture managers.

This process of growing venture managers can be promoted by ensuring that human resource managers use appropriate criteria in hiring and evaluating employees. For instance, the corporation can stimulate innovative activity by assessing entrepreneurial and innovative initiatives as part of the performance evaluation program. Human resource managers can provide invaluable help in identifying, recruiting, training, compensating, and designing career paths for innovators and internal entrepreneurs.

To be effective at this task, HR managers need to understand the characteristics of opportunity-driven, entrepreneurial employees and recruits. Paradoxically, the very characteristics that distinguish such people are the same characteristics that sometimes mark them as "troublemakers" and frequently prevent their employment in large firms. But action orientation, self-direction, and the need for autonomy are not incompatible with the ability to function as part of a team. The presence of these characteristics can be detected by using the Myers-Briggs Type Indicator (1976) and the Schein Career Anchors Inventory (1985)—two test instruments that can provide valuable information but should be administered only by people trained to do so. Although the results of these tests can help an organization identify people with the characteristics necessary for effective venture management, senior managers should keep in mind that these characteristics alone are not sufficient and that promising test results are therefore no guarantee that a candidate will be able to build successful businesses.

The experience and accomplishments of potential candidates are the most important predictors of success, and if there exists a track record of accomplishment in challenging projects that required learning a lot quickly, team building, high energy, and resourcefulness, the choice is relatively easy. If no such record exists—as with entry-level candidates, relatively new people, or those who have been employed in traditional managerial tasks—testing can be very useful.

Product Champions and Venture Management

The most obvious choice for venture manager is often the product champion—the person who vigorously supports and promotes the venture idea to the point of approval. Although the product champion might sometimes be a good choice, actual experience is also important. Sykes' analysis of the Exxon Enterprises venturing experience (1986) showed that better results were obtained when venture management had specific experience in the market as well as a successful management track record. On the other hand, Sandburg and Hofer's study of 17 firms engaged in corporate venturing (1987) found no relationship between prior entrepreneurial experience or management experience in a related industry and venture performance. Clearly, the scope, scale, and nature of the venture, together with the nature and stage of development of the market and industry, will determine the experience and resourcefulness required. The one thing we're sure of is that knowledge of the business and the market combined with creativity, high energy, and management skills is a tough act to beat!

When making a venture management decision, it's hard to ignore the enthusiasm and drive of product champions, but putting them in charge of a venture does have some potential risks. In one study (Block and Subbanarasimha 1989), senior managers were asked to specify the relative weights of two key factors in choosing ventures—i.e., to what extent the decision was based on the business proposition itself versus the presence of a product champion. Firms with a poorer track record in venturing tended to select ventures mainly *because* of the presence of a product champion. Although it is obvious that most ventures would never see the light of day without a champion, it is also possible that as manager, the product champion may unnecessarily increase the company's losses by encouraging overly prolonged efforts to revive moribund ventures rather than killing them in a timely manner.

At the other extreme, choosing as venture manager an experienced administrative manager steeped in the practices and policies of the parent firm often leads to an excessive focus on administration as opposed to building a business. Such managers tend to follow organizational rules rather than find ways to get the rules modified or suspended in order to allow the new business to survive and grow.

Deciding whether to put the product champion in charge of the venture is just one example of the challenges involved in responding to the evolving needs of a new business as it progresses from an idea requiring approval to an actual startup.

EVALUATING THE PERFORMANCE OF VENTURE MANAGEMENT

According to traditional criteria, it makes sense to evaluate the performance of the venture team and its leadership by how close they come to achieving their objectives. But the problem lies in specifying what the new business is trying to achieve, because nobody really knows what the objectives are going to be. Furthermore, the initial objectives are quite likely to change. "There is no 'present' in which people know where they are going, what they are supposed to do, and what the results are or should be" (Drucker 1985, 188).

Although each venture can begin with clear objectives, experience shows that they must be modified to fit reality. In a sense, it is very much like a battle plan prepared before the outbreak of hostilities. General Norman Schwarzkopf described such a case in a spring 1991 address to West Point cadets in which he explained the careful planning done preparatory to engagement. Comparing the situation to that of an orchestra about to perform according to written music, the conductor (general) raises the baton, and "just at that point some son of a bitch with a bayonet jumps into the orchestra pit and starts chasing people all over the place, which plays hell with all the careful planning. . . ." Schwarzkopf made the point in response to planners unfamiliar with warfare who had criticized battle results for failing to meet planned objectives.

As we show in Chapter 7, business plan projections rarely, if ever, correspond with ultimate reality. About half of all ventures never even become profitable, and indeed, profitability is not always an objective. Furthermore, evidence indicates that the performance of a firm's entire venturing effort can be drastically affected by large losses in a single venture, so one objective must be to kill the fatally wounded as early as possible. (See Chapter 9, "Controlling the Venture.")

Evaluation Criteria

The evaluation criteria suggested in this subsection flow from one objective: to create a successful business if possible while at the same time protecting the parent organization against excessive losses and maximizing learning. These criteria are as follows:

- Actual completion of planned events
- Completion of events competently in a reasonable time and at a reasonable cost
- Quality of the conclusions drawn from completed events and alteration of assumptions and plans to fit new realities (i.e., evidence of learning and its application)
- Actual business results, judged both on an absolute basis and by comparison with projections
- Evidence of commitment (in terms of energy and hard work) to making the venture a success
- Evidence of team spirit

- Ability to obtain collaboration from other parts of the firm
- Ability to overcome internal obstacles and red tape without putting the firm at risk
- Minimal turnover of venture team members
- Parsimony in the use of resources
- Training and development of team personnel

These criteria are important at every stage of the venture's development, since they are the input factors that will produce the output results.

The most sensitive of these criteria is the evaluation of actual business results. In performing this evaluation, it is vital that senior managers fully recognize the venture's stage of development and take into account the reasonableness of the original expectations in light of unfolding experience and actual knowledge gained. The core of evaluation, however, involves the completion of events and the subsequent adaptation of plans and actions to reflect what has been learned. Performance deficiency can be defined as failure to complete an event and/or failure either to learn anything from the results or to apply what has been learned to future actions.

But it is crucial to avoid confusing mismanagement with misfortune. Take the example of a company that has the bad luck of launching a new business based on a technology that is suddenly and unexpectedly rendered obsolete by an even newer technological development. Mismanagement in such a case might very well consist of continuing the firm's high-energy, high-expense effort to grow that business (as happened with the Polaroid instant motion picture camera, which was displaced as a potential consumer product by the videotape recorder). Good management in such a case would consist of objectively recognizing the new realities and either changing the venture's direction significantly or closing it down. In this latter event, the venture manager should be rewarded for preventing additional losses in a hopeless cause.

The criteria presented in this subsection can be useful to senior managers in evaluating the efforts and input activities that affect a venture's success or failure and in deciding whether to change, train, or supplement venture leadership. They can also serve as result evaluation points, which can be employed as a basis for determining compensation and incentive payment.

COMPENSATING VENTURE MANAGEMENT

We start this section by discussing how compensation is related to venture performance, after which, we examine compensation strategies and practices commonly used by venturing corporations and consider what can be learned from venture capital compensation practices. In the last two subsections, we present the components of an incentive/reward program for venture management and show how a firm can develop an effective incentive program.

Does Money Really Talk?

There is no convincing evidence that any specific financial compensation and incentive plan is related to venture performance. Research seeking such relationships is sparse, and the results reveal little, although there is some evidence that the payment of bonuses is related to better performance both of individual ventures and of overall venturing programs (Block and Ornati 1987; Steele and Baker 1986).

Conventional wisdom holds that compensation is very important. A large majority of the managers we spoke to in three *Fortune* 100 firms (as part of a series of unpublished surveys) identified inappropriate compensation as a significant obstacle to venture success. Interviews with venture managers reveal uniformly that all would like to see compensation programs related to the venture's rewards to the firm, yet each person questioned stated that he or she would act no differently regardless of the compensation program.

Given the absence of data establishing a clear correlation

125

between compensation and venture performance, together with the strong feeling on the part of both venture personnel and many senior managers interviewed that compensation is a serious issue, it is difficult to reach firm conclusions about the significance of financial incentives and rewards.

It would appear that their significance depends on the characteristics and needs of the individual venture manager and the needs of the organization. In a competitive bid to hire a venture manager from outside the company or an effort to keep a highly visible manager from jumping ship, money can be a deciding factor. If an internal person must be wooed away from another major assignment in the firm, it can be decisive. (Tektronix, a high-tech firm, reports that financial incentives were required to get eminent scientists in the organization to join an entrepreneurial venture.)

If a venture management candidate just doesn't make enough to maintain an adequate standard of living, money can be crucial. If the candidate is already earning a high income and has no pressing financial needs but does have strong needs for independence and achievement, it will probably be less important. As a demonstration of appreciation for the value and contributions of the venture team, and as a simple matter of fairness, financial incentives and rewards can be very important, regardless of whether the team needs or desires them. And as compensation for the career risk being taken by venture managers, money may be very relevant.

In short, although incentives and compensation don't appear to have much of an impact on how a venture is managed, they may affect the organization's ability to retain outstanding people who are offered better incentives elsewhere as well as managers' willingness to take the career risks involved in venturing.

It is also possible no one has yet developed and tested a program of financial incentives and rewards that would have a positive impact on venture performance or that such a program, if it exists, has not been publicized. Finally, it would appear that no one has developed a program designed to prevent serious overcommitment to failing ventures.

Current Compensation Strategies and Practices

A survey by Block and Ornati (1987) involving 42 *Fortune* 1,000 firms gives an indication of the practices presently followed in compensating venture managers. This survey shows that:

- More than 30% of the firms compensated venture managers differently than other managers.
- More than 50% of all respondents, including firms without special incentives, believed that variable bonuses based on venture ROI should be used to improve venture management performance, and more than 50% of the firms with programs used this incentive.
- More than 50% of the firms using incentives believed that there should be a ceiling on incentives—ranging from 50% to 200% of salary.
- Internal equity was the major obstacle cited by firms that did not have an incentive program. Other obstacles included the difficulty of determining venture goals, concern about shareholder objections, and administrative complexity. In contrast, those firms that did have a program pointed to the difficulty of determining venture goals as the most significant obstacle. Internal equity was not regarded as an important obstacle in those firms.

The following sample of compensation arrangements for venture management shows the wide range of approaches to this issue—from extremely generous bonuses and percentages to no special compensation at all:

- *Milestone awards:* Tektronix reported using an incentive system that provides awards with a target of 4 to 5 times salary over five to seven years for venture leaders and 1 to 3 times salary for key people (Steele and Baker 1986). Awards are offered at four stages: upon product approval, upon engineering release, upon shipping release, and when production and profit maximization occur.

- *Risk levels:* ATT Technologies offered venture participants three risk levels (Kanter 1989), similar to those suggested by Block and Ornati (1987). The first level is standard compensation—for the participants' job level, unrelated to the venture activity; the second involves an agreement to freeze salaries until the venture generates a positive cash flow, at which point venture participants can receive a one-time bonus of up to 150% of their salary; the third involves participants' contributing up to 15% of their salary until the venture reaches positive cash flow and profitability. Payoff can be up to 8 times their investment.

- *Personal investment:* GTE, as part of an intrapreneurial program in one of its divisions, also offered a salary contribution program, with salary frozen. Up to 10% of salary would be contributed with no change in salary until a $100,000 profit is reached for a full year, at which time salary is restored to foregone income and frozen for another year. The maximum cumulative team award is $1,920,000. Other awards consist of "intracapital" funds, which the recipient can invest in another new venture. In its recently disbanded venturing activity, Kodak also had a program of salary reduction or investment, including a formula for potential return and a ceiling.

- *Percentage of profit:* DCA Food Industries, an industrial food ingredients firm, provided a percentage of gross profit earned from new ventures to the venture teams for a limited time period (five years). This sum could vary by 20% either way, depending on parent company ROI. There was no ceiling.

- *Discretionary bonuses:* Du Pont awards after-the-fact, discretionary bonuses to venture champions and teams.

- *Nothing:* At the present time, 3M provides no special compensation for venture managers or teams, although the record of former venture managers' becoming top executives, including CEO, is well known at 3M.

What Can Be Learned from Practices in the Venture Capital Industry?

Practices in the venture capital industry have significantly influenced the development of incentives for venture managers. Many firms have made an effort to design programs that can provide a capital gain path similar to that possible for independent entrepreneurs, although not with the same potential.

Is it a mistake for corporations to attempt to duplicate compensation systems used in the venture capital industry? As we noted earlier, there is very little similarity between the needs of a venture capital investor and a corporate investor in an internal venture. Regardless of their nobility of purpose, venture capitalists are primarily interested in making money by investing relatively small amounts in firms that will increase in market value and produce a profit for the venture capital partnership through the sale of shares within a five- to seven-year time frame. The potential for a five- to tenfold gain is often considered a prerequisite for investment.

Contrast this scenario with the interests of a prospective corporate venturer. Stock price is important, but for established corporations, performance is measured by return on investment, changes in market share, and reputation among customers. A corporation starts a new venture in order to improve its performance or protect itself against competition. The measure of a venture's success is its impact on ROI, market share, market position, growth rate, and reputation— not how much its stock can be sold for within seven years.

The risks faced by independent versus corporate entrepreneurs must also be weighed in developing an appropriate compensation system. Although, in many ways, it is much easier to start an independent business than a corporate venture because of corporate red tape, politics, and restrictions, the corporate venture manager takes less financial risk and has far more potential support in terms of knowledge and human and physical resources. Hypothetically, the risk of failure should be much less in a corporate venture, especially if the firm has some experience with the market and the technology. No directly comparable figures are available on failure rates in similar industries, but a recent study does indicate that on a percentage basis, the survival rate for corporate ventures may actually be greater than for private ventures (Block and Subbanarasimha 1989).

The personality characteristics and needs of corporate venturers versus independent entrepreneurs are also crucial. The motivation of entrepreneurs has received a great deal of research attention, and there is general agreement that they are driven by the need to find and fulfill opportunities and to realize a vision. Money is a measure and not a motivation, according to many studies. Entrepreneurs are very largely self-directed and require a high degree of autonomy (which also seems to be true of individuals who exhibit outstanding performance in many managerial tasks).

In contrast, entrepreneurs who choose to work in a corporate setting want interaction with and recognition by their peers, along with the relative safety of corporate sponsorship and employment. Our experience (albeit not supported by empirical data) has led us to conclude that corporate entrepreneurs have greater social needs than independent entrepreneurs, require greater social and political skills, and are rarely willing to personally risk everything on a new business. By functioning within an organizational framework, corporate venture managers are in fact demonstrating their willingness to accept more external control than their counterparts on the outside.

Even so, technical entrepreneurs leave existing firms and seek venture capital backing for a variety of reasons: frustration at not being supported in pursuing an opportunity of their choice, seduction by the prospect of obtaining very high rewards outside the corporation, and a growing need for greater independence than can be achieved within the corporation. An ironic corollary of the effort to generate internal corporate entrepreneurship is that the more successful the effort, the greater the firm's likelihood of losing good people. No company can support every proposal. The more proposals it generates, the more will be rejected—and as the rejection rate rises, so does the departure rate for proposers.

Potential Components of an Incentive/Reward Program for Venture Management

We now provide a menu of possible incentive/reward components, which will be followed by a model that can help senior managers design a system to fit their firm and venture.

The four possible types of incentives are:

1. Equity and equity equivalents
2. Bonuses
3. Salary increases and promotions
4. Recognition incentives and rewards

The following subsections examine each of these components in greater detail.

Equity and Equity Equivalents.   The rationale for using equity is clear and simple: it is an effort to emulate the independent entrepreneur's situation, in which the founder can share in the firm's gain in value and have a piece of the action (i.e., it enables the corporate venturer to be a pseudo-owner). Equity or equity equivalents can be provided as shares or options for shares in the parent firm, shares or share options in the venture if it exists as a separate corporate entity, or phantom shares or share options in the venture if it is not separately incorporated.

Equity awards may be made outright at the start of the venture, or they may be earned over a period of time. The time period for cashing out is usually specified, and there may be provisions for cashing out if the parent corporation changes strategy or discontinues the venture. Criteria for venture and venture management performance required to trigger any cash-out may also be included. And in the absence of market liquidity, the agreement should provide a formula for buyback by the parent that reflects any increase in the venture's value.

The essential characteristics of equity participation are that it is a relatively long-term incentive, and the upside gain potential is normally greater than with other forms of incentives.

Bonuses. The following are examples of the types of bonus programs used by venturing companies:

- Fixed amounts, known in advance, for achieving specified results in a specified time period (e.g., a sales level, cash flow result, profit level of ROI, and completion of milestone events)
- Variable, calculable percentages of results achieved in a specified time period (e.g., a percentage of sales or of surplus cash flow over a predetermined level or of profit based on ROI)
- Discretionary amounts awarded after the fact for major contributions

Bonus plans may involve a short- or long-term payout (or both), with the awards ranging from very modest sums to very large ones. (One venture manager accumulated 4 times the base salary within a two-year period through a bonus calculated as a percentage of gross profit in a new venture.) Bonus awards can be triggered by significant accomplishments, such as the milestones described in Chapter 7.

Salary Increases and Promotions. Incentive or reward programs involving salary increases and promotions are based on the premise that managing a new venture is no different from other corporate activities and should be compensated like any other job. In a firm whose basic climate has for years required innovation and continual generation of new products and new businesses, effective new-venture or innovation management becomes a standard requirement for advancement. As noted earlier in this section, one of the most successful venturing firms in the world, 3M, has no special compensation program for venture managers—but 3M's CEOs generally emerge from the ranks of those who have successfully managed new ventures.

Recognition Incentives and Rewards.   In many firms, and for many people, nonfinancial incentives may be more important than financial ones. Examples of nonfinancial incentives include recognition ceremonies and awards (sometimes involving money, as in Du Pont's case), increased autonomy (Pinchot 1985), sponsorship of sabbaticals and special studies, the opportunity to start more ventures, and recognition by peers. (A study of a telecommunications company's R&D unit revealed that innovators regarded peer recognition as more important than management recognition—since management was unable to fully appreciate the technical significance of most innovations!)

Such nonfinancial incentives are effective in companies whose culture is consistent with the awards ceremony. For instance, one highly innovative firm specializing in financial information pays salaries lower than the Wall Street market average. Not only does this firm tend to retain its innovative people, but those who do leave often return because of the firm's collegial climate and the sense of freedom it offers. Its annual innovation award ceremony, at which relatively modest sums are presented, is a highlight of the year.

Such incentives are not likely to be effective, however, if they are the organization's only manifestation of recognition and, more important, if the organization is unwilling to grant increased freedom of action to people who have earned it. Kanter (1989), reporting reactions from recipients of such

133

awards at Ohio Bell in its Enter-Prize program, states that "substantive attention rather than monetary reward was in some cases more highly prized" (256).

Developing an Incentive Model

The overall objectives of an incentive program are clear: to promote a venture's success and reduce the cost of failure if that should be unavoidable. Because the primary function of incentives is to attract and retain qualified people and enhance their morale, we need to examine the venture success factors that are both directly related to people and capable of being affected by an incentive program. Other critical success factors (such as having the right product at the right time for the right market and ensuring that that product is competently developed, produced, and marketed) are therefore beyond the scope of this examination.

Venture Success Factors, People Factors, and Compensation Strategies.   Table 5-1 provides an overview of the incentive plan features that affect each of the human factors considered essential to a venture's success: enthusiasm and continuing commitment, effective teamwork, organizational support, and recognizing and adapting to reality.

Enthusiasm and continuing commitment.   Both the venture leader and the team must demonstrate enthusiasm and sustained commitment to making the venture a success. Without this force to carry the venture through inevitable difficulties, it will founder. In this respect, corporations can learn from venture capitalists, who regard this factor as essential. Entrepreneurs seeking venture capital demonstrate enthusiasm and commitment through their sweat equity, through their financial investment, and often through their willingness to take a low salary out of the business during its early stages, in the confidence that the downstream gain will make such sacrifices worthwhile.

Table 5-1: Incentive Features Associated with People-Related Venture Success Factors

Success Factor	Incentive Features
Enthusiasm and continuing commitment	Significant earning potential Direct relationship between incentives and performance Competitiveness Financial and symbolic significance Rapidity of feedback Individualization
Effective teamwork	Teamwide incentives Fairness of distribution Team recognition
Organizational support	Perception of fairness Balance between potential risks and rewards
Recognizing and adapting to reality	Payment for results, not for strict adherence to plan Significant personal financial risk for venture managers

Note: Sykes (1992), summarizing his study of venture personnel-compensation practices of eight major corporations, suggests that the compensation plan should: match rewards against achievement and personal risk; provide congruence between individual, venture, and corporate goals; be flexible enough to adapt to changes in corporate strategy; emphasize team versus individual rewards; and be perceived as fair by those outside as well as those in the plan. Sykes, H. B. "Incentive Compensation for Corporate Venture Personnel," *Journal of Business Venturing* (July 1992): 253–265.

In designing an incentive program that supports enthusiasm and continuing commitment, the organization must consider the following incentive features:

- *Significant earning potential:* The very great odds that most (albeit not all) starting venture managers will not be around for very long should be taken into account. Hence, the incentive plan should be designed to reflect the actual possibility of achievement, and incentives should be considered which provide for replacing the starting manager at some future point.

- *Direct relationship between incentives and performance:* The venture's actual results or the extent to which it is meeting its plan should be assessed.
- *Competitiveness:* Keeping a firm's incentive program competitive does not necessarily involve financial considerations alone. Special attention should be given to providing autonomy and ensuring that the company's culture remains attractive to innovative and entrepreneurial managers.
- *Financial and symbolic significance:* The organization should consider both the financial needs of its venture managers and the symbolic value of the incentives offered.
- *Rapidity of feedback:* The faster the feedback, the better. All achievers, not just venture managers, want quick feedback. Handing out recognition awards long after everyone has forgotten what occasioned them frequently has the effect of annoying rather than encouraging recipients.
- *Individualization:* Depending on the manager's life status, cash may be more important than stock, fame may be more important than money, and promotion and greater responsibility may be more important than any of the other rewards. Since life status changes (e.g., kids start or finish college), the incentive plan should also be flexible enough to permit change— which makes more work for designers and negotiators but is essential to satisfy the plan's "customer."

Effective teamwork.   Big businesses cannot be built without committed and effective teams. A major advantage that large firms should have over independents is their access to a staff of highly competent professionals who have an appreciation of teamwork. This does not mean, however, that individual achievement and initiatives are hidden behind the facade of an anonymous team, any more than a star quarterback's performance is hidden behind the protection of a star lineman. Individual achievements must be recognized along with team achievement.

In designing an incentive plan, the organization can use the following features to enhance the effectiveness of team action:

- *Teamwide incentives:* For the past five years, Tektronix has provided incentives for every employee of its new ventures and is convinced that this promotes team effort. Similarly, venture capital investors usually like to see incentives made available to all key people, not just to the senior venture manager.
- *Fairness of distribution:* Although there will necessarily be differentials between senior venture managers and other team members, the division of incentives among the entire team must be fair. A scheme used by one product development organization involved accumulating a pool of funds based on a percentage of the margin contribution from the products developed by the unit. Each year, the pool was divided among all the unit's members in proportion to the salary received by each member as a percentage of total salaries paid. The only exception was the unit's senior manager, who received a higher percentage.
- *Team recognition:* Nothing turns a team off as much as seeing one team member singled out for a recognition award when many have contributed to the achievement. Providing recognition for teams as well as for individuals is critical to an incentive plan's effectiveness.

Organizational support.   The economic value of voluntary support, both formal and informal, from different parts of the organization is incalculable. At Du Pont, for example, this kind of support is part of the culture. Without it, a venture unit is doomed if it remains in the parent structure, despite the fact that separation from the parent would restrict the availability of know-how.

Although the factors that promote organizational support are generated outside of the compensation and incentive program, the wrong program can destroy such support. One sure way to undermine the parent company's support is to provide venture personnel with incentives that are perceived as unfair. The perception of unfairness can be reduced if the incentive plan realistically reflects the relationship between potential risks and potential rewards. Suppose the firm designs a plan whereby members of the venture team retain full company benefits, are assured that they can return to their former position, get the raises they would have gotten had they not left their former position, and stand to receive potentially high gains from the venture as well—i.e., a risk-free plan whose benefits are available only to the members of the venture team. Such a plan is unfair and will be so perceived within the parent organization.

This issue is serious and not easily resolved. One reason for separating ventures geographically and organizationally is that in order to attract and hold the best people, an organization may have to devise a special incentive program—a program that will be seen as, and may actually be, unfair. This, in turn, creates the problem of reducing the organization's ability to leverage its resources to help the venture.

If the incentive plan needed to get and keep key people conflicts with the corporate culture, the venture must be separated from that culture both geographically and organizationally. If the venture will require collaboration and support from corporate personnel under such circumstances, the parent corporation should either refrain from undertaking the venture or find an outside partner to run it.

Recognizing and adapting to reality.   The venture team's ability to recognize reality and adapt to it is the factor that determines whether the venture will be managed as a fruitless quest for fulfillment of the original venture plan—conceived in ignorance and constantly contradicted by new realities—or whether experiences will be milked for maximum learning and future plans and actions modified accordingly to achieve success. This factor will also largely determine how much will be lost in a venture that is neither redirected when it can be nor aborted when it should be.

Recognizing and adapting to reality are fostered when incentive payments are based on the venture's absolute results rather than on how closely it meets its plan. Mindless pressure to meet the plan, not only in connection with incentives but as part of a company's total value system, fosters desperation in spending and a tendency to ignore reality.

Venture managers' ability to recognize and adapt to reality is also directly related to the degree of risk they assume—i.e., to their stake in the venture. As noted earlier, venture capitalists usually require entrepreneurs to take significant personal risk—in terms of either money, sweat equity, loss of ownership interest, or all three. Clearly, internal entrepreneurs cannot be expected to risk as much money as the company does, but they might risk sums that are highly significant to them. If they don't have the money, the company might lend them some, or early-stage bonus money might be invested in the venture.

On the other hand, this limited personal investment could actually have the opposite effect. It might provide an incentive for venture managers to keep trying because of their financial leverage—one more dollar of theirs can leverage 10, 20, or more dollars of company investment, even if "ownership" is diluted. The key is to require significant personal investment, the loss of which would really make a big difference to the investor.

A plan requiring investment by venture management would probably have three effects: the higher reward potential associated with the venture would be less likely to be perceived as unfair elsewhere in the firm; the investors would find it economically counterproductive to keep a dying venture going; and fewer people would seek venture management positions. We believe that such a required investment feature could be effective in limiting potential damage only if the investment were economically significant to the venture managers.

This approach is clearly different from providing a safety net for venture managers, as suggested by Burgelman and Sayles (1986). Both approaches are probably valid—at different times and for different people. When a firm first initiates a venturing program, a safety net may be necessary, but if it is combined with a high reward potential, it will generate a sense of unfairness and can provide managers with an incentive to prolong the life of fatally wounded ventures.

A Sample Venture Incentive Plan. Although any incentive plan must of course reflect the unique realities of the parent corporation and the particular venture, what follows is a "generic" venture incentive plan consisting of strategies that have often proved effective at the various stages of a venturing effort.

- *Before commercialization:* Upon completion of the concept test and feasibility study, the organization may provide either a small discretionary bonus or none at all. The rationale for this recommendation is that a bonus should be awarded only if the recipient has added value to the results of a testing and feasibility study by innovatively modifying an idea or recognizing a new opportunity.
- *Product development stage:* A bonus may be awarded if product development is completed on schedule and within estimated costs, with the exact amount of the bonus being adjusted to reflect the extent to which actual time and costs vary from plan. Depending on the scale of the venturing effort, the bonus at this stage can be significant. Base bonus amounts should be known in advance. The base amounts can be increased on a discretionary basis for the addition of unusual value or for insights that affect the firm's approach to the business, including a wise recommendation not to proceed. The rationale for linking bonus awards to time and cost is to provide an incentive to get the job done as quickly and inexpensively as possible— without jeopardizing the quality of the end product. Quality protection provisions such as this must be built into any incentive plan.

- *Preparation of the business plan:* A discretionary bonus may be awarded for outstanding performance in key aspects of plan preparation. Examples include identifying critical assumptions and designing methods for testing them, and making a proposal not to proceed if that is justified by the facts.
- *Startup:* The firm may award a bonus calculated as a percentage of the difference between planned and actual startup expenses. For instance, the manager of a cable TV company was paid a percentage of the difference between the contractors' price and the actual amount spent on the construction of a cable system. The contractor also received a portion of the savings from the contract price, which gave him a higher profit on a lower bill—with the proviso that all performance and quality specifications had to be met. Because money was such a significant incentive to the cable system manager, he made an extraordinary effort to help the contractor get the job done at the lowest possible cost—resulting in the manager's earning a sum equal to 35% of his annual salary in a six-month period.

  Another incentive at the startup stage is a bonus calculated as a percentage of sales achieved, with the percentage declining as the elapsed time increases—for example, a 2% bonus if minimum sales of $1 million are achieved in six months; 1.5% if that level is achieved in eight months; 1% if it is achieved in ten months. The firm should provide for this bonus to be phased out after a specified maximum time period.
- *Ongoing sales and production:* A percentage of dollar-amount improvement over planned profit or loss can be put into a team pool for distribution. Significant amounts should be awarded for significant improvement, and the funds should be distributed within a relatively short time period—either quarterly or semi-annually, and certainly no less often than annually. The firm can use a formula that reflects both sales and

141

profit. This would be especially appropriate if the drive is to achieve market share within a specified cost, with a portion of the pool being calculated on each percentage point of market share achieved and another portion being calculated on the cost of obtaining that share as reflected in the venture's profit or loss. A predetermined milestone bonus for reaching profitability might also be employed.

General venture incentive strategies. Founder's phantom stock can be issued, with its starting value being completely arbitrary. The formula for appreciation can be based on the achievement of milestones within specified time periods, and after profitability is achieved, it can be based on ROI. If such stock is not convertible into parent company stock or is not publicly traded, then an internal "buyback" price schedule must be devised. In one case involving a new cable TV venture by a large, multinational firm, founder's stock was issued at no cost to attract key people, who had an opportunity to quadruple their salary when the first full year of profitability was achieved. A variety of forms of incentive mechanisms involving stock, stock options, phantom stock, and stock appreciation rights are described in some detail by Shuster (1984).

In another firm, not publicly traded, in which expenses were well controlled, a stock option plan was introduced to stimulate sales growth and market penetration. An arbitrary, but supportable, valuation of the stock price was made. The buyback formula was based on the established price multiplied by the sales growth rate—e.g., if sales doubled, then the stock price doubled if it was sold before a public offering or a sale of the company.

Providing for Changes. Any change in senior management or parent company ownership can result in venture shutdowns and alterations in plans and strategy, which can drastically affect venture personnel. Incentive and compensation plans should therefore provide a payout mechanism or formula for use in such cases.

A payout mechanism must also be devised for venture personnel who voluntarily leave or are transferred or discharged. It is desirable to establish a "vesting" schedule—i.e., a minimum length of time that a person must remain in the venture—before any special provisions are made. The vesting mechanism can consist of a gradually increasing percentage of participation in a bonus pool, stock options, or other forms of equity equivalents.

In short, the company must establish a flexible incentive plan that provides for changes in the plan in response to changes in the venture's stage as well as in corporate management and objectives.

CONCLUSION

The firm must understand the roles to be filled in the venture and make sure the right people are available to fill them. In particular, ventures need both a business innovator who can lead, integrate, and manage and an executive champion. Nor is it enough for the firm to pick the best qualified people to manage the venture; it must also make sure those people are committed and enthusiastic.

The organization can breed potential venture managers by assigning tasks with high uncertainty to promising people. Hiring and evaluation practices should be examined to ensure that potential innovators are being recruited and encouraged rather than rejected and discouraged.

The venture's success should be evaluated based on milestones, with the parent company's senior management assessing not only the actual completion of events but also the learning that has taken place. Besides the achievement of goals, senior managers must also consider more qualitative issues, such as the commitment and teamwork displayed by the venture group.

There is no sure-fire way to compensate venture managers; existing plans range from generous to nonexistent. Compensation programs should be shaped according to a careful examination of the characteristics of the firm and the venture's managers, and should be customized to individual situations insofar as possible.

The corporation can use equity or equity equivalents, bonuses, promotion, salary increases, and recognition awards to compensate and motivate members of the venture team. In general, rewards should be related to risk. The incentive arrangement must also provide for management turnover and possible changes in the parent company's strategy or ownership.

Guidelines

1. Ensure that new ventures have a business innovator as well as a product champion.
2. Grow potential venture managers by challenging promising people with tasks involving high uncertainty.
3. Evaluate individual performance according to what is learned and how that learning is applied—not according to blind adherence to a plan.
4. Compensate venture managers according to the venture's requirements, the firm's culture, and the venture management team's needs. Do not automatically assume that incentives will affect performance.
5. Assume that changes in venture management will someday become desirable or necessary and take that likelihood into account in making initial personnel assignments.

REFERENCES

Block, Z., and Ornati, O. 1987. "Compensating Corporate Venture Managers." *Journal of Business Venturing* 2, no. 1 (Winter): 41–52.

Block, Z., and Subbanarasimha, P. N. 1989. "Corporate Venturing: Practices and Performance in the U.S. and Japan." Working paper. Center for Entrepreneurial Studies, Stern School of Business, New York University.

Burgelman, R. A., and Sayles, L. R. 1986. *Inside Corporate Innovation*. New York: Free Press.

Drucker, P. 1985. *Innovation and Entrepreneurship*. New York: Harper & Row.

Greiner, L. 1972. "Evolution and Revolution as Organizations Grow." *Harvard Business Review* (July–August): 37–46.

Kanter, R. M. 1989. *When Giants Learn to Dance*. New York: Simon & Schuster.

Maidique, M. A. 1980. "Entrepreneurs, Champions and Technological Innovation." *Sloan Management Review* (Winter): 59–76.

"Myers-Briggs Type Indicator." 1976. Gainsville, FL: Center for Applications of Psychological Type.

Pinchot, Gifford. 1985. *Intrapreneuring*. New York: Harper & Row.

Sandburg, W. R., and Hofer, C. W. 1987. *Journal of Business Venturing* 2, no. 1: 5.

Schein, Edgar H. 1985. "Career Anchors: Discovering Your Real Values." San Diego: University Associates Inc.

Shuster, Jay. 1984. *Management Compensation in High Technology Companies*. Lexington, MA: Lexington Books.

Steele, B., and Baker, R. 1986. "Creating Entrepreneurial Pay Systems for Internal Venture Units." *Topics in Total Compensation* 1, no. 1: 37–55.

Sykes, H. B. 1986. "Lessons from a New Ventures Program." *Harvard Business Review* (May–June): 69–74.

———. "Incentive Compensation for Corporate Venture Personnel." *Journal of Business Venturing* (July 1992): 253–265.

6

Locating the Venture
in the Organization

This chapter addresses the crucial decision of where to locate a venture in the parent organization, with the key issue being the extent to which the venture should be separated from the organization's ongoing operations. Six major location options, involving progressive degrees of separation, are described and their pros and cons examined. These options range from simply assigning the venture to a line manager as part of his or her normal job to having the venture manager report to a new-business division or even directly to the CEO. It becomes clear from this discussion that there is no ideal place to locate a venture.

We then discuss the factors that influence how separated the venture should be, depending on the circumstances in which the parent company finds itself. Since the driving principle regarding the location decision is to ensure that the venture is placed in such a way as to protect it from any potential

147

corporate antagonism, we also present several safeguarding options.

Thus, there are a number of contingencies that must be taken into account in deciding where to place a venture within the organization. This short chapter provides senior managers with enough background information to enable them to determine a suitable (as opposed to universally optimal) location.

SELECTING THE VENTURE'S FORMAT

Before discussing the issue of venture location, however, we should point out that there are alternatives to simply creating a fully controlled internal corporate venture. A wide variety of format options are available—including selling an innovation off outright, licensing others to exploit it, starting an internal venture as a project team, forming a subsidiary to build the business, creating a joint venture (in which the parent company's ownership could range from a minority holding to 50/50 to a majority holding), acting solely as a venture capital source (either for an internally developed innovation or as a participant in a venture capital pool), or making an acquisition (either a foothold acquisition or a major one).

Why would a company choose to give up full ownership of a venture? The parent firm may be unable to provide the required expertise, principally involving technology or market, or it may need to obtain capital or share the risk. Other reasons include financing capacity (current and projected), an aversion to risk, timing needs, risk/reward potential, and fit factors. The shared ownership option may be rejected, however, if the parent company feels it must retain 100% ownership or is convinced it can meet all the venture's needs by itself.

Acquisition is used primarily to collapse time or sometimes to get the kind of management required and reduce the risk. The separate subsidiary approach can help the parent obtain and retain talented management and enable it to use innovative incentive and compensation arrangements without

148

alienating people in the core business. A joint venture, possibly with a minority holding, might be appropriate for a corporation that has a low capacity for risk, an urgent need to accelerate the venturing process, and a significant culture gap between the parent firm and the venture.

Of course, whatever the venture's starting format, it is unlikely to remain in that format permanently, particularly if strategic alliances or joint ventures are involved. Such agreements should contain exit provisions specifying the conditions under which the parties can exit, the pricing formula to be used in the event of buyout, and the process for handling unresolvable disagreement (e.g., arbitration).

A detailed discussion of the various alternatives to a fully owned internal corporate venture is beyond the scope of this book, however, and the remainder of this chapter deals only with deciding where to locate an internal corporate venture that is fully controlled by the parent firm.

VENTURE LOCATION OPTIONS

Venture location options range from totally embedding the venture in the parent company's ongoing operations to creating a completely separate new-venture division reporting directly to the topmost level of the organization.

The degree to which a venture is separated from mainstream corporate operations significantly influences a number of issues that are important for the venture's progress:

- *Focus:* The more embedded a venture, the less its chances of being the focus of attention in that location. Ventures placed in line operations tend to struggle to attract attention because line managers are distracted by day-to-day operating problems. So if focus of attention is important for the venture's success, a higher degree of separation will be needed.
- *Priority:* The more embedded a venture, the less likely it is to receive top priority insofar as the allocation of

resources is concerned. This is because the venture must compete for resources against established, large, and often much more profitable subunits in the organization within which it is embedded. Increasing the degree of separation therefore increases the venture's chances of receiving top priority.

- *Reliability of funding:* The more embedded a venture, the more unpredictable the availability of funds, since there is a tendency to respond to contingencies by preempting the venture's funding and diverting it to established operating units. Increasing the venture's separation increases the probability that needed funds will be forthcoming.
- *Coping with growth:* The greater the venture's separation from ongoing operations, the less built-in infrastructure and staff will be available to cope with the venture's growth. When a venture deeply embedded in existing operations needs to grow, the required systems, facilities, and staff are already in place. When a highly separated venture needs to grow, these resources must either be created or recruited, since they simply do not exist in that location. (The fact that resources are available in embedded locations does not necessarily mean that those resources will be forthcoming, only that they need not be created from scratch.)

In light of the preceding issues, an organization seeking to determine the initial location of a venture should ask itself where the venture can best be placed in order to ensure that:

- The venture obtains resources, know-how, and rapid processing of information.
- The venture is protected politically.
- The venture gets the necessary guidance, commitment, and attention.
- The venture gains optimal access to the target market.

- The venture enjoys a nurturing and supportive environment that includes appropriate controls.
- The parent firm is protected against major losses and other hazards (Tushman and Nadler [1978]; MacMillan and Jones [1986]; Hisrich and Peters [1986]; Mueller [1971]; Bart [1988]).

In the following subsections, we outline six major "levels" of location and list their main pros and cons. Note that each higher level represents an increasing degree of separation from the ongoing operations of the firm.

Level 1: Assigning the Project to a Line Manager. The venture project is assigned to a line manager to execute as all or part of his or her ongoing managerial responsibilities, with the line manager reporting to operating division management.

Pro: The venture enjoys maximum exposure to operations expertise.

Cons: This location maximizes the venture's intrusion into and disruption of the unit's present business while minimizing the attention it receives from line management. It also leaves the venture highly vulnerable to turf brawling.

Level 2: Creating a Separate Section in an Operating Division. The venture is assigned full-time to a line manager who reports to an operating division, and he or she assembles a team of full- and part-time people to get the venture going.

Pros: The venture gains political support, enjoys maximum exposure to corporate know-how, and has greater access to the organization's expertise in the business if it involves a familiar market. Subsequent integration into the division is facilitated (assuming that is the ultimate objective).

Cons: The venture has a low priority in terms of commitment, and its losses detract from divisional performance. It may be the first to suffer during periods of cost reduction; it faces the dangers of turf brawling and intrusion from the parent division; and it is susceptible to red tape.

151

Level 3: Having the Venture Report to R&D.   The venture is assigned full-time to a venture manager who reports to R&D, and he or she assembles a team of full- and part-time people to get the venture going.

Pro: The venture remains close to evolving technology and technical information that could prove crucial to its success.

Cons: The R&D division may become infatuated with the technology and be oblivious to market needs and timing—especially if it lacks business and marketing experience, orientation, and knowledge—and the evaluation of technical alternatives may be hampered by a "not invented here" attitude. This location also leaves the venture susceptible to red tape.

Level 4: Having the Venture Report to a Senior Staff Function.   The person in charge of the venture reports to a senior staff position (such as R&D or corporate development), either individually or as a venture manager in charge of a team of full- or part-timers.

Pros: This approach ensures dedication to addressing the key challenges of the venturing operation. Intrusion into existing operations is minimized, as is vulnerability to turf brawling.

Cons: The venture has little exposure to operations expertise and may suffer if the parent unit lacks business and marketing experience.

Level 5: Having the Venture Report to a New-Venture Division.   The venture manager reports to a separate new-venture division, which interacts directly with top management.

Pros: This approach ensures sympathetic nurturing of the venture, protection from corporate red tape, and a high level of attention focused on the key challenges facing the venture. Intrusions into the parent firm's operations are minimized, as is the venture's vulnerability to turf brawling.

Cons: The venture is removed from the corporate mainstream and competes for resources with mainstream businesses. Exposure to existing organizational expertise is minimized. The venture becomes a highly visible target, which increases its vulnerability to elimination.

Level 6: Having the Venture Report Directly to the CEO.
Pros: This arrangement guarantees maximum political protection, mainstream cooperation, and the availability of resources.

Cons: Strong support from the CEO can hamper objective evaluation of the venture's progress, and failures are likely to be more costly. Crown prince jealousy is also a possibility.

As can be seen from the preceding discussion, there is no ideal location for a new business—no single arrangement that can be universally suggested or applied. Each option has its strengths and weaknesses. Although selecting the right location will not guarantee venture success, selecting the wrong location can guarantee venture failure—and possibly very high-cost failure.

FACTORS SHAPING THE CHOICE OF VENTURE LOCATION

In the preceding section, we stressed that there is no evidence to indicate that any particular venture location option is either better than one or more of the others or generally superior. This is not to imply, however, that the decision is a toss-up. Rather, the appropriate venture location varies from one case to another, depending on the individual company and venture. Hence, although it is impossible to identify a universally superior venture location, it *is* possible to identify a location that is right for a given company and venture. To do so, senior managers should consider the following eight factors, which play a significant role in shaping the correct location decision:

153

1. *Acceptance of venturing and of the venture:* The level of acceptance within an organization, both of venturing as an activity and of a particular venture, varies from one firm to another. If most of the established organization is indifferent or hostile to the venture or to venturing in general, or simply does not believe in venturing, then the venture has a very great chance of falling prey to lack of support or deliberate obstructionism or getting chewed up as powerful vested interests engage in turf brawling. Clearly, when organizational acceptance is poor, there is a need to safeguard the venture, either by placing it in what Galbraith (1982) terms "a reservation" (a level 3 or level 4 location, described in the preceding section) or by creating one of the safeguarding mechanisms described in the following section.

2. *Experience with venturing:* An organization's experience with venturing can range from nonexistent to extensive. Even if the organization welcomes venturing, it may simply lack the experience base required to venture successfully. In this case, it is probably better to locate the venture where it can be protected from constantly having to account for differences between plans and results. Once again, it may become necessary to place the venture in a reservation (i.e., a level 3 or level 4 location).

3. *The venture's criticality:* The venture's importance to the firm and the urgency of its success must be considered in making the location decision. Highly critical ventures tend to need a location that reports to senior levels of the parent organization.

4. *Current organizational and divisional performance:* If the organization is performing poorly or is subject to great stress, the venture will wither on the vine unless it can command organizational attention, which means a level 3 or level 4 location. It is totally inappropriate to place a venture in any division that

is under stress because of environmental turbulence or internal performance disappointments.

5. *Organizational structure:* The organization's current structure also affects where a venture can be located. There are five basic types of organizational structure: functional, geographic, product, divisional, and hybrid. Highly functionalized firms tend to have extensive policies and procedures by which to coordinate cross-functional activities, whereas geographically dispersed firms tend to have similar policies and procedures to coordinate activities in various areas. In geographically dispersed firms, ventures placed in lower-level locations will tend to get strangled by "homogenizing" staff groups whose task it is to ensure that all units comply with corporate policies. In firms with such homogenizing bureaucracies, ventures should be placed in locations with a high degree of separation.

6. *Scale of the venture:* The venture's size is an important consideration in making the location decision. A major venture involving significant commitment of organizational resources and significant organizational effort will obviously require a large multifunctional team, which will probably be separated from the company's ongoing operations. The smaller the scale of the venture, the more likely it is to be located as a group or an individual embedded in some part of the organization.

7. *Stage of venture evolution:* There is no one location that will fit all the stages through which a venture passes as it evolves. The location needs of a venture in its very early stages differ significantly from those of a successful venture that is about to become a large component of the parent organization. It is quite conceivable for a venture to start as a one-person investigation in the development department, perhaps liaising with one or two sales and production contacts,

155

and then evolve into a large, separate operation as it grows. The key is for senior management to step back and reassess the location decision as the venture progresses, changing the location if it no longer fits the venture's current needs.

8. *The venture's anticipated future location within the firm:* If the new business will ultimately become part of one of the firm's existing operations, the initial location decision should be made in such a way as to minimize later integration problems. For example, in its new-venture program, ATT Technologies did not undertake any venture unless the business unit in which it would eventually be placed was represented on the venture advisory board and had agreed to accept the venture, since the company didn't want any orphaned businesses floating around. Although ATT Technologies did have a special group that helped launch ventures by providing the required initial nurturing and reducing red tape, venture participants understood at the outset where management ultimately intended to place each new business.

SAFEGUARDING THE VENTURE FROM ORGANIZATIONAL ANTAGONISM

It should be abundantly clear that the eight factors discussed in the preceding section are significant determinants of a venture's outcome and that certain combinations of these factors can lead to political and bureaucratic conditions that will guarantee the failure of a poorly located venture, no matter how great its intrinsic potential.

Although all eight of these factors are important, senior management's top priority in making the venture location decision should be, first and foremost, to place the venture where it will be safeguarded from organizational antagonism (that is, political and bureaucratic interference). There is no way a venture can survive simultaneous internal and external competition, so unless the venture can be protected from internal attack, at least in its early stages, it is doomed.

As indicated earlier in the chapter, the most effective way to seal a venture off from organizational antagonism is to separate it from ongoing operations, but this is not necessarily the only way to protect a venture that faces opposition. Here are some additional safeguarding mechanisms the parent firm can use as alternatives to separation:

- *Venture advisory board:* A significant measure of protection from organizational politics and bureaucratic attack can be achieved by creating a board comprised of important internal and even external advisers whose task is not only to provide the venture with technical and managerial advice but also to protect it. Particularly if one or more of the board's members are very senior executives of the parent firm, they will be in a position to overrule policies and procedures that may be obstructing the venture or discourage political moves against the venture manager.
- *Executive champion:* In addition to a venture advisory board, the organization should appoint a very senior manager as executive champion, with explicit part- or full-time responsibility for defending any ventures that come under political or bureaucratic attack. The challenge in filling such an assignment is to find a senior manager who is widely respected in all functional areas and possesses an entrepreneurial attitude and mind-set. And if the assignment is a part-time one, there is a question of whether the executive champion will devote enough attention to the ventures he or she is supposed to protect. On the other hand, appointing such an individual sends the rest of the organization a powerful signal regarding the seriousness of the firm's commitment to venturing.
- *Right of direct appeal:* The final and least costly safeguarding mechanism is to give the venture manager the right to appeal directly to the senior management

team or policy committee whenever he or she feels that the venture is being compromised by organizational issues. In theory, this should work fine. The question is whether the venture manager will risk challenging a powerful senior executive when the venture's needs conflict with the executive's wishes. The effectiveness of this mechanism depends to a great extent on the organization's experience with and acceptance of venturing as well as how critical the particular venture is to the organization.

In short, if a venture faces any danger of organizational antagonism, safeguarding it should take top priority in making the location decision. And no matter how compelling a particular location may seem, a venture facing hostility may require protection through the use of such safeguarding mechanisms as separation, a venture advisory board, an executive champion, or some right of appeal to top management.

CONCLUSION

When the issue of venture location is first raised, senior managers may wonder what all the fuss is about. Why not simply create a new-venture division or have the various venture managers report directly to the CEO? However, as we discuss in detail in Chapter 8, "Organizing the Venture," separating the venture from the rest of the organization could deny it access to valuable know-how, which, in turn could significantly increase the venture's cost and reduce its chances for success.

Thus, there is always a basic trade-off that must be made: If the venture is separated, it will be protected from antagonism and/or bureaucratic interference but its access to valuable know-how will be restricted, thereby compromising its success in one way; if the venture is embedded, it will be able to avail itself of that know-how but it will be exposed to organizational antagonism and/or bureaucratic interference, thereby compromising its success in a different way.

In the absence of antagonism, there is no reason why any particular venture location is superior to another—all have their shortcomings. What matters is whether the shortcomings of the particular location have been recognized and offset through the use of appropriate mechanisms (discussed in detail in Chapter 8).

Finally, as with every other design decision, the location decision must be reexamined on an ongoing basis and may require change as the venture evolves through its various developmental stages (startup, survival, expansion, maturity).

Guidelines

1. Exercise great care in positioning a venture in the firm, for this decision is a critical determinant of the venture's success.
2. Since safeguarding the venture from corporate antagonism is essential, take appropriate protective measures if need be. These include having the venture report directly to senior management, providing for an executive champion, creating a venture advisory board, or establishing the venture manager's right of direct appeal to the highest levels of management.
3. In determining the venture's degree of embeddedness or separation, consider the venture's needs in terms of priority in securing management attention, reliability of funding, and coping with growth.
4. Revisit and reassess the location decision as the venture evolves.

REFERENCES

Bart, C. K. 1988. "New Venture Units: Use Them Wisely to Manage Innovation." *Sloan Management Review* (Summer): 35–43.

Galbraith, J. R. 1982. "Designing the Innovative Organization." *Organizational Dynamics* (Winter): 5–25.

Hisrich, R. D., and Peters, M. D. 1986. "Establishing a New Venture Unit within a Firm." *Journal of Business Venturing* 1: 307–322.

MacMillan, I. C., and Jones, P. E. 1986. *Strategy Formulation: Power and Politics*. Saint Paul, MN: West Publishing.

Mueller, R. K. 1971. *The Innovation Ethic,* 114–140. New York: American Management Association.

Tushman, M. L., and Nadler, D. A. 1978. "Information Processing as an Integrating Concept in Organizational Design." *Academy of Management Review* (July): 613–623.

7

Developing the Business Plan

It is common knowledge that business plans for new ventures bear little resemblance to reality. This is a particularly distressing problem for corporations in which planning is such a vital part of management and plan fulfillment is so important in evaluating performance. But there is a better way to plan—one that can help companies develop more realistic expectations, evaluate progress more effectively, and improve their chances for venture success.

In essence, new ventures are projects with an experimental component. Their planning and performance can therefore be greatly improved through the use of project-planning methods—i.e., by establishing critical path milestones, identifying and testing key assumptions, and continu-

This chapter is an expansion of Z. Block and I. A. MacMillan, "Milestones for Successful Venture Planning," *Harvard Business Review* (September–October 1985): 4–8.

ally adapting to the new and surprising information that will inevitably emerge.

This chapter provides guidelines for developing a useful, realistic business plan for a new venture. In the first section, we describe the differences between the purposes of new-venture plans and plans for established businesses and show how those differences affect planning. The following sections examine the key elements of new-venture plans, the use of milestone planning, and the organization's strategic choices for entering the market. The chapter closes with an overview of the action steps that venture managers should take in developing a new-business plan, together with the questions that senior managers should ask in evaluating such a plan.

NEW-VENTURE BUSINESS PLANS VERSUS TRADITIONAL BUSINESS PLANS

This section, which contrasts planning done for new ventures with planning done for established businesses, examines the following questions:

- What is the planning/performance paradox, and what is it about new ventures that creates this paradox?
- What are the purposes of new-venture plans, and how do they differ from the purposes of traditional business plans?
- Is new-venture planning actually necessary? If so, can it be done effectively?
- What planning process should be used? (Who should do the planning, when, and how?)

The Planning/Performance Paradox

Venture folklore states that the three keys to a successful new business are a good business plan, a good business plan, and a good business plan, and most courses in entrepreneurship focus on the development of a business plan. Yet new-venture business plans often have more in common with advertising than with effective management. Usually, there is little or no connection between what is projected and what is delivered. All the concrete numbers and detailed analyses contained in the typical business plan belie the fact that forecasting the performance of nascent ventures is even harder than predicting the weather.

In cases where traditional business-planning methods have been applied to new ventures, the correlation between planning and performance has been pretty tenuous. A study comparing projections with the results of ventures funded by a leading venture capital firm found that actual costs, functional benefits, competitive action, and, most especially, sales bore little or no relation to plans or expectations (Sacher and Wolterbeek 1987). These findings were confirmed by a group of 25 venture managers from a *Fortune* 100 company at a seminar on new-venture planning as well as by virtually every one of the managers we interviewed from other firms.

The most accurate prediction that can be made about any venture plan is that cost and time estimates will be achieved or exceeded and revenue estimates will not. Even in the case of roaring successes, the disparity between plans and performance can be great. One new-venture plan projected sales of $3 million for the following year, whereas the actual sales turned out to be $40 million. Although the surprise was not unwelcome, it nonetheless created a financing crisis.

To make matters worse, despite the recognized limitations of business plans, corporate managers often use them to pressure venture managers to achieve impossible results, ultimately leading to unnecessary losses.

Why do new-business plans fall so far short of reality? One reason for the gap between projections and performance is the competition for funding, causing what one venture manager calls "a lying contest." This is a somewhat harsh, but not entirely inaccurate, characterization of the "best-case scenario" approach to planning.

163

This approach doesn't fool everyone. Indeed, it may not fool anyone. A former IBM marketing executive reported that when new-venture projections were evaluated during his time at IBM, the reviewers made it a practice to double the costs and halve the sales, and if the proposal still looked good, they would seriously consider it.

In a 1986 study by MacMillan, Block, and Subbanarasimha, many of the obstacles to new-business development identified by venture managers were related to the planning process: imperfect market analysis; underestimating the competition, the venture's riskiness, and the required funding; the company's impatience to get results; and lack of contingency planning.

What is it about new ventures that creates the planning/performance paradox? Quite simply, the fact that they are new—not necessarily to the world but to the venturing company. If the parent firm lacks experience in relevant technologies, products, and markets, it can only roughly estimate the rate at which any new venture will develop, the market acceptance, the costs, and the competitive response—and those estimates are sure to be significantly inaccurate. In the case of truly new technologies and markets that have yet to be developed, the level of uncertainty is far greater. It is not rational to expect certain quantitative outcomes from a fundamentally unpredictable situation.

Purposes of New-Venture Plans versus Traditional Plans

A new venture can be regarded as a project that must be funded, and therefore, an initial objective of the business plan is to sell the investor, the corporation itself. The plan must provide a basis for determining whether to invest, and it is almost always evaluated in competition with other proposals.

The outstanding and distinguishing purpose of a new-venture plan is to learn whether and how to conduct the new business, and such a plan can be designed to ensure that the necessary learning occurs. Other purposes of the plan are to attract key personnel, apprising them of where the venture is intended to go and how it will get there, and to stimulate contribution to and implementation of the plan.

These purposes are quite different from those of a plan for an established business—where the nature of the business is clearly defined, where the unit's managers have developed the ability to work together as a team, where the risks have probably already been identified and managed to some degree, and most important, where the premises and assumptions on which the business is based have long since been identified and tested through experience.

The most important difference of all is this: The plan for an established business is designed to produce predictable performance extremely accurately, with the actual performance record being used as a basis for evaluating the business's management and with people being rewarded or punished based largely on how close they come to fulfilling the plan. In contrast, a primary purpose of the plan for a new venture is to help get the business going in a situation in which predictability is virtually impossible because the business has no history, the people are new to the particular project, and the plan must be based mainly on assumptions rather than facts. Since an established business has a past, it possesses a wealth of information regarding existing customers, known competitors, and previous levels of sales and profit. Hence, when such a business and its environment are relatively stable, business planning is more straightforward, and there is every reason to expect performance according to a well-developed plan.

The Feasibility of Effective New-Venture Planning

Given the formidable difficulties of creating a credible new-venture plan and the virtual certainty that the plan will be inaccurate in many respects, some may wonder whether such planning is actually necessary and, if so, whether it can be done effectively. In our view, new-venture planning is both absolutely essential and entirely feasible—assuming managers abandon traditional notions of planning as if for an established business. Although planning is possible, a high degree of long-term predictability cannot be achieved, at least not in a venture's early stages. The actions to be taken are predictable, and in a broad sense, their probable outcomes are reasonably predictable, but precise outcomes certainly are not.

In short, a new-venture plan is not a static document designed to enable the parent company to accurately forecast results. Rather, it is a dynamic tool designed to enable the company to determine whether the proposed business is possible and worth the effort and, if so, to yield the knowledge the firm needs to run and build the business while its operations are actually under way.

Because new ventures face a relatively unknown and unstable environment, they must deal with shifting assumptions, and in the case of new businesses, these assumptions take the place of a track record. In a venture's early stages, the plan provides a strategy for testing these assumptions. As the venture develops and information is compiled, assumptions are altered, with many of them ultimately being replaced by facts—a process that gradually leads into more traditional planning.

The Recommended Planning Process

The process that should *not* be used is for senior management to request a business plan immediately after a venturable idea is first discussed.

The recommended process is based on the concept that a new-venture plan must *evolve* in a corporate setting. The first step leading toward a business plan is the opportunity identification and evaluation process described in Chapter 4, which is followed by feasibility evaluation, product development, pilot operations, and market testing. During the course of these steps, more and more facts are learned, and initial assumptions are verified, modified, or dropped. Before the company makes a major investment in a new business, a formal and reasonably complete proposal—the document generally referred to as "the business plan"—is warranted and needed. But because this document will still contain major assumptions that have yet to be tested, it will need to be changed as experience is gained. Thus, the planning process will continue throughout the first phases of the new venture's development until the business becomes somewhat established.

The planning itself must be done by the venture team. For its part, senior management must understand the dynamic nature of the new-venture planning process and encourage venture managers to make appropriate changes to the plan rather than pressuring them to fulfill initial projections that are no longer valid.

ELEMENTS OF A NEW-VENTURE PLAN

In addition to an executive summary, a new-venture business plan should contain the following major sections:

1. Description of the proposed business—precisely what it will do, including its unique characteristics and clear objectives
2. Strategic relationship between the new business and the parent firm
3. Target markets—including their description and size, market trends, why customers will buy, and the specific accounts to be targeted initially
4. Present and anticipated competition—including the identity of specific competitors and their characteristics, competitive advantages, and market share
5. Go/no-go assumptions and the basis for them
6. Definition of failure

7. Action plans and objectives, with defined milestones designed to test the go/no-go assumptions in each functional area
8. Necessary resources—money, physical, and human—and how they will be acquired
9. Principal risks and how they will be managed
10. Sensitivity analysis—an assessment of how certain contingencies might affect the venture
11. Financial projections and objectives, together with the assumptions on which they are based, including profit and loss and cash break-even points
12. Description of the venture's management and the compensation methods that will be used

A number of these sections require no further explanation here, since they involve topics discussed in earlier chapters. However, most venture plans and planning guides we've seen do not include sections on the definition of failure, go/no-go assumptions, and action plans with milestones; they also tend to be casual about identifying the principal risks and how they will be managed and frequently omit sensitivity analysis.

Such omissions and oversights are understandable when people are competing for funds and may therefore have an incentive to gloss over certain aspects of a proposal. But unless senior management insists on the inclusion of the aforementioned topics (which are discussed in the following subsections) and then uses that information to decide which projects to support, it will make very costly errors in selecting projects and venture management.

Definition of Failure

The plan's section on the definition of failure should simply describe the conditions under which the project will be dropped, liquidated, or otherwise disposed of. The most valid condition is when the fundamental assumption on which the business idea was based has become untenable—due, for example, to a technological leapfrog by the competition, the disappearance of a need, or a change in a government regulation that makes the business uneconomic or even illegal. The least valid condition (albeit a very common one) for terminating a project is the failure to achieve a specified economic objective within a prescribed time period—even though the factors that produce the opportunity remain unchanged and the opportunity itself still exists. That kind of "failure" may simply reveal an inability to make accurate predictions or a need for the firm to either change its approach to the business or obtain allies to share risks and losses.

Principal Risks and How They Will Be Managed

The primary areas of risk are financial, technological, market, and management. An example of a financial risk would be the cost of building a factory in anticipation of a demand that has yet to materialize. One way to manage such a risk would be to outsource the product until an appropriate level of demand has been achieved and then build the factory. Although technological risks cannot always be managed, approaches that may minimize such risks include continuing to develop existing technology, licensing potentially competing technologies, or establishing a sufficiently strong patent screen.

Sensitivity Analysis

Sensitivity analysis is the "what if" section of the plan, and the technique for performing this analysis is well known. For example, in a new-venture proposal for a medium-sized company that involved a major capital expenditure requiring borrowed funds, the following questions were asked: How much would projected sales have to drop before the firm would become unable to repay the debt on schedule? If gross margins dropped by specified amounts, how would cash flow be affected? The key to sensitivity analysis is to avoid generating pages and pages of unintelligible Lotus printouts that no one will read and instead focus on a few realistic possibilities.

Go/No-Go Assumptions

Behind any new business, there are a wide variety of assumptions, both about the business itself and about the environment within which it will operate. Assumptions must be made regarding the following areas:

- *The market:* growth rate; size; target segments; factors affecting purchase decisions; usage levels; the effectiveness of distribution channels; sales closing time; order size; marketing costs; marketing mix requirements; pricing; distribution costs
- *The product:* functions; competitive advantages and their duration; service requirements; switching costs; quality level; quality control limits; potential enhancements and extensions; costs; materials; availability of labor and skills
- *Technology:* development time and costs; scaleup time and costs; proprietary protection; ability to coordinate with marketing and manufacturing; availability of required know-how
- *Economic:* break-even point; upside gain; downside risk; dollars needed to reach cash break-even (fixed assets, startup costs, operating negative cash flow) or profit break-even; margins; all cost categories; age of receivables and payables; financing method; interest rates
- *The competition:* present and future; timing of expected responses in the areas of quality, pricing, service, delivery, marketing strategy, and product characteristics
- *The organization:* financial and nonfinancial support,

including limitations on the use of organizational funds and time; freedom of action; staff interference or support; availability of an executive champion; political protection; satisfactory compensation and incentives for venture team members; cooperation from existing operations when needed; control of publicity

- *The environment:* government regulations; international relations; trade and business barriers and opportunities; social and lifestyle trends; probable major technological changes; industry restructuring; internal organizational limitations and opportunities; takeover effects

Why so much emphasis on assumptions? Essentially, every new venture is an industrial experiment (with the assumptions being the hypotheses), and the experiment must be designed to ensure that these hypotheses are tested.

We define a go/no-go assumption as a hypothesis which must be correct in order to justify getting into the business at all, that is: If correct, it's "go" and if false, no-go." These and other key assumptions are the basis for the planning of the business. Changes in these assumptions based on emerging facts must be examined to decide whether to redirect the business, change the plan, or abort the effort entirely. Therefore, managers must not only articulate the important assumptions, especially those on which the existence of the business depends, but also develop a business plan which includes actions for the purpose of testing those assumptions, even if those actions have no other purpose than that test and thus force learning to occur.

What's the best way to do this? Scheduling periodic reviews of the venture's progress can lead to learning. But this approach does not reflect the importance of completing actions and events in a required sequence nor of completing actions that have been deliberately designed to test critical assumptions.

It is very difficult for new businesses to grow in an efficient and orderly manner. Development costs are often incurred before a concept is tested; plants may be built before development and pilot operations are completed; and marketing programs begin before product is available—all of which can result in high cash burn and enormous losses. Competitive pressures sometimes necessitate such chaos, but that is not always the case.

Like any complex project with many unknowns, ventures benefit from *critical path milestone planning,* as was the case with America's lunar exploration and landing program. This planning method identifies the actions, event completions, and results required *in the sequence required*—i.e., the completion of each event is linked to previous events whose completion was a prerequisite to it and to future events that depend on its satisfactory completion.

Viewed in this manner, it is obvious that new-venture plans must be changed to reflect what is learned at each milestone and to ensure that necessary sequences are maintained. This does not mean that the venture's central objective must be changed (although it might), but that its pace, direction, actions, and schedules are very likely to be changed, along with the projected numbers related to time. Nor does this mean that periodic budget reviews should be completely abandoned, but the primary emphasis must be on learning and on modifying plans and budgets based on the completion of planned events.

In certain cases, it may be crucial for the schedule to become a driving force if time demands make parallel activity essential. A limited window of opportunity, a contractual obligation, an anticipated change in regulations (particularly involving taxation), or a competitive race for market position may dictate that the firm take more risk than would otherwise be desirable. The firm may have to compromise the assumptions-testing process and simply gamble on some key assumptions' being right, trusting that the required events can occur on time.

The following example illustrates the risks inherent in such an approach: A new venture was initiated to produce a computer enhancement component. According to the business plan, development would be completed in March of 1987, the manufacturing plant would start up in September of that year, and marketing would begin nationally in October. Development had been under way for some time prior to 1987. Because training time was needed for the marketing people, and offices were required in a number of locations, the company began to employ sales and marketing people in June 1987 and had opened offices by September. Land was acquired for the projected plant as well.

Here's what actually happened: Development was completed in October of 1987 rather than March. The company was unable to obtain zoning approval for the plant, which could not be built on the land it had acquired. The marketing people were hired, however, and the offices opened. The cash burn rate was $500,000 per month. When the product was finally developed, the company had to have it assembled by an outside supplier, and sales were at last able to begin—in March of 1989.

We are unable to judge from our vantage point whether this business was actually faced with a clear-cut choice between using such an approach or losing the opportunity, but we do know that the venture management group did not consciously consider the choice in those terms. The moral is: "Don't let time pressures dictate planned actions unless external factors make it unavoidable."

Building Assumptions Testing into the Plan. In our investigations of underlying critical assumptions that companies have made about new ventures, we have found that management often: (1) makes unconscious assumptions, (2) makes conscious assumptions but fails to articulate them, (3) fails to test articulated assumptions, and (4) fails to use the results of assumptions testing to change plans. (See Figure 7-1.)

When a company makes any of these oversights, it loses the underlying premise for rational new-venture control, which can result in spectacularly expensive failures. Chapter 9, "Controlling the Venture," provides dramatic examples of this point.

Figure 7-1: The Process of Recognizing, Articulating, and Testing Go/No-Go Assumptions and Making Necessary Changes

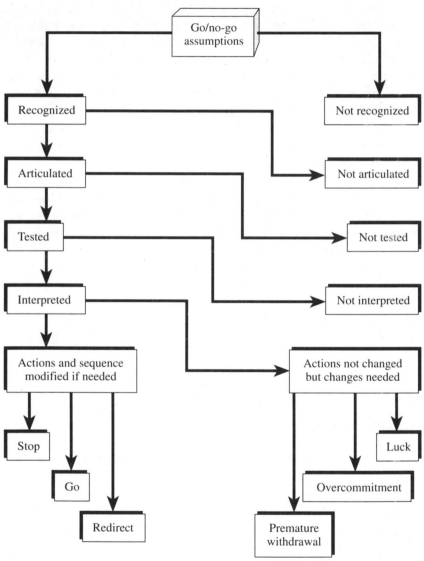

Business plans must include built-in, systematic methods for identifying and testing assumptions, particularly go/no-go assumptions. The lengths to which an organization should go in testing these assumptions are determined by the potential significance of the risks and rewards associated with the venture and the timing needs.

At each stage of the venture development process, managers must ask the following questions about their assumptions:

- What is the current basis for this assumption?
- How can this assumption be tested?
- Would the business be pursued if the assumption turns out to be incorrect and is not replaced either with facts or with a new assumption that, when tested, justifies pursuing the business in one form or another?

Checking for Hidden Assumptions.   In any new business, there will always be unarticulated or unconscious assumptions. The more these hidden assumptions can be ferreted out, the less likely it is that the new business will be blindsided by one of them. Pinpointing these hidden assumptions requires vigilance and consultation with people who are knowledgeable about the business, the industry, and the organization but are not directly involved in the new venture. They can be asked, "Do you see us making any unstated or implicit assumptions whose validity is fundamental to the venture's success?"

In its oil shale venture, which resulted in a \$4-billion loss, Exxon made the articulated go/no-go assumption that the price of oil would stay at more than \$35 per barrel and wisely exited when the price dropped, invalidating that assumption. But Exxon also made the unconscious assumption that conservation efforts would have no significant effect on the demand for oil and that OPEC would continue its monopolistic control of oil production. If the assumption about the effects of conservation measures had been articulated and tested, perhaps by tracking what was happening to demand,

175

Exxon might have been able to make a much earlier and less expensive exit.

USING MILESTONE PLANNING

Figure 7-2 shows the stages through which a venture may pass on its way from idea to established business. In milestone planning, our objective is threefold: (1) to relate each stage to the assumption(s) that can be tested at that stage, (2) to plan actions that might not otherwise occur in order to test assumptions that are important to the venture's success, and (3) to plan actions in a critical path so that the feedback from earlier actions can be used to modify later ones.

Although each venture has a unique pattern of growth and development, many stages are common to all ventures, and we will regard them as potential milestones for assumptions testing, as shown in Figure 7-2 and described in the following subsections. Each of these milestones gives the company an opportunity to decide whether to continue with the business as planned, redirect the effort, or bow out. Milestones 1 through 6, which are substantially investigative, offer the best opportunities for testing the assumptions, refining them, and learning.

At each stage, venture managers should ask the following questions about the new business:

- What assumptions did we make?
- How have they changed?
- In light of these changed assumptions, what actions do we need to take (including abandoning the idea)?

Milestone 1: Completion of Concept and Product Testing

Product testing, which can sometimes be done with a low-cost model, gives the firm an opportunity to test the idea before getting into more expensive product development with

Figure 7-2: Milestones and Events for Assumptions Testing

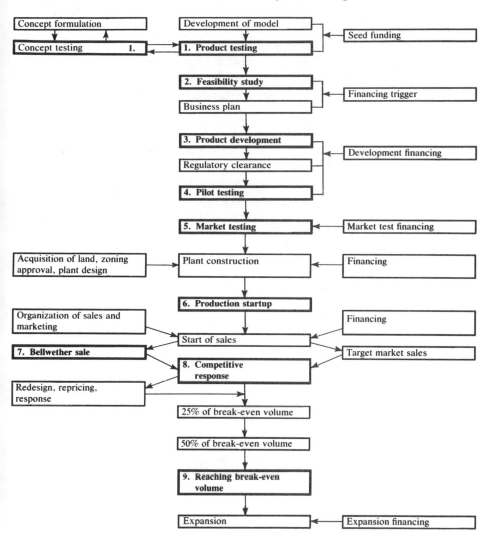

a fully developed or engineered prototype. If a model can't be created and product development is expected to be expensive, then the concept alone can be tested. This testing can validate or alter the assumptions that have been made about who is likely to buy and why, assuming specific product characteristics and anticipated price. In the case of an industrial product, early and direct discussions with potential customers can help the company formulate a project in such a way as to increase the likelihood of the product's acceptance. Without such discussions, the company will have to make assumptions about the customers and their needs, spend lots of money on development, and then hunt for uses that may not be found or may take too long to develop.

Of course, customers don't always know what they need. Some needs are so profound that consumers may be unaware of them until they are presented with potential solutions. Examples include telephones, televisions, gene splicing, semiconductors, transistors, and other major technological innovations that have changed both industries and the world. Firms that attempt to develop products like these must recognize the assumptions they are making and realize that it takes deep pockets and a great deal of time, persistence, and patience for such projects to succeed.

These technology-driven, high-impact, and high-risk projects should be consciously labeled as such and treated differently from typical new businesses. These are the ventures that can be enormous winners or losers. Like any highly volatile substance, they should be handled with care. It is especially important in such projects to plan for the earliest possible testing of concept acceptance and to obtain input from potential customers in shaping the venture's objectives. Unavoidably, these events will probably occur only after significant R&D money has been spent.

The concept- and model-testing stage provides the first data for verifying assumptions about the target market, reasons for purchase, and required product or service characteristics. The importance of such testing in evaluating ideas is illustrated by the experience of a food company that supplied prepared doughnut mixes to bakers. The firm's R&D department believed it would be possible to produce a doughnut significantly lower in fat and calories than the usual product, and in the mid-1970s, the firm attempted to develop such a product. But since development costs would have been significant to the company, it assembled a focus group from the target market to pretest the concept. The group's response was overwhelming: "It's impossible. Such a product couldn't be tasty." This led to the assumption that consumers might purchase a good-tasting, low-fat doughnut if it could be developed.

The company could have acted on that assumption by abandoning the idea or by proceeding, at great expense, with development, assuming that once consumers tasted the product, resistance would melt. But instead, the company did another concept test. It repackaged existing doughnuts with very high consumer acceptance in dummy cartons that presented them as low-fat and low-calorie and then offered them to another focus group. The group judged the doughnuts to be poor-tasting, confirming the earlier opinion that such a product couldn't possibly be any good! Therefore, the revised assumption was that the market would not immediately accept any such product labeled low-calorie and low-fat. Realizing that it could spend an awful lot of time and money trying to convert attitudes, the company dropped the project. (Since then, however, consumer preferences have shifted, and many products engineered for lower fat and calorie content—e.g., frozen desserts, salad dressings, "cheeses"—have been introduced and successfully marketed.)

Upon completion of concept and product testing, the company can make one of the following decisions: change the concept and retest it, put the project on the back burner for later consideration, abandon it, or proceed with a feasibility study, including prototype development. The back-burner option is appropriate if the reasons for postponement involve lack of market and technological readiness. When the company determines that the reasons for postponement have been overcome, the project can be brought back on line.

Milestone 2: Completion of the Feasibility Study

The feasibility study helps the company improve the determination of whether the business's objectives are achievable and whether the underlying assumptions should be changed. Whereas the concept test is an initial examination of the likelihood of market interest, the feasibility study, at the very least, should provide the information needed to develop a business plan, if the results warrant doing so. The feasibility study is designed to enable the company to estimate or determine what it will take in time, money, and people to develop the product or service; possible material, production, selling, and service costs; selling prices; competitive offerings and the venture's possible competitive advantage; physical resources needed to get into production; the range of investment (preliminary estimate); possible formats; the availability of needed supplies and potential suppliers; and the availability of distribution channels.

The completion of the feasibility study should enable the company to make a more objective estimate of development time and costs, the functional characteristics and probable quality level that can be achieved, and possible competitive advantage and also give it some idea of production costs.

Milestone 3: Product Development

Since product development almost always takes longer and costs more than planned, it is particularly important to establish submilestones within the product development phase itself and to review assumptions at each of these intermediate milestones.

This frequent monitoring is essential to minimize the risks of losses at this stage. For example, a medium-sized machinery manufacturer saw an opportunity to develop a device that would turn out 40 widgets per minute. It would carry a price tag of $40,000 and yield a 25% ROI to the widget producer. The feasibility study indicated that the machine could be developed for $150,000 and that there was a probable market for 100 machines per year at $30,000 apiece. Production costs were estimated at approximately $12,000 per unit. Based on these data, the company decided to proceed with development.

After spending about $60,000 on design costs, the firm learned that the device would require metal with different characteristics than had originally been assumed, raising material and machining costs to $25,000 per unit (and boosting the price tag to $60,000 per unit). It also learned that development costs would hit $400,000.

Clearly, the entire venture required re-evaluation. What was the market for machines costing $60,000 instead of $30,000? Should the production rate objective be altered? Again, the fundamental questions had to be asked: Shall we redirect the effort, abandon it, or proceed with no change in direction, timing, or planned action sequence? In this case, the project was ultimately abandoned, since it was clear that there was no significant market for the higher-cost machine.

The product development phase is a time when managers can also test assumptions about the product development strategy itself—that is, the magnitude of the undertaking and the product characteristics to be achieved. Canon's entry into the personal photocopier market is an example of a major effort to develop a new market for copiers. Because the potential market was so large and copier competition so strong (i.e., from Xerox, Minolta, and Kodak), the high risk of a development effort involving more than a thousand engineers over a five-year period was considered well worth taking.

The Canon case is also an illuminating example of a development strategy involving the reassessment of assumptions. The basic problem was to develop a product with minimal service requirements because of the impracticality of providing service to the target market. In order to solve this problem, every feature of both existing products and the production process had to be reassessed. In the Canon case (Nonaka and Yamanouchi 1989), the copier's entire design concept was changed to minimize service requirements. At the same time, design was integrated with production to ease the design-to-production transition. As firms seek to reduce product development cycle times, they are increasingly employing this strategy of expanding development teams to include those who will be responsible both for designing and operating the production processes and for marketing.

To apply the lessons from product development, venture managers must answer the following questions:

- What assumptions did we make about development time and costs, and how have those assumptions changed? Why?
- What impact should those changes have on plans and timing with respect to new hires, plant construction, or marketing? How do they affect needs and timing with respect to financing?
- What has been learned about the costs and availability of labor, materials, and equipment, and how does this affect pricing plans?
- Do the observations and assumptions about the target markets still hold? If not, how have they changed, and how should those changes affect plans for each succeeding event, with respect to objectives, timing, and resource utilization?
- Do the product's characteristics fit the original concept and plan? Have any new opportunities been identified? How should actions be modified as a result?
- Are assumptions regarding significant competitors and the characteristics of competitive products still valid?
- How should investment requirements be changed?
- Are assumptions about suppliers and distributors still valid?

Milestone 4: Pilot Testing

Feasibility testing and product development provide many answers needed to validate assumptions, but until the product or service is actually produced, those answers are still theoretical. The pilot-testing stage will provide hard information about the suitability and costs of materials, processing costs and skills, investment requirements, personnel training needs, reject levels and costs, quality control requirements, the uniformity of materials from suppliers, supplier reliability, processing specifications, and maintenance requirements.

In the pilot phase, products are sometimes found to have unsuspected values. One such case occurred during the development of a process for producing onion rings from diced onions. Pilot testing revealed that the product was much more durable than expected—so much so that hand packaging, the industry standard, was not required. This discovery made it possible to use fully automated packaging at drastically reduced costs, thus greatly increasing the economic value of the process, which was to be licensed to frozen-food manufacturers, and justifying much higher royalties than had been considered likely. Furthermore, the product's stability made it feasible to employ transparent film packaging, which made the product more attractive to consumers and resulted in a significant expansion of the consumer market for onion rings.

Milestone 5: Market Testing

Market testing is the time to examine assumptions about the venture's target market. It is also a critical turning point, because from here on out, investment in the venture increases exponentially.

The questions that venture managers must ask at this stage are:

- Have target market customers demonstrated that they'll buy the product? With what frequency? Why? Why not?
- Is the product really different from and superior to the competition?

- Are the pricing assumptions still valid in light of emerging information about costs?
- Does the product perform well in various field applications? What problems are occurring and why? What are the positive surprises, and how can they be exploited?
- How should estimates of achievable market share, size, and target markets be modified?
- Are servicing assumptions accurate?
- What impact does the foregoing information have on planned goals, actions, and timing?

Milestone 6: Production Startup

The production startup milestone tests the revised assumptions about production resulting from pilot testing. The sequence and timing of planned actions should provide for changes in those assumptions, particularly with respect to marketing actions, commitments to customers, and rigidity of pricing. The failure to build in some time between production startup and delivery may result in excessively high startup costs due either to high reject levels or to attempts to squeeze production out of a plant or services out of a service organization before the facility is fully ready. Planning for production startup can best be managed by making a separate critical path milestone plan for the startup and by providing for the accumulation of a specified quantity of inventory before shipments begin.

At this stage, it is critical to compare production costs and quality levels with the cost and quality profile of competitors. After constructing a cost profile of its competitor in a developing new market through product analysis, supplier information, trade journal articles, and company annual reports, a packaging manufacturer learned that its costs were, and would continue to be, higher because the competitor had the advantage of a proprietary production process. As a result, the manufacturer decided that it needed to utilize its greater flexibility, rapid changeover capability, and higher quality to compete on the basis of fast delivery (and hence, lower inventory requirements for customers) plus superior quality. With this approach, it is now successfully building a significant share of this new market.

Milestone 7: Bellwether Sale

The bellwether sale is the first substantial sale to a major account. The business plan should specify the first five sales that will be made, identifying target accounts by name, and at least one of them should be a potential bellwether account. In the case of an industrial product, the target should be a respected leader in the industry; in the consumer product area, it should be a respected leader in retail marketing or distribution, such as a top supermarket chain for a food product. Establishing credibility is crucial for the new venture's success, and there are few better ways to build that reputation than by selling to an account whose very act of buying is a statement of belief that the new entrant has something significant to offer.

The bellwether sale will tell venture management how the product really compares with the competition, whether its characteristics and functions are significantly superior, what the service requirements are likely to be, whether a satisfactory level of quality control has been achieved, and whether the selling methods need to be altered.

Milestone 8: First Competitive Response

Although a company has no way of knowing in advance exactly how the competition will respond to a new product or service, it can envision possible alternatives and design tests to evaluate them. It is worth real effort and self-discipline to answer such questions as: Which competitor(s) will be hurt the most by the new product? What are the strengths and weaknesses of the competitor(s) that will be most significantly affected? How would our firm react under similar circumstances? What information is available on previous competitive responses to threat?

Competitors have various options for responding, which include lowering prices, controlling the supply of a critical material, closing off vital distribution channels, adding features that the new product lacks, stealing key people, or initiating a lawsuit (valid or not).

What can your firm do to prevent or counteract the competitive response? Much can be learned from the experience of the GD Company, which supplies materials to chemical manufacturers. GD developed a new process for producing a commonly used material. This process—which did not require, but could use, GD's raw materials—was patent-protected, and GD decided to license the process nonexclusively. A royalty percentage plus an initial payment and a minimum license commitment period were formulated.

GD did not know what its major competitor's response would be but was concerned about it, particularly because of the royalty level. To smoke out competitive reaction, GD presented its program to a very loyal customer of the competitor with which it had little or no hope of doing business. The customer quickly notified GD's competitor, which advised the customer that it would be able to supply a royalty-free alternative in 90 days. Given this information, GD altered its program by eliminating the minimum commitment period and guaranteeing return of the initial payment if the licensee chose to replace the program with that of a competitor within a six-month period. This action completely blocked the competitor's attempts to stop GD's progress. Although the customer first approached by GD never became a licensee, the information GD obtained in dealing with it proved extremely helpful in marketing the process to other customers.

Although a company may not always be able to get a competitor to tip its hand as GD did, it *can* conceive possible competitive responses to the new product or service. In attempting to answer key questions—e.g., What might the competition do? How can we find out? How can we prevent or counteract it?—the firm can plan actions to elicit competitive response.

The alternatives—either blithely assuming superiority over the competition or sitting back and waiting without making any effort to learn and devise contingency plans—can be very dangerous. A financial services company found this out when it introduced a new service that offered protection to large-scale bond investors. Although the service had a significant drawback, in that it failed to provide investors with hard-copy confirmation, it was very useful and at first grew rapidly without competition. However, a competitor subsequently introduced a similar service that included hard-copy confirmation, which customers wanted, as the originator of the service was aware. This improvement allowed the competitor to obtain leading market share. Too late, the first firm chased after the competition in an attempt to catch up, but failed and is now a secondary provider.

Milestone 9: Reaching Break-even Volume

A new venture's break-even volume often turns out to be greater than planned—assuming it is planned at all. If a company lets events take their course and then learns that the planned break-even volume is too low, it ends up either scrambling to learn why or, as so many firms do, just recalculating a higher break-even point. Clearly, it is preferable to avoid this scenario by testing assumptions that can affect the break-even volume. Assumptions about costs and losses should be examined at intermediate volumes such as 25%, 50%, and 75% of planned break-even (or at any intervals that make sense for a particular venture) and testing built into the business plan.

A common source of miscalculation and delay in reaching break-even and profitability is the company's assumption regarding the time interval between the initiation of a sales effort and its consummation. (And in some markets, overly optimistic assumptions regarding how quickly customers will pay have resulted in entirely unrealistic time estimates for cash break-even, as has occurred with businesses based on the hospital market, where payment tends to be very slow.) Among the major factors, usually uncalculated, that cause delays in achieving break-even are: the risk to customers in switching to the new product/supplier, actual switching costs incurred by customers, customers' internal timetable for when funds are budgeted for the category of product being offered (capital equipment, for example), unexpected service requirements, customers' internal approval process required for selecting a new product or an alternate supplier of a product, and reorder cycle.

If the corporation has done its homework, if it has carefully identified the important assumptions and used milestone planning and evaluation up to this point, it will have recognized many of these potential challenges long before it reaches this final milestone. In fact, a number of them will have emerged during the feasibility study and plan preparation and particularly during the market-testing stage.

STRATEGIC CHOICES FOR ENTERING THE MARKET

When should a firm plan to enter a new business on a large scale aggressively, taking high risks, and when should it plan to make a slower, less aggressive entry? Although milestone planning is desirable and necessary in either case, there are circumstances in which timing requirements may force the company not only to abandon the critical path approach, but also to enter the market with maximum effort and resources in order to reap potentially high rewards, or to protect its existing market position.

The following guidelines can help a company decide on the degree of aggressiveness appropriate to an individual venture.

For **maximum aggressiveness** (i.e., high expenditure and effort in every area—investment in facilities, marketing, development):

The *market* is established and growing or emerging with great potential and is highly competitive; *resources* are ample and affordable; *salience* to the firm is high; *diversity* from the existing business is not great; *competition* is strong or potentially so; *proprietary protection* is present; the *corporate culture* is supportive and not excessively risk averse; a large *critical mass* is needed in order to start the venture.

For **minimum aggressiveness:**

The *market* is in an early state of development, its rate of development is unpredictable, and the firm does not have the resources to persevere, or the market is a niche market; *resources* are relatively sparse and early large losses are not affordable; *salience* to the firm is relatively low; *diversity* from the existing business is significant; *competition* is not present or weak; there is strong *proprietary protection;* the *corporate culture* is risk averse, not strongly committed to venturing; a large *critical mass* is not necessary in order to start the business.

Any one or a combination of these factors may be sufficient to dictate the level of aggressiveness of entry. For example, if the firm is highly risk averse and uncommitted to venturing, it is foolhardy to enter at the maximum risk level inherent in an aggressive mode. Similarly, a resource-limited firm without a major sustainable competitive advantage in its new venture would be foolish to aggressively enter a slowly emerging market with major potential which will attract powerful competition with deep pockets.

What the company should avoid is selecting an entry strategy that disregards the critical factors of market, competition, and risk affordability, or simply assuming that success is dependent on maximum aggressiveness of entry.

CREATING AND EVALUATING
THE NEW-VENTURE PLAN

This section provides short overviews of the processes used in developing and evaluating a new-venture business plan.

Action Steps for Planners

The following list summarizes the key steps to be taken by venture managers in developing a business plan:

1. In the business plan, identify the important events and actions that must occur in order to achieve the venture's objectives.
2. Determine which events or actions are prerequisites to others—that is, establish the necessary sequential links between events or actions.
3. Develop a critical path milestone chart that displays the sequence graphically.
4. Identify the significant, go/no-go assumptions on which the venture's success depends.
5. Ask whether the events or actions on the milestone chart will test each of the critical assumptions. If not, design one or more testing steps and insert them into the chart. Specify the information needed to validate each assumption and how it will be obtained.
6. As each event occurs and assumptions are replaced with facts, review planned future events, changing their nature and sequence as necessary.

Evaluation Questions for Senior Managers

The key questions senior managers must ask in evaluating business plans are:

- Does the business fit the firm's strategy?
- Does the plan clearly specify the critical assumptions being made about the market, competition, costs, product or service functions, pricing/margins, investment and timing requirements, and regulatory and environmental factors? Are actions planned to test, or achieve control of, each of these assumptions?
- Does the plan state the potential downside risk and upside gain?
- Does the plan clearly define financing triggers?
- Are success and failure defined?
- Does the venture's proposed format meet the needs of the new business and provide the resources (people, knowledge, physical requirements, money) necessary for its success? (Refer to Chapter 3 for a discussion of establishing a good match between venture needs and corporate capabilities.)
- Have relevant internal and external political factors been considered?
- Does the plan provide a credible possibility of achieving the promise that led the company to investigate the business idea in the first place?
- Is the management team capable of supplying the factors needed for the venture's success?

CONCLUSION

New-venture plans are based largely on assumptions rather than facts. If these assumptions are unknown or untested, the parent company can spend a lot of time and money to find out that it is headed in the wrong direction. For that reason, effective new-venture plans must include activities designed to test the critical assumptions underlying the effort.

Since many of these assumptions will prove to be inaccurate, the business plan will have to be revised on an ongoing basis to reflect new information. Such changes may involve sequences of actions, timing, funding, target markets, pricing, intensity of effort, and possibly abandonment of the venture.

Because it is based largely on assumptions and not facts, new-business planning must necessarily differ from planning for established businesses. Venture managers and their senior management must clearly understand and accept these differences or pay the penalty of misguiding new ventures to expensive failure or only limited success.

The point is to build a business if possible, not to adhere obstinately to a plan conceived in ignorance and preserved intact no matter what is learned along the way.

Guidelines

1. Since the first rule of new-business planning is that plans and results almost never match, recognize and accept the fact that plans will and must be changed.
2. Articulate, understand, and test the critical assumptions on which the new venture is based.
3. Include in the business plan actions and events deliberately designed to test critical assumptions—that is, make sure the plan provides for learning as well as doing.
4. Because the results of assumptions testing may dictate changes in the nature and sequence of future actions, use the critical path approach for action planning, in which certain actions must be completed before subsequent actions based on their outcome can begin.

   (Note: Guideline 4 does not apply in cases where a company must undertake a high-pressure race to market in order to achieve share or preempt competitive entry and where the potential stakes are high enough to warrant taking the greatly increased risk of abandoning a more systematic and cautious approach.)

192

5. In preparing a new-venture plan, focus primarily on event completion, not strict adherence to schedules— unless analysis of competitive factors indicates that a specific time is of the essence.

REFERENCES

Bangs, David, Jr. 1988. *The Business Planning Guide*. Dover, NH: Upstart Publishing.

Brandt, S. C. 1986. *Entrepreneuring in Established Companies*. Homewood, IL: Dow Jones–Irwin.

————. 1987. *Strategic Planning in Emerging Companies,* Chapters 6 and 7. Reading, MA: Addison-Wesley.

Burgelman, R. A., and Sayles, L. R. 1986. *Inside Corporate Innovation*. New York: Free Press.

MacMillan, I.; Block, Z.; and Subbanarasimha, P. N. 1986. "Corporate Venturing: Alternatives, Obstacles Encountered and Experience Effects." *Journal of Business Venturing* 1, no. 2 (Spring): 177–192.

Nonaka, I., and Yamanouchi, T. 1989. "Managing Innovation as a Self-Renewing Process." *Journal of Business Venturing* 4, no. 5 (September): 299–315.

Sacher, W., and Wolterbeek, M. 1987. "A Comparison of Venture Capital Backed Business Plans versus Business Results." Applied Business Project Report. Graduate School of Business Administration, New York University.

Timmons, J. A. 1990. *New Venture Creation,* 329–397. 3d ed. Homewood, IL: Dow Jones—Irwin. (This book is particularly recommended for its detailed instructional material and good examples.)

Welsh, J. A., and White, J. F. 1983. *The Entrepreneur's Master Planning Guide*. Englewood Cliffs, NJ: Prentice-Hall.

8

Organizing the Venture

This chapter addresses the two key decisions in venture organization—namely, the venture's focal activity (i.e., the fundamental activity that drives the rest of the activities in the venture) and the key linkages that should be established between the venture and the rest of the organization. The crucial variable that shapes these two organizing decisions involves the degree to which the venture's product, market, and technology are related to the parent organization's product, market, and technology. The more unrelated the venture, the greater the learning challenges facing the firm; the more related the venture, the greater the potential for capturing know-how available within the organization.

The different combinations of product, market, and technology relatedness give rise to seven distinct types of ventures, each with its own unique pattern of learning challenges, opportunities for capturing know-how, and potential for the venture to intrude into various aspects of the parent firm's ongoing operations. The guiding principles for organizing ventures involve designing the focal activity with the aim of meeting the learning challenges and designing linkages with the rest of the organization with the aim of capturing know-how—but without permitting the venture to intrude excessively into the established business.

As we argued in Chapter 7, "Developing the Business Plan," the key to venturing success is to focus on learning—on converting initial assumptions into commercializable knowledge. In organizing a venture, learning remains the primary challenge, and the new business should therefore be organized in such a way as to maximize learning.

For the purposes of discussing venture organization, let us define *learning* as "the process of obtaining information and discovering solutions to problems." This includes developing the capability to identify and solve problems "automatically," as a matter of organizational routine. Thus, all ventures have major learning requirements associated with them, for until a venture has pinpointed the problems facing it, and developed and fine-tuned protocols and procedures for solving these problems, it has little hope of reaching a state of sustained growth and profitability. The challenge for the venture manager is to organize the new business in a way that enables such learning to be achieved as rapidly as possible.

At the start of the chapter, we said that organizing a venture involves two major sets of decisions: (1) what the focal activity will be and (2) what the linkages between the venture and the parent firm will be. Before we begin a detailed discussion of how to organize a venture, however, it would be productive to briefly consider some key principles for deciding on focal activity and linkages:

- *Decisions on focal activity:* The firm must determine which activity (development, production, or sales/service) should be the venture's focal point and major driver, which is determined by what major challenges must be met if the venture is to succeed. For instance,

if the major challenge facing the venture is to understand and enter a new market, then the focal activity
will be dedicated sales and marketing.

- *Decisions on linkages:* The firm must exploit and capture existing corporate know-how that may be useful
to the venture. Therefore, it is important to establish
mechanisms to link the venture's focal activity with
those parts of the organization that possess the required expertise.

Furthermore, in any venture, there will always be unan-
ticipated and unpredictable contingencies—those events,
good or bad, that suddenly need to be dealt with by different
functions in the organization. So the two purposes of linking
mechanisms are (1) to facilitate the transfer of information
and know-how to the venture and (2) to supply the knowledge
and assistance required to deal with the contingencies that
will inevitably arise as the venture gets under way. Those
contingencies vary in predictability (for instance, manufacturing glitches are an absolute certainty, whereas a regulatory
problem is merely a possibility) as well as in frequency, and
the relative frequency of various contingencies can be guess-
timated.

Galbraith (1982), has suggested linking mechanisms
based on different combinations of frequency, predictability,
and scope of the contingency, which we have summarized
in Table 8-1. The precise nature of the linking mechanism
described in each quadrant of the table depends on whether
linkage is required between only two parties or between various parties. To illustrate, in quadrant I, if only two departments are involved, it will suffice to name just one contact
person in each department; if more than two departments are
involved, a task force is the recommended mechanism.

Starting in quadrant I, if the contingency involves a
highly predictable situation that is not expected to arise too
often, all the firm must do is design an appropriate contingency plan, agree on what events will trigger this plan, and
then leave it to the responsible parties to carry out the plan's

Table 8-1: Linking Mechanisms to Handle Contingencies

	Low Frequency	*High Frequency*
High Predictability	I Contingency plan is activated.	II Preassigned liaison or "SWAT" team takes action.
Low Predictability	III Contact person or task force investigates and recommends action.	IV Program manager or management team monitors and coordinates.

provisions when the triggering events occur. An example of such a contingency would be the loss of a major source of supply—in which case, a plan can be devised ahead of time to switch to alternate sources or alternate materials. All that needs to be done is for the responsible parties (say, people from manufacturing, distribution, and sales) to be notified of the loss of the original source of supply, and they can carry out whatever actions have been assigned to them.

The next level (quadrant II) involves contingencies that are both highly predictable and expected to occur frequently. Examples of such events would be an unplanned plant shutdown, an unforeseen shortage of supplies, or a sudden rush order from distributors or customers. The organization knows these events will happen, and rather often; the only question is when. The contingency tool suggested here depends on whether just two departments are involved or more than two. In the case of two departments, all the organization must do is identify a liaison person in each department. Whenever the contingency occurs, these liaison people get in touch with each other and decide on which of a prearranged set of actions they will take. In the case of a contingency involving multiple departments, each department selects a liaison person who is a member of a "SWAT" team assigned to the task of handling the contingency by selecting and coordinating whatever actions they have prearranged.

At the next level (quadrant III), we have contingencies whose predictability and frequency are both low—i.e., the firm cannot tell in advance when these contingencies will occur and cannot be sure except in general terms what they might consist of. Examples of negative contingencies would be an unexplained decline in a new product's quality or a sudden rise in customer complaints about the product. A positive contingency would be the discovery that a new product is performing much better than anticipated.

There are no predetermined actions that can be worked out ahead of time in such cases. Hence, for a situation involving two departments, the firm needs to identify a contact person in each department and designate the two to work together whenever a level III contingency arises—to investigate the problem or opportunity and deal with the contingency. These individuals may be the same as the liaisons named to respond to level II contingencies, or they may be people higher up in the organization. If the contingency involves more than two departments, each department assigns a representative to serve on a task force that will investigate the problem or opportunity and determine an appropriate response.

Note that although the individuals assigned to serve on the task force are "permanent representatives," they are mobilized only when a contingency arises; the task force disbands when the contingency has been handled and does not reassemble until the next contingency arises. The task force members can, of course, enlist experts or obtain input from knowledgeable contributors as necessary. Note, too, that as in other cases, the contingencies dealt with by the task force need not be negative ones. Positive phenomena such as unexpectedly high market penetration or unexpectedly outstanding product performance are equally worth investigation, to ensure that these benefits are sustained.

The final level (quadrant IV) involves low-predictability contingencies that are expected to occur with high frequency, which usually happens at the start of a venture. In this case, the firm must assemble a project team led by a project manager whose sole task is to orchestrate information flows among the various departments and call on project team members for help on an as-needed basis.

RELATEDNESS—THE CRUCIAL ORGANIZING VARIABLE

In organizing a venture, it makes a huge difference whether the venture's product, market, and technology are very similar to or very different from the parent company's existing products, markets, and technology. Therefore, by far the most important factor to consider in venture organization is the relatedness between the venture's business and the established business.

Those features of the venture that are highly unrelated to the rest of the organization pose the major challenges for organizational learning. Those features that are highly related offer the major opportunities to capitalize on existing corporate know-how, for they represent areas where the firm's past experience and current relationships can be used to maximum effect to enhance the venture's chances of success.

Therefore, the concept of relatedness provides the basic framework for deciding what the venture's focal activity should be and what linkages should be established. The venture's managerial focus should be on the activity where the greatest amount of learning must occur if the venture is to succeed. It is this area that should receive the most attention. On the other hand, linkages need to be designed to enable the venture to tap any useful know-how the firm already possesses.

In terms of priority, we suggest that when making the trade-off between maximizing learning and maximizing the capture of existing know-how, maximizing learning should take precedence. For example, if the primary lack of expertise involves market knowledge, but the firm knows the product and technology well, then the venture must be organized around a dedicated marketing and sales team, with a good marketing generalist as program manager to maximize market learning. To capitalize on available corporate know-how, this marketing generalist should be supported by key liaison people in operations and development who can provide input on major product, process, systems, and design issues that affect the marketing thrust.

Whether the venture has high or low relatedness with the parent firm's products, markets, and technology largely determines the learning challenges the venture will face and the opportunities it will have to capitalize on existing corporate know-how—so much so that different combinations of product, market, and technology relatedness lead to seven distinctly different types of ventures, which are discussed later in the chapter. The most important issues for organizing each type of venture are what specific learning challenges are faced given various *low* levels of product, market, and technology relatedness and what specific know-how can be exploited given various *high* levels of product, market, and technology relatedness.

LEARNING CHALLENGES ASSOCIATED WITH LOW RELATEDNESS

Table 8-2 lists the major learning challenges that tend to be associated with low relatedness between the venture's product, market, and technology and those of the parent firm.

To maximize learning effectiveness, venture managers should start by carefully scanning Table 8-2 to identify which of the learning challenges associated with unrelatedness might apply to their particular venture. They should then supplement this list with whatever additional new-product, new-market, and new-technology learning challenges can be identified by thinking through the specific venture.

The final step is to identify what must be learned as the venture progresses, decide how to capture that learning as it occurs, and assemble a venture unit that will best be able to focus on the learning needs that have been identified. In the

Table 8-2: Learning Challenges Associated with Low Relatedness

Area of Low Relatedness	Types of Learning Challenges
Product	Operations turbulence New processes and systems Trial runs and reject rates Debugging problems Lack of product and supply standards Lack of service standards Greater selling effort Switching cost disadvantages High customer returns
Market	Selling uncertainty New customers and channels Lack of relationships Lack of customer and channel tolerance and empathy Poor understanding of industry protocols New salesforce Lack of experience in servicing the product
Technology	New processes or systems Reliability New equipment suppliers New material suppliers Debugging problems New skill requirements New product, systems, and process standards

case of a project that primarily requires new-product learning, for example, there is no point in locating such a facility in one of the existing operating divisions, since little can be learned from the firm's present production or systems operations. On the other hand, much of the necessary learning *can* occur if the firm creates a dedicated operating facility specifically for test runs, debugging, product evolution, evolution of standard operating procedures and training therein, and development of satisfactory supply, product, and service standards.

The following subsections provide brief overviews of the specific learning challenges often associated with low levels of product, market, and technology relatedness. We make no claim that these lists are exhaustive. However, any venture that involves creating a highly unrelated new product, new market, or new technology will surely face one or more of these learning challenges, among others. It is up to the organization to identify which learning challenges the particular venture will face and decide how the venture can best be organized to meet those challenges.

Low Product Relatedness: New-Product Learning

The following are among the major learning challenges that may arise when a venture's product is very different from the parent company's existing products:

- *Operations turbulence:* When a new product is being produced, the operations producing that product are subject to tremendous turbulence. This creates an operations climate characterized by high uncertainty and extreme pressures, and can generate an environment in which the entire work force is tired, demoralized, and lacking in confidence. Maintaining energy and morale can become a serious problem.
- *New processes and systems:* The organization must learn to deliver quality product with new processes and systems. Considerable "burn-in" experience is needed before these processes and systems can be operated without frequent shutdowns, and it usually takes longer than anticipated to achieve stable operating conditions.
- *Trial runs and reject rates:* While learning to make a new product, a venture is often forced to undertake large numbers of short trial runs accompanied by enormously high reject rates, which is both costly and disruptive.
- *Debugging problems:* Since new processes tend to be

poorly understood, the sources of breakdowns and operating failures may at first be only vaguely comprehensible.

- Production/systems operation could therefore be plagued by serious debugging problems.
- *Lack of product and supply standards:* If the product is very new, there could be a complete lack of clarity regarding what the standards should be, both for the product and for material and equipment suppliers. Even if the product is not new to the world but is simply new to the parent company, the venture must learn what standards should be imposed on suppliers. This standards vacuum creates a great deal of uncertainty as to what the product, production, and supply characteristics should be. The challenge is to identify, create, or fine-tune these standards.
- *Lack of service standards:* Since the firm is unfamiliar with the product, it is equally unfamiliar with the need for product servicing and therefore enters the market uncertain of what it will take to service the product and what its service standards should be. Particularly in the venture's early stages, while the production process is being burned in, demands for service can be inordinately high, as can the level of customer dissatisfaction if service is not delivered.
- *Greater selling effort:* When it first attempts to sell a new product, the salesforce simply does not know what customers really want. In fact, if the product is very new, neither do the customers. Sales reps therefore have to make a much greater selling effort for the new product than for their existing product portfolio.
- *Switching cost disadvantages:* If the new product enters the market against existing competition, the challenges facing the salesforce might be compounded by the fact that a competitor's offer is preferred and that there are significant switching cost disadvantages of which the firm is unaware. It could take serious effort

to identify and overcome these switching cost disadvantages.

- *High customer returns:* The problems of greater selling effort and switching cost disadvantages are then further compounded by the fact that in the venture's early stages, as the production system is being burned in, there are inevitable problems with customer returns. This can place a serious strain on the comfortable relationship that derives from selling existing product to customers, thereby providing a disincentive for the salesforce to sell the new product.

Low Market Relatedness: New-Market Learning

The following are among the major learning challenges that may arise when the market for the venture's product is very different from the market for the organization's existing products:

- *Selling uncertainty:* The newer and more unrelated the market, the greater the level of selling uncertainty that the organization faces. Little is known about the customers' real needs, who makes their purchasing decisions, what usage patterns are common in the industry, and what risks the customers take if they switch to the venture's product.
- *New customers and channels:* In many cases, it is unclear what the true target customer group is and which channels should be used to reach it. The firm may know very little about the reliability and quality of service of various existing channels, nor whether a particular channel will actually promote the product. Often, a firm is forced to create entirely new customers and/or attempt to reach them through entirely new channels.
- *Lack of relationships:* When the company serves ex-

isting markets, relationships are created between the salesforce and the channels/customers—relationships that perpetuate conditions of trust, loyalty, and emotional switching costs. When the company enters an entirely new market, those relationships do not exist, and it takes a tremendous amount of learning to understand what is needed to develop and sustain such relationships in a new market.

- *Lack of customer and channel tolerance and empathy:* When the company is operating in well-known markets and has good customer relations, there is a level of mutual tolerance and empathy between the customers, the channels, and the provider. Because of past experiences and mutual trust and loyalty, each party has developed a willingness to tolerate and empathize with the others when they are experiencing transient difficulties. In new markets, no such tolerance or empathy exists, and every failure to deliver on a promised transaction is viewed with suspicious intolerance if not outright destructive distrust.

- *Poor understanding of industry protocols:* Every industry has its own protocols regarding how things are done in that industry—who is called on, in what order, how the buying decision is made, how the sale is pitched and closed, how the product is delivered, and what demands can or cannot be made by buyer and seller. Failure to understand the requisite protocols often puts a new entrant to a market at a serious disadvantage.

- *New salesforce:* The more unrelated the market, the less knowledge the firm has about the best ways to select, train, motivate, and remunerate the salesforce. Many firms make the blunder of using the same principles as they use for the existing salesforce—principles that can prove fatal in new markets—or they attempt to use the existing salesforce when, as is often the case, it is essential to develop an entirely new salesforce dedicated to the new market.

- *Lack of experience in servicing the product:* The newer the market, the less aware the entrant is of the specific service expectations of the channels and customers, and the less aware it is of how much effort will be required in order to meet those expectations. Once again, the venture's service force may have to be selected, trained, motivated, and remunerated very differently from the service force for the company's existing businesses.

Low Technology Relatedness: New-Technology Learning

The following are among the major learning challenges that may arise when the venture's product employs a technology that is very different from the technology employed to produce the organization's existing products:

- *New processes or systems:* Movement into an unrelated technology inevitably creates the learning challenge of designing and developing new processes (in the case of manufacturing) or new systems (in the case of service).
- *Reliability:* After the design challenge has been met, there still remains the challenge of nursing the fledgling process or system along until it becomes a reliable, predictable operation. This challenge is compounded by the highly disruptive debugging of process problems or systems operating problems that typically occurs as a new design is being burned in.
- *New equipment suppliers:* As the new process or system is being developed, the company faces the problem of identifying reliable manufacturers of the equipment required for the process or system. It would be unwise for the firm to assume that new equipment suppliers will necessarily match the standards of quality, reliability, and service being delivered by its current suppliers. Particularly in cases involving a new-to-the-

207

world technology, the suppliers may be experiencing their own problems, first in determining what the appropriate standards for their industry are and then in meeting those standards.

- *New material suppliers:* In addition, since a new technology often requires very different materials than the ones currently being used, reliable new sources of material must be identified. And the standards and protocols being used with the existing group of suppliers will probably not apply among the new group.
- *Debugging problems:* As the new technology is being burned in, the debugging problems occurring in the evolving production process or in the evolving product itself tend not only to disrupt the organization's internal systems but also to disrupt and cause major problems for channels of distribution and customers. The organization must rapidly develop an understanding of what external disruptions its debugging problems are creating and mobilize solutions to channel and customer problems, for if it fails to do so, it will lose their support.
- *New skill requirements:* As the new technology begins to be deployed, there is a dramatic increase in the need to recruit and/or train a work force that will be capable of using this new technology or incorporating it into ongoing operations. If the new technology is to become cost-competitive, the firm must manage to steadily drive down the skill levels needed to use it. New technologies that require a large number of highly skilled people to keep operations flowing smoothly will end up either being too expensive or being obsoleted by less costly competitive technologies.
- *New product, systems, and process standards:* As the new technology develops, it is essential that the company find ways to at the very least meet, but preferably exceed, the standards of quality, reliability, and

Table 8-3: Opportunities to Capture Know-how from High Relatedness

Area of High Relatedness	Types of Know-how That Can Be Captured
Product	Predictability and stability of operations Operating confidence Operating processes/systems Long runs and systems reliability Low customer returns Supplier trust and confidence Supplier relationships Understanding of service needs Service delivery capability Switching cost advantages
Market	Customer trust and loyalty Channel trust and loyalty Seasoned salesforce Customer and distributor relationships Understanding of industry protocols Customer and channel tolerance and empathy Experience in servicing the product
Technology	Understanding of product design and redesign Understanding of process and systems design Knowledge of reliable equipment suppliers Good relations with equipment suppliers Knowledge of industry standards for equipment and materials

service being delivered by existing products, systems, and processes.

OPPORTUNITIES TO CAPTURE KNOW-HOW ASSOCIATED WITH HIGH RELATEDNESS

Table 8-3 lists a number of places where a venture may significantly benefit from the know-how associated with high relatedness between its product, market, and technology and those of the parent company. Once the venture's focal activity has been identified, the venture manager can review Table 8-3 and decide what expertise the firm may possess stemming from relatedness. Mechanisms can then be devised to link the venture manager with those parts of the firm that might be in a position to provide useful input.

To continue the example presented earlier of a company that undertakes a venture requiring high product learning and sets up a dedicated operating facility to develop a new product, let us further assume that the product will use existing technology and be sold to existing customers. In that case, it makes sense to set up a team of key line personnel in the existing marketing, sales, and development operations to serve as points of liaison with the new venture. This team can facilitate the transfer of know-how to the venture and work with the venture manager to address problems as they arise.

As you can see from the list in Table 8-3, a venture stands to gain significant benefits from the know-how associated with existing products, markets, and technologies; hence, if there is any way of deploying this know-how to support the venture, some effort should be made to do so. Therefore, in organizing a new business, it is important for the venture manager to carefully consider where the parent company possesses expertise relevant to the particular venture and devise linking mechanisms that will enable the venture to tap that know-how. For instance, the venture manager might recognize that his or her firm has significant service know-how, which could lead the manager to arrange for one of the firm's experienced service managers to assist in designing and monitoring the venture's service program.

The following subsections provide brief overviews of the specific opportunities to capture know-how that are often associated with high levels of product, market, and technology relatedness. Again, we make no claim that these lists are exhaustive, but any venture whose product, market, and/or technology is closely related to one of the parent company's current products, markets, and/or technologies will surely find itself able to tap one or more of these types of organizational expertise, among others. It is up to the firm to identify those areas possessing valuable know-how and decide what linkages need to be established in order to enable the venture to capture that know-how.

High Product Relatedness: Capturing Know-how from Existing Products

The following are among the major types of expertise that can be tapped when the venture's product is closely related to one or more of the organization's current products:

- *Predictability and stability of operations:* It is difficult to underestimate the tremendous benefits that derive from well-honed, smooth operations. Established operations, if well managed, have a rhythm to them—the operations people know the rhythm of their own operations as well as the rhythm of the supply industries, the customers and channels, and the service requirements, and they can anticipate and cope with the shifts in this rhythm as the business goes through its cycle. If this know-how can be deployed to assist the venture, it will provide an invaluable stability, particularly in the new business's earlier stages.
- *Operating confidence:* There is an underlying confidence associated with production and operations know-how. The responsible people have learned what problems will be experienced by the suppliers, customers, and channels and have found ways to solve those problems.
- *Operating processes/systems:* Those responsible for operations are also knowledgeable about the operating system. They have fine-tuned the system and know how to maintain and adjust it and when to replace worn-out components.
- *Long runs and systems reliability:* Operating managers know how to achieve consistent reliability and quality during long production runs and how to adjust and fine-tune operations to ensure that reliability and qual-

ity are maintained. If the venture can capture this know-how, it will be able to keep reject rates to a minimum, thereby holding down the cost of operations.

- *Low customer returns:* The parent company has developed procedures and protocols for responding expeditiously to customer complaints and returns; hence, it is able to handle those few complaints and returns that it does receive in a way that maintains high customer satisfaction.

- *Supplier trust and confidence:* Established operations have evolved high levels of mutual trust and confidence between the suppliers and the company. This tends to elicit significant tolerance and empathy on the sporadic occasions when either party is experiencing difficulties.

- *Supplier relationships:* In many cases, there have evolved over time powerful relationships between the firm and its suppliers—relationships that will make the suppliers extremely willing to go the extra mile when called on to do so.

- *Understanding of service needs:* Through past experience with the operations of the business, the firm will have developed an in-depth understanding of a product's service problems and their solutions. It will also have a clear idea of how often service is likely to be required.

- *Service delivery capability:* An established company will also know when and where service is important, based on the service pattern and demands of the customers and their channels, and have developed the capacity to deliver this service.

- *Switching cost advantages:* Significant switching cost advantages will be in place. Customers and channels will have major investments in supporting the firm's current product offerings and will have developed economic and psychological dependencies as a result.

212

High Market Relatedness: Capturing Know-how from Existing Markets

The following are among the major types of know-how that can be captured when the market for the venture's product is closely related to the market for the organization's existing products:

- *Customer trust and loyalty:* One of the major benefits of doing business in existing markets is that as a result of years of mutual interaction, adjustment, and evolving understanding, the customers have learned to trust the firm, and thus, significant customer loyalty may have developed. If the new venture can tap this trust and loyalty without disrupting it, the venture's progress can be greatly accelerated. Loyal customers can more easily be cajoled into accepting new products and/or trying out products based on new technologies.
- *Channel trust and loyalty:* As is the case with customers, years of mutual adjustment and understanding can create channel trust and loyalty that will cause the channel to go the extra mile or tolerate temporary difficulties the firm may face. This goodwill can be used as a lever to persuade the channel to distribute products from the new venture.
- *Seasoned salesforce:* If the firm's current salesforce can be deployed and motivated to support the new venture, tremendous benefits can be derived. The current salesforce possesses a wealth of product knowledge, understanding in great detail what the product can or cannot do; it also has an in-depth understanding of the needs, concerns, and requirements of both the customers and the channels of distribution.
- *Customer and distributor relationships:* In addition to its knowledge of product characteristics and customer and distributor needs, the salesforce may have built up significant relationships with both individual cus-

213

tomers and channels based on personal understanding and empathy. If the venture can use these relationships advantageously, its progress can be accelerated.

- *Understanding of industry protocols:* A seasoned salesforce is familiar with the whole pattern of protocols for its industry. It does not make the mistakes common among novices—e.g., failing to understand who should be called on, what is expected when a sales call is made, how a deal is closed, and what the peripheral and implicit agreements are when a deal is closed.

- *Customer and channel tolerance and empathy:* As a result of long-standing relationships with customers and channels, the firm and these parties develop a high level of mutual tolerance and empathy that can be of enormous benefit to the venture. Because of these relationships, customers and channels will (within limits) tolerate the disruptions that are inevitably associated with product or technology innovations.

- *Experience in servicing the product:* The firm has an in-depth understanding of what the service expectations are in the industry and what is regarded as acceptable in terms of service standards and product reliability.

High-Technology Relatedness: Capturing Know-how from Existing Technology

The following are among the major types of know-how that can be captured when the technology employed in the venture's product is closely related to the technology employed in the organization's existing products:

- *Understanding of product design and redesign:* By working with an existing technology, the firm develops a rich base of design and rapid redesign capabili-

214

ties that can be deployed to speed up the venture's progress.

- *Understanding of process and systems design:* In addition to the product design know-how, the firm may also have significant skills in developing processes and systems to deliver the product.
- *Knowledge of reliable equipment suppliers:* As it works with existing technology, the firm develops expertise regarding the quality, standards, and reliability of various equipment suppliers. By tapping that expertise, the new business can avoid a host of problems associated with obtaining equipment.
- *Good relations with equipment suppliers:* In addition to the technical know-how just discussed, the firm may have established powerful relationships with top-notch equipment suppliers. Based on their high confidence and trust in the firm, these suppliers may be prepared to go to extra lengths to assist the fledgling venture.
- *Knowledge of industry standards for equipment and materials:* If the venture is using an existing technology, the parent firm will have a pool of expertise involving standards of supply in the industry for both equipment and materials. Knowing what standards of quality and reliability to expect from vendors can be of great use to the venture manager in designing a new process or product.

VENTURE INTRUSIONS INTO THE FIRM'S ONGOING ACTIVITIES

However attractive it may be to the venture to tap existing know-how, the venture manager must recognize that in tapping that know-how, he or she may be perceived, rightly or wrongly, as intruding into and interfering with the firm's major ongoing activities. There are two types of perceived intrusiveness/interference that must be taken into account in organizing a venture:

1. *Passive intrusions:* These are intrusions in which the venture's interaction with the mainstream business is seen as a distraction to the ongoing activities and treated as a nuisance; the manager is therefore disregarded when attempts are made to tap know-how or secure support. We call them passive intrusions, since no real harm is done. The manager's problem is to overcome the resistance to providing the needed support or expertise.

2. *Active intrusions:* These are intrusions in which the venture's interaction with the mainstream business actually disrupts the ongoing activities of the firm. We call them active intrusions, since real harm is done. Intrusions of this second type must be avoided, and the venture should be organized in a way that prevents them—even if it means sacrificing the opportunity to capture know-how.

The two major areas where ventures tend to intrude in the parent company's ongoing activities are (1) operations and (2) sales and service. The types of passive and active intrusions that can occur in these areas are listed in Table 8-4 and discussed in the following subsections. In pursuing know-how, the venture manager must recognize, and be appropriately sensitive to, the potential for such intrusions.

Operations Intrusions

The following subsections provide a brief overview of the passive and active intrusions that may result if a venture manager seeks to tap existing operations expertise.

Passive Intrusions. In designing linkages between a venture and the parent company's operations function, the ven-

Table 8-4: Possible Venture Intrusions into Existing Operations

Areas Intruded Upon	Aspects Affected
Operations	*Passive Intrusions*
	Operations
	Operations predictability and stability
	Long runs and low reject rates
	Business and customer rhythm
	Customer returns
	Active Intrusions
	Systems and operations
	Supplier relationships
	Morale
Sales and service	*Passive Intrusions*
	Order-taking mentality
	Routine selling
	Customer complaints
	Service demands
	Active Intrusions
	Customer and channel relationships
	Sales and service
	Morale

ture manager may have to overcome resistance to providing requested know-how in cases involving the following aspects of the established business:

- *Operations:* If the problems of process and systems burn-in disrupt ongoing operations, this will generate resistance to cooperation.
- *Operations predictability and stability:* If the venture attempts to tap operations know-how in ways that require the people in operations to disturb their comfortable and predictable manufacturing or systems routines, they will be inclined not to do this, so the challenge is to find ways to ensure that the venture gets the necessary attention.
- *Long runs and low reject rates:* Likewise, people in

ongoing operations are uncomfortable with disrupting the scheduling of long runs to attempt trial runs, with their accompanying high reject rates. The tendency to resist this must be managed.

- *Business and customer rhythm:* If the venture makes demands on operations that disturb the even, well-honed, and well-understood rhythm of business with customers and channels, this will be seen as an intrusion. The venture manager should therefore be alert to how the interventions he or she is attempting impact and adversely affect this rhythm.
- *Customer returns:* If the firm starts to experience an increase in customer returns resulting from the venture's activities, this will generate discomfort and thus resistance to cooperation.

Active Intrusions. In designing linkages between a venture and the parent company's operations function, the venture manager must recognize and avoid intrusions involving the following aspects of the established business. These are the cases in which the contemplated intrusion would be so harmful to the parent that the firm should forego any attempt to tap existing internal expertise and instead either find other means of acquiring the necessary know-how or abandon the venture entirely.

- *Systems and operations:* There is no conceivable reason why a new venture's interactions with the parent company should be permitted to seriously compromise ongoing systems and operations. If it becomes apparent that the attempt to extract know-how will precipitate disruptions to these fundamental activities, it may result in a justifiable suggestion that the venture be disbanded.
- *Supplier relationships:* There is also no reason why an attempt to tap expertise should be permitted to precipitate serious conflicts with suppliers and thus compromise important supplier relationships.

- *Morale:* The venture's interaction with ongoing operations must not be allowed to generate conflict that will in any way undermine morale and discipline in the parent firm's affected functions.

Sales and Service Intrusions

The following subsections provide a brief overview of the passive and active intrusions that may result from attempts to capture existing sales and service expertise.

Passive Intrusions. As the venture manager tries to establish linkages to tap know-how available in the parent company's sales and service functions, the following aspects of the established business could be affected in ways that generate resistance to cooperating with the venture:

- *Order-taking mentality:* If the venture is to use the parent company's existing salesforce, then it is important to establish whether an order-taking mentality prevails among the sales reps. If so, it will be extremely hard to persuade them to shoulder the burden of the additional effort that will be required to sell the venture's output.
- *Routine selling:* Another problem can arise if handling the venture's output will in any way disrupt the existing salesforce's selling routines—sales routes, sales call requirements, steady commissions. If such disruption is foreseen, suitable incentives must be designed to motivate the salesforce to sell the venture's product under such conditions.
- *Customer complaints:* The inevitable increase in customer complaints associated with the venture's product will be perceived as a burden by the recipients of those complaints. Any effort to tap the know-how of those recipients will meet with scant cooperation.
- *Service demands:* If the venture attempts to capitalize

on the firm's existing service capabilities, the service force may actively resist the increase in both the amount and the unpredictability of service demands placed on it by the venture.

Active Intrusions.   When the venture manager attempts to establish linkages to tap the parent company's sales and service expertise, he or she must ensure that the linkages are designed in a way that avoids active intrusions into the following aspects of ongoing operations. Such intrusions are so detrimental to the firm that they cannot be tolerated, and if they are unavoidable, either the opportunity should be sacrificed or the know-how should be obtained by some other means.

- *Customer and channel relationships:* Any attempt to capitalize on the organization's sales and service capabilities must not be allowed to lead to serious customer and channel conflicts.
- *Sales and service:* Any intervention by the venture designed to tap sales and service expertise cannot be condoned if it might seriously compromise the delivery of sales and service to channels and customers.
- *Morale:* If the venture's interaction with the ongoing sales and service functions is likely to precipitate conflict that will in any way damage morale and discipline in the established business, then it is probably better to forego the opportunity to tap know-how.

SEVEN MAJOR VENTURE TYPES

Table 8-5 shows the seven major venture types, each of which has a characteristic pattern of relatedness levels, learning challenges, exploitable know-how, and potential for intruding into the firm's ongoing activities if the venture manager tries too hard to capture existing know-how.

Type 1 venture: product augmentation.   Product augmentation ventures are characterized by low product relatedness and high market and technology relatedness. They involve introducing a new product into an existing market using known technology. GE's move from making plastic moldings for automobile interiors to manufacturing exterior moldings, such as bumpers, provides an example of this type of venture. Both these categories of product require molding technology and serve exactly the same market, but the kind of plastic needed for the two applications is completely different. From Table 8-5, we can see that the venture's greatest learning needs are in the areas of production and operations and that the firm already possesses know-how regarding sales, marketing, and technology development. However, if the venture demands excessive interaction with the marketing department, this could create intrusions into and disruptions of the firm's existing sales and service activities, which should be guarded against.

Type 2 venture: product development.   Product development ventures are characterized by low product and technology relatedness but high market relatedness, an example being Anheuser-Busch's move into the production and distribution of bar snacks. In this case, the venture requires both product and technology learning, whereas marketing know-how already exists within the firm and simply needs to be tapped by appropriate linking mechanisms. Once again, excessive exploitation of the parent company's marketing expertise could lead to the disruption of ongoing sales and service activities.

Type 3 venture: technology innovation.   Technology innovation ventures are those in which only technology relatedness is low, but the company knows the products and markets well. Examples would be IBM's move from mainframe computer technology to microprocessor technology and Citibank's move from a teller-driven service distribution system to one based on automated-teller machines. In these cases,

Table 8-5: Seven Major Venture Types

Venture Type	Relatedness			Learning Challenges (Table 8-2) (The focal activity—areas requiring a separate, dedicated function)	Exploitable Know-how (Table 8-3) (Areas where linkages should be established)	Areas Subject To Intrusion (Table 8-4)
	Product	Market	Technology			
1. Product augmentation (e.g., interior to exterior auto plastics)	Low	High	High	Operations	Marketing and development	Sales and service
2. Product development (e.g., beer to bar snacks)	Low	High	Low	Development and operations	Marketing	Sales and service
3. Technology innovation (e.g., teller-based system to automated-teller machines)	High	High	Low	Development	Marketing and operations	Operations, sales, and service

				Marketing	Development and operations	Operations
4. Market augmentation (e.g., gas turbines to aircraft engines)	High	Low	High	Marketing	Development and operations	Operations
5. Vertical integration (rare) (e.g., beer to beverage cans)	High	Low	Low	Marketing and development	Operations	Operations
6. Technology commercialization (e.g., solar cells to calculators)	Low	Low	High	Marketing and operations	Development	None
7. Blue-sky (e.g., oil refining to office equipment)	Low	Low	Low	Marketing, development, and operations	None	None

the learning challenges primarily involve technology development. The firm has significant operations and marketing know-how at its disposal, although the venture manager must recognize the danger of the venture's intruding in operations, sales, and service if the connections to operations and marketing are overexploited.

Type 4 venture: market augmentation. Market augmentation ventures involve taking existing products and technologies into unrelated markets. GE's move from gas turbines to aircraft engines is a case in point. Here, the major learning challenge lies in marketing, whereas the venture can tap the firm's existing know-how in operations and development.

Type 5 venture: vertical integration. In the (rather unusual) case of vertical integration ventures, the parent company has high product relatedness but low market and technology relatedness. An example was Anheuser-Busch's decision to externally market the cans originally manufactured as containers for its own beer. The firm's major learning challenges were to develop its own can-manufacturing technology capability and an in-depth understanding of the can market, but it could draw on its experience in making the product itself.

Type 6 ventures: technology commercialization. A technology commercialization venture is one in which the firm pushes an existing technology to commercial exploitation, as Sanyo did in deciding to use newly developed solar-cell technology to manufacture light cells for calculators. The learning challenges lie in the areas of operations and marketing, whereas existing know-how can be found in the area of development.

Type 7 ventures: blue-sky. Blue-sky ventures—which involve entering an attractive market despite low product, technology, and market relatedness—are the most challenging for the venturing firm. An example would be the decision by

Exxon, an oil-refining company, to enter the office equipment business. In such a situation, there is absolutely no existing know-how to be exploited, and the firm faces significant learning challenges in the areas of development, operations, and marketing in spite of foothold acquisitions which may be made.

ORGANIZING THE VENTURE

Based on the foregoing discussion, we can now propose the following four principles for organizing a corporate venture:

1. *Organize to maximize learning:* The major benefits of organization derive from the ability to create a dedicated activity focused on those areas where the greatest learning must take place. The organization's first priority is therefore to organize the venture in a way that maximizes learning.

   If learning is required in multiple areas, learning about market takes precedence over learning about technology or product. Thus, if the organization does not know the market, it is crucial to have a dedicated marketing group to drive all other activity in the venture unit. In contrast, if the organization knows the market but does not know the product, a dedicated production group is needed to drive all other activity.

2. *Organize to maximize the capture of know-how:* If the venture has areas of high relatedness to ongoing operations, the firm's second priority is to identify those functions whose expertise will be of value to the venture and organize linking mechanisms to ensure that their know-how is applied to the new business.

3. *Organize to minimize or manage intrusions:* After ensuring that the venture is organized to maximize learning and the capture of know-how, the company's

225

third priority with regard to design is to minimize the danger of active intrusions into ongoing operations. It is also important to identify passive intrusions and design mechanisms for overcoming resistance to them.

4. *Use the simplest possible coordinating mechanisms to meet the venture's linkage needs:* The preceding three principles primarily involve creating coordinating mechanisms—for instance, to link those departments possessing know-how with those managers dedicated to the venture's focal activity. Table 8-1 (see page 198) showed various coordinating mechanisms used for handling contingencies. These same types of linking mechanisms are also used to facilitate the transfer of know-how from the parent company to the venture. In designing coordinating arrangements, the firm should avoid organizational overkill and instead employ the simplest possible mechanism appropriate to the challenge of the particular linking task.

Earlier in the chapter, we listed the learning challenges associated with low product, market, and technology relatedness (Table 8-2); the opportunities to capture know-how from high product, market, and technology relatedness (Table 8-3); and the aspects of the established business that a venture may intrude upon in the areas of operations and sales and service (Table 8-4). And in Table 8-5, we listed the seven major types of corporate ventures and provided an overview of their key characteristics.

We would strongly suggest that managers actually involved in organizing a new venture scan the information in this group of tables to identify the critical issues that must be addressed and the key decisions that must be made in designing their particular venture. These tables can be used as comprehensive (but by no means exhaustive) checklists for organizing specific programs designed to maximize learning or capitalize on existing corporate know-how or avoid intrusions into ongoing operations.

To illustrate how this group of tables can be used in venture organization, we shall work our way through one detailed example, which involves identifying the major issues and decisions that managers may face in organizing a product augmentation venture. Readers should then have no trouble using the tables to extract guidelines for designing other types of ventures.

Let's start by referring to the first row of Table 8-5, which identifies the key characteristics of product augmentation ventures. Since these ventures have low product relatedness, little would be gained by locating them in or linking them with existing operations. Since the major learning challenge involves new-product learning, the focal activity should be operations—which suggests that a dedicated operations facility be created, separate from the firm's existing operations, to ensure that maximum attention is given to developing the operations skills the new business will need.

Whether the venture should be embedded in an ongoing sales or development group or be completely separated from ongoing sales and development activities is a function of what safeguarding the venture needs, but it is essential for the firm to create linkages that will enable the new business to capture both market and technology know-how.

Suppose for the moment that from an organizational standpoint, it seems advisable to put a skilled manufacturing person in charge of a separate new-product unit. The question is how this manager will capture the firm's existing technology and marketing know-how. Depending on the venture's size, scope, and criticality, marketing and development managers can either be permanently assigned to the venture or be named as task force members to liaise with the venture manager. At this stage, though, simple, informal contacts will not suffice.

According to Table 8-5, the primary learning challenge for a product augmentation venture involves operations. Interested managers can refer to Table 8-2 for a list of some of the specific types of learning challenges commonly faced by ventures with low product relatedness. Although the actual challenges any venture will face are a function of the particular venture and the particular firm, it's a good bet that the venture will need to address one or more of the challenges listed in Table 8-2. The venture manager must work with development and marketing, first to identify which of these challenges apply to the venture and then to decide how to respond appropriately.

Let's say the major challenges foreseen for this particular venture involve new-process development and switching cost disadvantages. This would indicate the need for two major efforts—the first, in collaboration with the firm's development person, to design and debug a pilot production system and the second, in collaboration with the marketing person, to attack the problem of switching costs. A list of significant milestones, complete with plans for verifying assumptions, would be developed as part of each of these efforts.

According to Table 8-5, opportunities for the venture to capture know-how lie in the areas of marketing and development. Interested managers can refer to Table 8-3 for a list of some of the specific types of expertise that can be tapped in cases of high market and technology relatedness. Once again, the actual opportunities depend on the particular firm and venture. The venture manager, in collaboration with the task force members from marketing and development, should identify all the possible areas where existing corporate know-how could help the venture.

Suppose that the key market opportunity involves capitalizing on customer trust and loyalty and the key technology opportunity stems from the fact that the firm has good relations with equipment suppliers whose reliability standards are exceptionally high. To capitalize on the first opportunity, linkages with key customers could be used to help shape the standards that might erode competitors' switching cost advantages; to capitalize on the second, linkages with the supplier could be forged to help in developing the production process and product standards.

According to Table 8-5, sales and service are the functions that face the greatest risk of being intruded upon by a product augmentation venture. Interested managers can refer to Table 8-4 for a list of some of the specific types of passive and active intrusions that can affect sales and service. Once again, the actual disruptions will depend on the particular firm and venture.

Let's say the major problem posed by the venture is that members of the current salesforce will have to increase the number and frequency of their sales calls and expend greater selling effort during those calls. This means that the marketing liaison needs to work with senior sales management to develop a suitable incentive program that will elicit the desired behavior from the sales reps.

CONCLUSION

In this chapter, we presented some key concepts of organization, from which we derived a number of basic principles for organizing ventures. We also identified the major venture types, based on how closely the venture's product, market, and technology are related to the firm's existing offerings. We closed the chapter by showing venture managers how to use this information to identify a number of key issues and decisions that should be considered in organizing each of the major types of venture.

Guidelines

1. Analyze the relatedness between the venture's activities and the firm's ongoing activities—i.e., how closely the venture's product, market, and technology are related to the parent company's product, market, and technology.

2. Identify the key learning challenges and the key opportunities to capture know-how.
3. Priority 1: Organize to maximize learning. Create a dedicated activity focused on those areas where maximum learning is needed. If learning is required in multiple areas, learning about market takes precedence over learning about technology or product.
4. Priority 2: Subject to priority 1, create linking mechanisms to maximize the capture of know-how.
5. Priority 3: Subject to priorities 1 and 2, organize to minimize the danger of active intrusions. Identify passive intrusions and design mechanisms for overcoming resistance to them.
6. Priority 4: Use the simplest possible coordination tools.

REFERENCES

Fast, N. D. 1978. *The Rise and Fall of Corporate New Venture Divisions*. Ann Arbor, MI: UMI Research Press.

Galbraith, J. R. 1982. "Designing the Innovative Organization." *Organizational Dynamics* (Winter): 5–25.

9

Controlling the Venture

Since plans for a new venture should focus on learning and evolve, the parent company must use control methods that ensure that learning occurs and is applied. Conversely, the parent must *not* use control methods that actually prevent learning and change.

In this chapter, we start by explaining how and why traditional control methods are inappropriate, then present the objectives and elements of a venture control system and show how such a system can be created, and close by clarifying the distinct roles of venture management and senior management in the venture control process. How a venture is structured and designed at the outset, how the corporation's policies and procedures are applied to the venture, how feedback is built in and used, and how budget controls are applied determine how well the venture is controlled and whether venture management will have the flexibility and freedom that are absolutely essential for venturing success.

TRADITIONAL CONTROL METHODS AND THEIR INAPPROPRIATENESS

Almost nothing has been written in any detail about the special control needs of new ventures. Yet every major researcher in the field of innovation and corporate venturing has pointed out that traditional control methods are inappropriate, and they advocate—in our view, correctly—granting a high degree of empowerment and flexibility to venture managers. This is hardly arguable. The venture's survival and success depend on rapid adjustment to the unexpected, and those closest to the situation are best qualified to judge what must be done. All the reasons that can be cited to justify decentralization, delegation, and empowerment in established businesses are even more valid in the case of new businesses.

Yet red tape—in the form of multiple-level approvals and many handoffs and sign-offs—is more often than not an integral part of corporate operation. The complex approvals, reports, procedures, and policies are an important—albeit unwanted—element of the parent firm's control system. They are holdovers from an earlier period characterized by less intense competition and greater market stability. But this red tape can strangle the efforts of new ventures (as well as the efforts of established businesses, as many companies are learning) in various ways: it hampers their ability to respond to threats and opportunities, it creates a need for political maneuvering and negotiation in order to obtain approvals, and most important, it generates a sense of demoralization and outright disgust on the part of venture managers who want to build a business and are dragged down by work that is seen as (and often is) irrelevant to the task that needs to be accomplished. (One venture manager, shaking his head in dismay at the delay in getting a relatively small sum approved for a capital expenditure, observed, "I can cost the company millions by making a wrong pricing decision, which I am authorized to do, but I have to go through this [expletive] to get approval to spend $100,000 on equipment that we need in a hurry to keep up with growing demand!")

The supposed purpose of such controls is to minimize the risks associated with new ventures. Some of these controls are designed to protect the corporation against the risk of violating safety regulations and other laws as well as the risk of damaging its reputation, both with the public and with existing customers. Other controls are designed to protect the corporation against the most common risk associated with new ventures—i.e., financial risk, the possibility of incurring prolonged, unplanned, major losses that damage the firm. Yet the evidence indicates that traditional control mechanisms neither ensure venture success nor protect the parent firm from substantial, and often unnecessary, venture losses. Otherwise very well managed organizations such as Time-Life, Federal Express, Exxon, and Polaroid have all experienced enormous venture losses, despite traditional controls.

Traditional control mechanisms are based on *comparing performance against plans*. In a normal, well-established organization, a nearly universal control mechanism is comparison of performance with projections using variance reporting. For even tighter control, *line-item budget control* is used. Other common strategies for maintaining control are establishing *head-count limits* and requiring special procedures to get exceptions approved; periodic review meetings; and linking incentives and compensation to performance against plan or budget. The application of *policies and procedures,* enforced by staff personnel, is an attempt to ensure equity and uniformity across the entire corporation.

These practices are often absurd and can be dangerous and expensive; they may provide motivation for ignoring emerging reality and attempting to achieve plans and projections that are rapidly becoming obsolete. In fact, we suggest that the planning and control mechanisms normally used are a principal *cause* of large losses rather than merely an obstacle to venturing success. Given the high degree of unpredictability of new ventures, it is neither logical nor effective to use a control system designed for the reasonably predictable circumstances of a normal, ongoing business with an established track record.

But we are not arguing that venture managers should have absolute freedom. Far from it. A new business does require control, but it must be *a different kind of control*—suited to its unique needs. The venture requires control mechanisms that provide enough flexibility and freedom to allow it to grow, but at the same time, it requires enough contact with and interest on the part of senior managers to give them the information and understanding that will enable them to make the necessary decisions and furnish the venture with the necessary help.

Damage control must be an essential part of any control system. Recognizing serious problems and knowing when to pull the plug on ventures that are headed toward large losses is one of the biggest challenges corporations face in managing ventures. In a survey by Block and Subbanarasimha (1989), 41% of 328 ventures achieved profitability within a six-year period, but only one firm in eight reported a return on investment from its combined venturing activities equal to or greater than from the firm's core business. As noted in Chapter 1, this disparity between the ROI results and the number of profitable ventures can be explained by one big loser wiping out the gains from many smaller winners. Thus, a major objective of a venture control system is to limit the damage from the inevitable losers while maximizing the gain from those ventures that do survive.

The control approach we describe in the following section is designed to ensure that venture management has maximum flexibility while the parent retains outer-limit controls. One way to picture such a control system is as a "playpen," with the size of the pen's floor and the height of its surrounding walls defining the area within which the fledgling venture enjoys freedom of action. This "playpen" type of control system can be contrasted with the more restrictive "harness" approach, which discourages initiative and resourcefulness, hampers flexibility, and precludes a sense of fun—so necessary for venture success.

A CONTROL SYSTEM FOR NEW VENTURES

The objectives of any system designed to control corporate ventures are as follows:

- To maximize the venture's success
- To minimize the costs of failure
- To provide a basis for evaluating the performance of the venture's staff
- To provide a basis for making decisions about the venture's future

These objectives can be achieved through what we characterized in the preceding section as a "playpen" approach to venture control. The parameters of such a "playpen" are formed by the following key control points, which are discussed in the balance of this section:

- The design of the venture itself—including the management team's composition, incentives, and compensation; organizational positioning (i.e., the venture's location within the firm); the choice of format and entry strategy; and the selection of milestones to trigger financing
- Modified application of corporate policies and procedures

235

- The design and use of a feedback system to test major assumptions
- The use of modified budget control methods

Design of the Venture

As W. Edwards Deming, the man who revolutionized the quality of Japanese industrial output, has shown in manufacturing, the design of products and processes has a major impact on controlling quality. The same holds true for new ventures, for design is just as important to controlling the quality of a venture's performance as it is to controlling the quality of a product. Design alone, to an enormous degree, will determine both the relative difficulty of operating the venture and the probability of its success. By *design,* we mean how the venture is set up: who manages it, to whom the venture team reports, what format is used, the choice of entry strategy, and the choice of milestones that trigger successive rounds of financing. Venture design is what can enable the firm to avoid a preventable failure whose postmortem concludes, "It was set up wrong."

As important as the initial design structure is, flexibility must be built in to allow for change. Furthermore, senior management must understand the processes and signals that indicate that change is required. The two dynamic forces that dictate the need for change are: the problems that develop during the startup and the evolution of the venture through its life-cycle stages. Senior managers have to adjust to these forces and modify the venture's design when necessary.

Design changes can be triggered both by progress and by problems. If the new business is growing rapidly, changes will be required in order to manage that growth successfully. If the business is doing poorly, design changes may be made in an attempt to turn the situation around. No matter whether the business is flourishing or withering, some kind of design changes will surely be needed.

In the following subsections, we examine the control implications of three key aspects of venture design: (1) the selection and compensation of venture management, (2) the new business's format and its location within the organization, and (3) the use of a milestone achievement system to trigger financing.

Management Selection and Compensation.   One of the central challenges of venture design is to ensure that the venture has the right management at the right time. As we discussed in Chapter 5, the management skills needed to launch a venture are very different from those needed to grow it successfully. This issue must be addressed at the outset.

A startup requires venture management that is highly entrepreneurial, flexible, and resourceful. As the business grows, management must delegate decision-making responsibility, use more formal controls (Roberts 1986), and achieve direction through coordination, which may call for a rapid switch from entrepreneurial management to more "professional" management skills. (See Chapter 10 for further discussion of early transitional stages and the requirements for different management skills.) Transitions can be difficult, often for psychological reasons rather than for lack of ability. It is important for senior management to be alert to these changing needs and act appropriately—from supporting the venture team to providing needed training to replacing one or more team members.

If the startup manager is interested in developing the skills required to manage the new business over the long haul and is personally adaptable, there may be no need for a change in managers. However, many venture managers are simply not interested in running the ventures they begin and will prefer to start new ventures. This means there will come a time when the venture's management must be changed. Corporate management has the responsibility of preparing for this transition, recognizing when it is necessary, and taking appropriate action.

Senior managers also need to ensure that the startup venture manager understands this situation from the beginning. Venture capitalists face a similar challenge in supporting new ventures. One leading venture capitalist, when asked how he handles the problem, said he discusses the matter with the entrepreneur before the venture is financed. The discussion goes something like this:

> Venture Capitalist: You know, sometimes we find that the person who starts a business is neither interested in building the business beyond a certain point nor capable of doing so. What if we find this to be the case?
>
> Entrepreneur: Don't worry, if I find that I'm getting in over my head, I'll be the first to let you know. After all, it's in my economic interest to ensure the business's success.
>
> Venture Capitalist: But what if we think a change is needed before you do?

The venture capitalist then discusses the developments that they can mutually regard as warning signs requiring action—for example, administrative foul-ups; inability to attract and hold good people or, conversely, to let go of people who can no longer contribute; inability to handle the growing work load; or unacceptably slow growth.

The situation is especially difficult in corporate ventures because venture managers rarely have continuing ownership interest in the venture that they will no longer be managing, so it is not to their economic advantage to initiate a change; moreover, a change is likely to be regarded as a sign of failure on the managers' part. For these reasons, there may very well be a conflict between the needs of the venture, the interests of the venture manager, and the interests of the parent firm.

These conflicting interests, if overlooked, can create a situation with a high potential for producing large venture losses or delays in profitability. Compensation and incentive schemes can help to bring the needs of the venture manager, the venture, and the parent into closer alignment, although a major factor in the venture manager's mind will be the sensed attitude of the corporation toward a proposed change.

For compensation and incentives to be effective control mechanisms for venture managers, the venture's stage of development must be considered. There's no point in establishing a profit incentive for a manager of a venture that isn't expected to make a profit for five years—by which time, the manager will probably be long gone. Also, as described in Chapter 5, the incentive must have the potential to significantly affect the recipient's standard of living. The upside gain that may be achieved through venture management can be designed to be commensurate with the downside loss being risked. Venture management can be given an opportunity to invest in the venture and thus share in the risks as well as the rewards.

But even if venture managers share some risks, there is an enormous difference between the potential gains and losses of independent and corporate entrepreneurs, which leads us to wonder how the losses of parent firms would be affected if intrapreneurs had more to lose through venture failure.

Although venture managers and corporate senior managers almost always place great emphasis on incentives and compensation, how important are these factors from a control standpoint? As we have shown in Chapter 5, there is no evidence that incentives, except for milestone bonuses, are correlated with venturing performance. Unfortunately, however, there are no data on the effect of compensation and incentives in preventing big losses. Furthermore, the overwhelming majority of the compensation or incentive schemes we studied could not have made a significant difference in the recipients' standard of living.

To provide effective control, compensation and incentive plans should be tailored to the venture's changing objectives. One plan, for example, provided a cash bonus for completing plant construction, with the bonus's size depending on the time and cost involved. This was followed by a percentage of the positive cash flow, with the percentage increasing with increased cash flow within a specified time period. Finally, this was succeeded by a percentage of profit, calculated after a threshold return on investment. This plan reflected the venture's evolving priorities while providing protection against opportunistic compromises of quality or failure to achieve market share. In this case, the venture manager doubled his income in six months while creating a highly successful business.

Format and Organizational Positioning.   The venture's format can have a major impact on both the control and ultimate success of the venture. For instance, a joint venture might be appropriate in the early stages of a new business, but as the venture develops, the original reasons for having chosen the joint venture format might become invalid because, say, the venture team has acquired certain key skills formerly needed from one of the partners, the period of maximum risk has passed, the risks have increased to the point where one of the partners can no longer afford them, or unresolvable disagreements have developed. To cite another example, a venture that begins as an internal division may develop to the point where it needs to be included in an existing operating unit.

Organizational positioning is a particularly changeable element. What starts as an R&D project may best be continued as a new-business unit in a venture division or an operating division, or it may evolve into a new division of the company or be consolidated with an existing operation. The venture's scale and self-sufficiency may dictate where it should be located in order to get the necessary resources and controls.

Because a new business's format and positioning have a very high probability of requiring change, these aspects of the venture's design should provide for flexibility and be subject to periodic review.

Milestones to Trigger Financing.   The release of financing for the venture should be tied to the achievement of milestones and should be changed when the facts support doing so. The losses anticipated before break-even may climb to a point where the risk can no longer be borne by the parent alone, which would call for a change in format. For example, Sprint started as a foothold acquisition by GTE, but after years of losses, it was changed to a joint venture in which GTE had 50% ownership, then to an investment in which GTE had only a minority interest, and finally GTE disposed of it completely.

In short, the venture's original design provides the basis for achieving senior management control. And for that design to remain effective, it must be reviewed frequently and altered when needed.

Modified Application of Corporate Policies and Procedures

It is not reasonable to expect a fledgling venture—which requires nurturing, flexibility, and relief from the costs of expensive corporate staff—to blindly adhere to all corporate policies. Nor is it reasonable to expect the corporation to put itself in legal jeopardy or put its reputation at risk as a result of the venture's violating important policies. Therefore, what is needed is some way to protect the parent without crippling the venture. For example, a particularly sensitive area is incentives and compensation methods that are necessary for venturers but appear to conflict with the policies of the firm.

There are many ways of allowing the new venture to have different policies than the parent company. The corporation may spin off ventures, which are then operated independently; it may enter a joint venture; or it may appoint a high-level executive champion to act as an arbitrator on policy issues. This champion can protect both the venture and the firm by deciding which policies and procedures can be modified or bypassed altogether.

With the guidance of an executive champion, staff personnel can provide significant assistance to venture management by simplifying procedures. For example, in an organization that requires the use of the central engineering staff for plant design, the executive champion could make or expedite the decision to go elsewhere if the service will be faster and perhaps more specifically expert, while engineering staff executives could help in searching for and evaluating such an outside source. This is not an idyllic dream. The IBM PC could not have been developed as quickly as it was without such protection and collaboration.

Much of the control in large organizations is exercised through policies and procedures, which affect hiring procedures, the number of people hired, the job classification scheme on which compensation is based, promotion practices, adherence to the law, publicity about the venture and the firm, purchasing, the relationship with customers of other organizational units, leases, contracts, the use of staff functions, and a myriad of other practices that must be standardized in big firms.

Venture managers often regard these policies and procedures as obstacles: they cause delays, inflexibility, and higher costs than would be incurred by a freestanding business. To illustrate the frustrating impact of such bureaucracy, consider the following experience of a venture manager in a multibillion-dollar corporation: When the venture was initiated, office space was provided in the firm's headquarters. The venture manager wanted to move his furniture from his previous location, which was deemed acceptable. As a result, however, wooden furniture previously used at the new location was freed up. The venture manager wished to allow another member of the venture team to use that furniture and contacted the staff person responsible for furniture allocation to arrange this. The proposed transfer was disallowed because the team member was not at a high enough grade to warrant wood, and company rules called for metal! The venture manager asked, "Are you telling me that I have to go out and spend money on new furniture when we have a surplus of furniture available?" The response was, "That's the company rule." The venture manager declared, "I'm not going to do it," whereupon the staff person told him that a previous similar incident had been referred to the corporation's executive committee and put on the agenda at one of its meetings, at which an exception had been permitted. It took the involvement of the firm's CEO and a number of other senior executives to obtain a simple agreement to permit resourcefulness.

Yet this same company is purportedly seeking to encourage entrepreneurial behavior! How can a firm expect venture managers to be concerned about costs and losses and retain a sense of urgency when faced with such blind application of a policy? Emerson was so right when he observed in his "Self-Reliance" essay that "A foolish consistency is the hobgoblin of little minds."

On the other hand, it would be foolhardy for the organization to suspend all policies for new ventures, even if the venturing activity is totally separated from the parent firm. Nevertheless, an understanding of how such policies can damage venture development will help senior management to minimize the blanket application of parent company policies to new businesses.

Policies and procedures reflect the accumulated learning of a corporation (Sykes and Block 1989). For a business to grow into a large organization, delegation is necessary, and effective delegation requires decision rules that are consistent with the firm's philosophy, goals, and aspirations. Those rules are a codification of the firm's specific experience. The new venture, in contrast, doesn't have experience, and the time for delegation has not yet arrived. But even if delegation has occurred, the decision rules are not clear enough, and even if the rules were clear, they would be different from those of the parent firm.

Organizations that cannot accept such differences had better remain as close to their present business as possible. It is the inability to make this adjustment that contributes to the conclusion that companies should stick with what they know best—especially those companies that, like old dogs, find themselves unable to learn new tricks! It may very well be true that certain organizations fail in diversifying new ventures not because of what they don't know but rather because of what they do know that isn't relevant to the situation—and because of their inability to learn.

Design and Use of a Feedback System to Test Assumptions

Once again, we emphasize that the economic success of a firm's overall venturing activity may and probably does depend on minimizing the losses from failures as well as maximizing the gains from winners. Venture management is responsible for building a successful business, but in a corporate framework, senior management must provide the required resources and limit serious losses.

How can such losses be prevented? Although venture managers must control operating expenses, serious losses do not occur as a result of minor variations in operating expenses or sales revenues, nor are they prevented by diligent bean counting or high-level line-item budget control. We suggest that major losses are caused by continued pursuit of a venture in a predetermined direction even after the fundamental basis for the venture has turned out to be invalid. In other words, the venture is based on incorrect assumptions (which does not necessarily mean that mistakes were made in arriving at the original assumptions, just that those assumptions have proved wrong in light of emerging experience). If the firm fails to recognize these now-wrong assumptions, it will often fail to recognize the need for change—in design, direction, or objectives, including, but not limited to, abandoning the effort—and will instead continue pouring money into the venture.

Since assumptions are at the heart of venture planning, if senior managers are to control a venture, they must understand the assumptions that underlie it and make sure that mechanisms have been devised to test those assumptions. This is part of the "playpen" approach to venture design, discussed earlier in the chapter, and it requires review, analysis, and decisions upon completion of the assumption-testing events. The following three subsections illustrate the damage that can result from overlooking, ignoring, or misreading assumptions.

Polaroid's Polavision.   Introduced in 1977, Polavision was a system for taking home movies that could be viewed in 2 minutes. In 1978, the press reported that test marketing was successful. In January 1979, however, it was reported that the system faced obsolescence. The $7 soundless Polavision cassette, which lasted for 2.5 minutes, was not faring well against the $20 videotape with sound, which lasted for 2 hours. Later in 1979, Polaroid announced the addition of a sound feature. By September of that year, Polaroid had taken a $68-million write-off on Polavision. The company reportedly spent over $200 million for research, production, and marketing.

Whether articulated or not, the following assumptions seem to have been the basis for Polaroid's entry into this business:

- Consumers wanted or would accept instant movies.
- A 2.5-minute cassette costing $7 would compete effectively against a videotape costing less than one-fifteenth the price per minute.
- Polavision provided acceptable quality.
- Selling and marketing would enable Polavision to overcome the superior quality of videotape competition.

Clearly, the second assumption, about Polavision's cost-effectiveness as compared to the competing videotape product, was unlikely to have been articulated. Had it been, Polaroid would not have required $68 million to test it.

Time-Life's *Cable Week*.   This venture, whose history has been chronicled by Byron in *The Fanciest Dive* (1986), introduced a weekly guide to cable television programs customized for specific systems. Between its start in 1983 and its termination in 1984, the venture reportedly lost $47 million.

According to press accounts, demand estimates were based on computer simulation, not market tests.

Before the *Cable Week* venture was initiated, the following assumptions were made:

- Time-Life had the technology to process the data on cable programming fast enough to ensure timely printing and distribution.
- Enough cable operators and cable consumers would accept the publication to generate an adequate level of advertising sales.
- *Cable Week* would compete effectively against *TV Guide* and capture part of that market.

None of these assumptions turned out to be true. However, the biggest problem was that even though the *Cable Week* venture's original proponents had clearly stated that the idea was based on assumptions that needed to be tested, those tests were not performed for political reasons. Instead, the pressure was on to meet the plan, which had been widely announced. And expenses were increased even more because new offices were constructed for the venture before there was any evidence that they would actually be needed.

Federal Express's ZapMail. FedEx's ZapMail venture is reported to have lost $657 million in the aggregate, including the final write-off. The ZapMail system, which delivered facsimile copies anywhere in the nation in two hours, initially required transmission exclusively to and from Federal Express facsimile machines. However, when the service was introduced in 1984, many companies already had competitors' fax machines, and the use of such machines was growing rapidly. In September 1986, Federal Express terminated ZapMail. The stated reason was that the venture would have required an additional several hundred million dollars for network and customer equipment.

Whether articulated or not, the fundamental assumption underlying this venture appears to have been that enough companies would be willing to use ZapMail service to support the business, despite the rapid increase in the number of firms purchasing their own fax machines. Unfortunately for Federal Express, companies selling competing fax machines were improving quality and lowering costs. And Federal Express added nothing of value for firms that already had fax machines. FedEx could not possibly have articulated this assumption, for had it done so, the assumption would surely have been tested or rejected as invalid.

Taking Appropriate Action in Response to Feedback. In the preceding examples, the key problem is not that incorrect assumptions were made or that some new ventures failed, but rather that they were allowed to fail in an unnecessarily expensive manner. This high level of expense appears to be related to the failure to articulate or test basic assumptions combined with internal corporate pressures that prevented venture management from altering the venture plan or aborting the effort.

When should management pull the plug? Kanter and Fonvielle (1987) suggest that a project be continued as long as there is still a demonstrable need for the product or service, internal support, and evidence that the project can work. However, actions to prevent large losses must be taken long before a termination decision is made. Not only will these actions reduce the cost of a possible failure, but they can also enable the firm to redirect the venture to increase its chances of success. Here is what assumptions tests can tell the organization about the actions needed:

- The time to pull the plug is when a go/no-go assumption is found to be invalid and it is not replaced either with facts or with a new assumption that justifies continuing the business.
- The time to modify the venture's direction or strategy is when basic assumptions have changed or the firm has obtained new facts that indicate the need for change.

247

The value of testing assumptions is illustrated by the case of a textile-manufacturing company that had developed a new material and was approaching the point of taking orders based on approval of a sample produced by a pilot plant. The managers had assumed, unconsciously, that they could produce the fiber without difficulty in one of the firm's two existing plants, since pilot operations had given them great confidence in their knowledge of the process. In an exercise designed to ferret out hidden assumptions in their plan, they became aware of this assumption as well as others regarding quality control, available capacity, and costs.

Members of the venture team decided that they had better test their assumptions about production capability in the plant they had selected. After a series of test runs, they realized that the plant was not suitable for producing the new fiber. As a result, they changed the time of their first delivery, tested their other plant, rechecked costs, and adjusted prices. That is, the venture's actions, sequence, and timing were altered to fit the newly learned reality, thereby avoiding major problems for the new business. If the firm had not deliberately articulated and tested its basic assumptions, customer dissatisfaction might have set the venture back by months.

In another case, a food company developed a system for providing supermarkets with frozen doughnuts that could be reheated to produce hot, fresh doughnuts with little on-site labor. The system required a significant investment in each supermarket outlet, as well as the construction of a central bakery and freezing operation to serve the outlets. The viability of the entire venture was based on two clearly stated critical assumptions:

1. A required minimum weekly sales level would be achieved.
2. Service personnel would be available in each store.

The assumption regarding sales was derived from historical data on doughnut sales in supermarkets and retail doughnut shops. The assumption regarding the availability of service personnel was based on the fact that the new system would be placed next to the existing deli operations, whose personnel were expected to be on hand as needed. To test these critical assumptions, the corporation established a pilot production facility and ran a six-month test in 6 supermarkets. The results were encouraging but inconclusive. A larger test was then conducted in 50 supermarkets, with the costs of the test being shared by the food company and the supermarket chain. The results of the larger test showed that neither of the two assumptions held.

At that point, the company had a choice of enlarging the product line and retesting, or stopping the program. It decided to stop the program because, simultaneously, the environment had moved toward scratch baking operations in supermarkets. What might have been a very costly failure had the firm adhered to the original business plan and doggedly pressed for more customers was converted into a relatively inexpensive experiment. The pilot facility, which had been expanded to serve the 50 stores, was then diverted to a planned backup use.

In both these cases, senior management exercised control by reviewing the results of assumptions tests and revising planned actions accordingly. Once again, here are the critical questions senior managers must ask about each go/no-go (i.e., major) assumption. The first two questions are asked prior to assumptions testing; the last four, after testing has taken place.

1. At what point will this assumption be tested? (This should be specified in the business plan.)
2. How will it be tested?
3. What are the test results?
4. How do those results affect our original assumption? Should it be changed? To what?
5. What are the implications of the change for the project's timetable, costs, investment, resource requirements, action sequence, and critical path strategy?
6. In light of the test results, should we slow the venture

down, speed it up, change design elements, redirect it, or terminate it?

In many firms, even if assumptions are identified and tested, internal pressures, described by Staw and Ross (1987), may prevent managers from exercising the most potent form of control over the new venture—pulling the plug on it. Here are some examples of such pressures:

- Certain pressures are endemically cultural. In many organizations, persistence is equated with leadership, and the failure to persist is seen as a personal or organizational weakness.
- Persistence is expected in order to meet the projections of a business plan, even though most projections are no more than fantasies quantified by Lotus and cannot be met.
- A project may become highly symbolic of the firm's stature and competence—a self-imposed test of its vitality.
- Some projects are continued because there is no way to recover the firm's investment unless they are completed (for example, a large construction project such as a tunnel). Rather than cutting its losses, the firm continues the project in the hope of some kind of recovery.

In short, designing and using a feedback system to test critical assumptions will do a firm little good unless it then takes decisive action based on that feedback.

Use of Modified Budget Control Methods

If, as we have observed, budget projections for new businesses are rarely accurate, what is the point of budget control? The budget is the financial expression of the business plan, and although both the plan and the budget will inevitably require change, operating budgets and budget reviews will help the firm pinpoint the factors that necessitate changes. An understanding of these factors, coupled with growing knowledge about the business, will or should result in an increasingly reliable budget control system.

Tracking the cost of getting from one point to the next in the venture plan is a more effective means of control than monitoring monthly expenditures. Let's take the example of a project in which R&D costs are budgeted at $50,000 per month, with a target of completing product development in 12 months. Normal control methods would focus on the $50,000 in planned monthly expenditures, with variances being reported and investigated. If product development had not been completed at the end of 12 months, more time and money would be provided.

A step toward a more realistic budget control approach would be to earmark a lump sum of $600,000 for the completion of product development. Rather than conducting monthly reviews, the firm would conduct stage reviews—for example, upon completion of the following events: formulation, process design, process testing, development of quality control procedures, and development of specifications for raw materials and finished product. In building the $600,000 budget, the firm would estimate the cost and time required to complete each stage in the product development process. Either upon completion of a particular stage, or at some earlier or later point, the cost to reach that stage would be compared with the estimate and used to determine the impact on the cost of completing future stages. This budgeting process can be carried through for each stage of business development.

Here's a case involving the production of a motion picture that provides a very good example. An independent producer attempted to raise additional funds to complete a film, which, at the time, consisted of raw, unedited footage containing many scenes that required reshooting. In seeking funding, the producer (whose first film this was) requested an amount that would supposedly suffice to completely finish the film. An experienced film producer was consulted and was asked, "What percentage of the total cost of a film is usually spent to arrive at this film's current stage?" The answer was 25%. Yet the sum requested by the neophyte producer was based on the estimate that more than 75% of the film's total cost had already been incurred and that only 25% of that estimated total was still needed. Additional funds were raised, but the amount was increased enough to reflect a more realistic estimate of the cost of completing the film.

To cite another example, a venture's budget calls for achieving $1 million in sales during the first year of commercial sales and shows cumulative project costs of $2 million. Of that $2 million, the budget calls for $500,000 to be spent in the first year to achieve the sales, with that sum covering all costs, including selling costs. By November 15, though, it is clear that sales for the year will reach only $500,000, but $1 million has already been spent. The budget review should focus on the reason for these variations. Should any assumption be changed? If the company were budgeting now, on November 15, how would it change the selling cost/sales/ time numbers? Is the variation in the cost required to reach the event one that will affect all future projections? The senior manager to whom the venture manager reports must ask these questions and dig for causes and work to identify needed changes. The venture manager must have done likewise and be ready to make or have already made the required changes in strategy or actions.

On the other hand, let's say the sales result was exactly as indicated in the preceding paragraph, but just $250,000 was spent in that year. In this case, the only variation involves the time, and the only important questions about this variation are whether the venture's competitive position is endangered by the delay, when the venture expects to achieve future sales, and how the budget and plan should be changed to reflect this new knowledge about timing—especially the sequence and timing of future actions.

(Note: In preparing estimates, it is very common to underestimate how much time will elapse between the first offer to a customer and the first purchase. This is especially true in the case of industrial products or services, or capital equipment, or when a prospective customer must change its procedures in connection with the purchase. The venturing firm really has to understand the market practices to make any reasonable estimate of the required selling time.)

It is during the budget review process that destructive pressures can be brought to bear on venture managers, causing them to concentrate on meeting timetables and justifying costs based on line-item review rather than on completing key events and objectively analyzing the costs required to do so.

Again, we want to make it clear that this systematic approach is not applicable in the case of certain high-risk ventures in which, for example, entry barriers to competition are very low, there is little or nothing proprietary about the firm's venture position, and seizing market share rapidly is the key to venturing success.

CONTROL ROLES: VENTURE MANAGEMENT VERSUS SENIOR MANAGEMENT

Senior management's role, which is to control corporate risk, may be filled by a corporate or operating unit responsible for a number of ventures, by an operating unit of the firm, or by senior corporate executives, all external to the venture itself. Venture management's role, which is to manage and control the venture, is filled by those directly responsible for operating the venture, who are inside the venture itself.

The ever-present and universal dilemma is to find the right balance between allowing venture management to have the necessary freedom and enabling corporate management to exercise the necessary controls. (Table 9-1 illustrates the distribution of control tasks between parent and venture management.) The suggested basic principles for senior parent management are to permit venture management to run the venture within specific outer limits, to clearly identify the go/

253

Table 9-1: Distribution of Control Responsibility

Control Tasks	Venture Management Responsibility	Senior Management Responsibility
Design		
Select venture management	—	Primary
Design compensation/incentives program	—	Primary
Select format/entry strategy	Secondary	Primary
Determine organizational positioning	Advisory	Primary
Establish financing triggers	Secondary	Primary
Propose business plan	Primary	Approval
Feedback Implementation		
Articulate assumptions	Primary	Secondary
Design assumptions tests	Primary	Secondary
Review test results	Secondary	Primary
Modify business plan	Primary	Secondary
Approve plan changes	None	Primary
Budget Control		
Prepare budget	Primary	Advisory
Approve budget	None	Primary
Conduct line-item review	Primary	None
Prepare event completion budget	Primary	None
Conduct event completion review—budget versus actual	Primary	Primary
Policy/Procedure Control		
Identify obstacles	Primary	Remove them
Identify necessities	None	Primary
Permit exceptions	None	Primary
Fate of the Venture		
Decide the venture's fate	Secondary	Primary

Note: "Primary" means having the decision-making responsibility. "Secondary" means having the responsibility for providing input and participating.

no-go assumptions and the events that will be used to test them, to review the results of those tests carefully, and to assure that appropriate action is taken based on those results. Aside from the issue of control, senior management must supply the required support, as described in Chapters 2 and 8.

CONCLUSION

Traditional control methods—i.e., line-item budget reviews, variance from projections, and time-centered budgets unrelated to the completion of events or the achievement of milestones—are not effective either for promoting the success of new ventures or for preventing large losses from venturing.

The most important control instruments are the design elements of the venture itself—who manages it, where it is positioned within the parent firm, what its format is, the key milestones chosen to trigger the release of financing, and the venture's strategy and plan. These elements are what must be altered when necessary to achieve the desired control.

Control can also be achieved by modifying how corporate policies and procedures are applied to the venture; identifying key assumptions, testing them, and making appropriate changes based on the test results; and using modified budget control methods suited to the unique requirements of a new business.

The goal is to devise a system that enables senior management to maintain an adequate degree of control without stifling the venture and at the same time enables venture management to have the necessary freedom and flexibility without putting the parent company at risk.

Guidelines

1. Design the venture to provide freedom for venture management within outer limits. That is, use the "playpen" approach to venture control rather than the "harness" approach, and redesign the "playpen" as the "baby" grows!

2. Designate a senior executive champion or facilitator to cut red tape and modify the application of policies and procedures.
3. Use budget controls that focus on the completion of events or the achievement of event-related milestones rather than on line-item control related to the calendar; compare actual results against budget; and use what is learned to determine how much should be budgeted for subsequent events.
4. Make sure critical assumptions are identified and tested and that test results are used to determine whether and how to redirect and/or redesign the business.
5. Dispose of the venture (i.e., sell or liquidate it) when a go/no-go assumption is found to be wrong and cannot be replaced with a satisfactory substitute assumption, for this means the firm no longer has any basis for staying in the business.

REFERENCES

Block, Z., and Subbanarasimha, P. N. 1989. "Corporate Venturing: Practices and Performance in the U.S. and Japan." Working paper. Center for Entrepreneurial Studies, Stern School of Business, New York University.

Byron, C. 1986. *The Fanciest Dive*. New York: New American Library.

Kanter, R. M., and Fonvielle, W. H. 1987. "When to Persist and When to Give Up." *Management Review* 76, no. 1 (January): 14–16.

Roberts, M. J. 1986. "Managing Growth." Note #9-387-054. Boston: Harvard Business School.

Staw, B. M., and Ross, J. 1987. "Knowing When to Pull the Plug." *Harvard Business Review* (March–April): 68–74.

Sykes, H. B., and Block, Z. 1989. "Corporate Venturing Obstacles: Sources and Solutions." *Journal of Business Venturing* 4, no. 3: 159–167.

10

A Survival Guide for
Venture Managers

This chapter is specifically addressed to those who lead
the way toward the creation of new businesses and who manage ventures: the product or venture champion, who promotes the venture internally; the business innovator, who is
responsible for the project (the venture manager); and the
executive champion, who acts as the venture's internal protector and buffer. A large part of the battle to establish a
successful venture capable of long-term survival depends on
managing the internal relationships and expectations of the
sponsoring parent organization. (Too often, this is a case of,
"With friends like these, who needs enemies?") The key
problem faced by the venture group, and especially the venture manager, is to achieve enough credibility so that they are
free to concentrate on the new business rather than negotiate
constantly with their parent. The information in this chapter
is designed to help them meet that objective.

The need to manage the internal relationships and expectations of the parent firm arises because every corporate venture is an assault on the status quo. It is a dangerous mission to the frontiers of corporate culture and management, often pushing the limits of both. Survival in this environment depends on a finely tuned instinct and a different set of rules than those that apply to established businesses.

Venture managers cannot always turn to others in the organization for guidance, because what works for managers of mature divisions may not work for the venture. Nor can venture managers look to independent entrepreneurs for guidance, because corporate entrepreneurs (i.e., intrapreneurs) must consider more varied and more numerous constituencies than those dealt with by independents; they have less control over the money, people, and physical resources needed than do independent entrepreneurs (however sparse the independents' resources might be); and they must be effective internal advocates and politicians, and must manage the expectations of a variety of audiences (with senior management being chief among them). Unlike their counterparts outside the firm, corporate venture champions who initiate high-reward/high-risk ventures are engaged in what, from their personal standpoint, is an inherently low-reward/high-risk activity.

Survival in this corporate environment is not easy. Under the best of conditions, the venture is created within a culture that supports and rewards innovation and entrepreneurship. But such an ideal situation is rarely encountered. And even in the best-managed firms, would-be innovators face a number of significant obstacles, including the competition for resources. Successful venture champions know how to use the system to overcome such obstacles and advance their project.

Despite the drawbacks, there are plenty of people who are internally motivated to innovate. Unwilling to wait for their organization to change, they either leave the firm (with or without venture capital support) or learn how to operate effectively within a relatively hostile environment. The forces driving such people vary enormously, but most common are the urge to see an idea come to fruition and the need for greater autonomy—not too different from the forces driving independent entrepreneurs.

In many cases, these innovators provide the impetus for a new venture and then move on to the next innovative effort. They tend to be out of the picture by the time the venture is operating profitably, with some being transferred, others promoted, some replaced, others discharged. At the other extreme, some innovators are kept in the venture management role too long, resulting in severe, and often fatal, damage to the ventures as well as to the intrapreneurs' career.

This chapter, which is designed to help intrapreneurs achieve greater venturing success in a corporate environment, shows what they can do to minimize such organizational and professional risks and to maximize both the performance of their ventures and their own career development. Achieving venturing success requires a fundamental strategy of undercommitment and overperformance, as we discuss in the following section, after which, we offer ten survival principles that intrapreneurs can use to implement that strategy.

THE GOLDEN RULE OF VENTURING: UNDERCOMMIT AND OVERPERFORM

The greatest need and greatest deficiency of new-venture managers is credibility. Remember, constant *uncertainty* is the only sure thing about new ventures. This means that venture managers have to adapt rapidly to new information, but in order to do so, they must be given great freedom and a high level of empowerment—far more freedom and empowerment than are typically given to managers of stable business units. Yet senior management does not easily grant such latitude to people whose credibility has not been established and who tend not to fit the normal corporate profile. (A remark by Peter Drucker at one of his symposiums neatly sums up the reason why corporate innovators often have to work hard to earn the trust of senior management. When asked, "How do you identify the entrepreneurs in the organization?," Drucker responded, "Look for the troublemakers!")

The best way to earn credibility is to have a track record of making and meeting commitments. Seasoned managers, who have such a track record, have credibility, but venture champions are usually not seasoned managers. Hence, the largely untested innovators who lead new ventures need to gain as much credibility as possible as quickly as possible, and they have to earn that credibility during the creation of the venture. Using the planning method described in Chapter 7—which begins early in the game with clearly visible action targets that have a relatively high probability of being achieved and gradually aims for more ambitious targets as more is learned—increases the odds of achieving credibility.

In building this credibility, it is essential for venture managers to understand that nobody cares how well they do in an absolute sense—only how close they come to meeting their projections (or budget or commitments or expectations). This is particularly evident in stock market reaction to company performance, which, in turn, may be responsible for senior executives' low tolerance for surprise.

A dramatic example was the 10% decline in the price of McDonald's stock on July 23, 1990, despite the fact that the company's sales and income were increasing at the time. As *The Wall Street Journal* explained: "McDonald's failed to meet Wall Street's earnings expectations" (A-7). In fact, earnings per share were $0.59 for the second quarter versus an expectation of $0.60! Furthermore, sales were 9.9% higher than the previous year, and net income was up 10.2%! Yet when U.S. Healthcare reported quarterly earnings of $0.65 a share instead of the expected $0.45, several analysts felt that they had been misled, which the company strongly denied. On May 6, 1991, *The Wall Street Journal* headlined its story: "Low Balling: How Some Companies Send Stocks Aloft" (1). Both of these stories illustrate the point that analysts seem to attach more significance to meeting expectations than to actual performance. Additional evidence is provided by the widespread use of incentive plans that are linked to making or beating budget—i.e., to meeting the financial performance commitment. Under such plans, even if absolute venture results are outstanding, the manager can be penalized if those results fail to meet expectations.

Because meeting commitments is more important than absolute performance, a fundamental rule for venture managers is to undercommit and overperform. This will enable them to develop a track record of consistently meeting commitments, which, in turn, will build credibility. This rule is particularly applicable when it comes to predicting the level of sales to be achieved by a given time, which tends to be the most unreliable prediction in any plan. Thus, it is advisable for venture managers to predict the lowest sales level at which the plan will be accepted, even if that level is lower than their private expectations. In the case of industrial products or services, no matter what commitments have been made by prospective customers, those commitments should be discounted in making sales projections, since many unknown factors can intervene between such commitments and the actual sales.

On the other hand, Conner Peripherals (which grew from sales of $0 in 1986 to $113 million in 1987 to $705 million in 1989) has successfully followed an unusual strategy for launching major new products: sell, design, and build—in that order! This strategy moves the unpredictability to the design and build area, which is subject to better control than sales (Kupfer 1990).

For most new ventures, the recommended strategy of undercommitting and overperforming is easier said than done. How can venture managers meet their commitments in a situation in which uncertainty prevails and surprise is the norm? How can they get an idea accepted if its potential value is unknown? How can they state an idea's potential value conservatively and still obtain resources if their idea is competing with other ideas or other demands for investment, particularly if the value of those other proposals is either more predictable or stated less conservatively? How can they maintain credibility with consistent undercommitment and overperformance?

These challenges illustrate the difficulty and impracticality of absolute rules. Precisely how far to undercommit must be weighed in the context of each situation: What will it take to get a project approved? And what level of performance can actually be achieved? We do *not* recommend dissimulation or falsification. Rather, managers can be direct about making a *commitment* to no more than a certain level of performance while at the same time indicating that a higher level of performance is possible, although that higher level is more to be aimed at and hoped for than to be banked in advance.

Despite the difficulties of following the "undercommit and overperform" strategy, this approach is far superior to overcommitting, which ensures underperformance and loss of credibility. And as we show in the next few pages, the shorter the time span of the commitment the venture manager makes and the smaller the action he or she commits to completing, the greater the likelihood that the commitment can be met.

GUIDING PRINCIPLES FOR THE SURVIVAL OF VENTURE MANAGERS

This section discusses the following ten principles, which are drawn from our experiences and the experiences of venture managers and champions whom we have studied and with whom we have worked:

1. Don't pursue an idea unless the potential reward justifies the potential risk.
2. Ask for the smallest possible decision at each stage of development.
3. Find and use allies, especially an executive champion.
4. Be your own first and most rigorous critic as you change your plan.

5. Recognize your own weaknesses and act decisively to compensate for them.
6. Avoid premature publicity, both internal and external.
7. Do not automatically decide to sacrifice profit and cash flow for market share.
8. Recognize and adapt to the venture's life-cycle stage.
9. Convince senior management that new ventures need different policies and procedures than the more mature parent organization.
10. Provide leadership as well as management.

In conjunction with the overall strategy of undercommitting and overperforming, these principles can help venture managers survive and thrive in a corporate environment.

Don't Pursue an Idea Unless the Potential Reward Justifies the Potential Risk

The need to assess the risk/reward potential before proceeding with an idea may appear self-evident, but such an assessment is often overlooked, or an idea's benefits are assumed without verification, or the idea may seem promising at the outset but the promise doesn't materialize in practice. In moving from concept to reality, three questions must be answered with increasing confidence at each step: (1) Is the idea feasible? (That is, can the project be done?) (2) What are the potential upside gain and downside risk? (3) Does the idea fit the firm, or can it be made to do so?

Answering these questions is a step-by-step process. There is no way these questions can be answered with a high degree of confidence at the beginning of a venture, but at each stage, the answers should become more definite and refined. Therefore, this principle combines the need to find the answers with the need to move the idea forward as far and as fast as emerging reality (i.e., performance) justifies.

Ask for the Smallest Possible Decision at Each Stage of Development

The venture manager should strive to keep the magnitude of decisions required by higher authority as small as possible for as long as possible consistent with achieving the venture's objective. In keeping with the need to establish credibility, the venture manager must concentrate on achieving a first small step that shows the value of the idea or the proposed new business rather than seeking support for the total project at the outset.

Even getting approval for the first step can be a major hurdle at some firms. The process usually begins with proposing a new-venture idea and obtaining funds or time for concept testing. A common procedure is for the idea generator to write up the idea and present it through "proper" channels. An uncommon, but by no means unknown, procedure is to bootleg this first step—to find a way of accomplishing it without multiple levels of approval.

In one company, five different approval levels were required for any expenditure relating to a new idea. A snowball has a better chance of surviving a trek across the Sahara than an idea has of making it through this process. And yet the top management of this *Fortune* 500 firm constantly bemoaned the dearth of innovation in the organization. Even so, innovation happens *in spite of* the system. For example, the senior executive of a highly innovative and economically successful division of the firm refused to give his subordinates permission to explore new ideas, replying simply, "Don't ask me. Just do it."

Doing battle with the corporate bureaucracy can be daunting. In a large telecommunications company, the usual response was, "Let me see a business plan," or outright rejection. One idea generator in this firm spent an entire year writing and revising business plans based on a single idea, only to have the idea rejected. His comment was, "How can I be expected to write a business plan when I don't know anything yet?"

The following subsections offer a few suggestions for how astute venture managers can advance incrementally but steadily, even through the thickest bureaucratic jungles.

Don't Ask for Permission. Some innovators have found clever ways to avoid dealing with the system altogether, eliminating the need for permission. A computer programmer with an idea for a new, marketable program for her firm bought the necessary hardware, used her own time to verify probable need/value by checking with a few potential industrial customers, developed a program prototype at home, and presented management with her results. The firm bought the hardware from her, recognized her contribution with a bonus, and then allocated the funds for complete development.

Use Suppliers. Suppliers can be enlisted as allies in the process of testing an idea. At one firm where getting approval for a capital expenditure required three levels of sign-offs and several months, an innovator convinced a supplier to help establish a new quality control method. At the innovator's urging, the supplier lent the firm the testing equipment in order to establish both how it would function and the magnitude of the process cost savings that might be achieved. No in-house permission was needed except from a friendly plant manager. After the tests had been completed, a request for funds was prepared and justified by specifying the amount of money that would be *lost* every week if the equipment were returned. The expenditure was approved within days, despite some mild mumbling about "not following procedures."

Use Customers (They Have More Credibility Than You Do). Customers can be the venture manager's most effective allies in the effort to secure approval for testing new ideas. An interested prospective customer can demonstrate the need for an innovation to reluctant management and create pressure for rapid approval of the idea. One research VP of an industrial food company regularly colluded with customers to request specific developments. This was also a very useful step in determining the likelihood of a market for the proposed innovations.

Scrounge, Borrow, Beg, Seduce. In other cases, people have used money diverted from another budget to fund a concept test. Bootlegging has become so common that some firms positively encourage it.

The preceding examples show resourcefulness in action and, if necessary, a willingness to beg for forgiveness rather than ask for permission. Some of these strategies entail risk to the individual implementing them, particularly if the idea doesn't pan out, but the venturing game is not for those who are unwilling to take necessary risks.

In most situations, such extraordinary tactics are not necessary to get approval for testing an idea. In these companies, the innovator should still maintain a focus on the first stage—testing the concept. But to gain corporate support for initial testing, the concept must be described. This corporate support is particularly important in the case of consumer products, for which concept testing requires professional design and may also require research to determine the size of the potential market—which can involve significant out-of-pocket costs.

Develop Support—Step by Step. The method we recommend for creating support for a project involves first writing a proposal, then proposing a feasibility study, and finally building a business plan.

Step 1: Write a proposal. The process of generating support begins with writing a proposal, which can then be presented for approval. The proposal should contain the following elements:

1. A description of the idea that needs to be concept-tested and how it fits the company's strategy.
2. Either a rough guess of upside gain, downside risk,

feasibility, and fit or a statement of the need for testing to provide data on which to base a first estimate.

3. The anticipated target market segments and their rough potential.
4. A statement of the need or want to be fulfilled.
5. A statement of the possible benefits to the firm.
6. Competitive advantages that may be obtainable.
7. A description of the concept test.
8. A statement of the test's objective: to determine whether to proceed with a feasibility study, modify the concept, or drop it.
9. The funds and time required for the test. (If producing a model—*not a prototype*—would be relatively easy and inexpensive [e.g., a food product, a simple mechanical device, an information service in printed form], funds for this should be requested as well. If producing a model would involve significant cost, time, and effort, the concept test results should be obtained before proceeding with the production of a model.)

In order to clarify the objective of the idea proposal and help build credibility, the proposal's *tone* should be a combination of enthusiasm and inquiry. The proposal is for an *experiment,* to determine whether the firm should proceed to the next step or whether the concept might need to be changed and retested. The test's objective is not to "prove the concept" but to give senior management the information it needs in order to determine what the next step should be. No approval is to be sought for that next step at this time.

Step 2: Propose a feasibility study.   When the first step is completed, the innovator is in an improved position to obtain approval for the next, more expensive, feasibility verification step, assuming the innovator has met his or her commitment to get the answers within the specified time frame and cost and the results warrant further action. The innovator's credibility is enhanced if he or she exhibits objectivity and is willing to modify or reject the concept if necessary. A negative concept test result does not always lead to abandonment; it can also be used as an analytic tool for modifying the concept or the target market.

If the concept test results are favorable with respect to the upside gain, downside risk, apparent feasibility, and fit, the next step is exploratory product development and market research to get approximate information regarding the following issues:

- How much it will cost and how long it will take to complete the development process
- Cost/price range of the product, service, or business
- Market acceptance and size, which should be examined in greater depth at this time
- Investment requirements
- Competitive position—in terms of quality, costs, and functions
- Quality requirements and possibilities

The purpose of this step is to get enough information to enable senior management to make a sound decision about proceeding with the much more expensive step of development. The proposal for feasibility verification should therefore include a plan for obtaining all the required information. The proposal's tone should still convey a spirit of learning and enthusiasm. Its aim is to achieve the stated purpose in the stated time at the stated cost.

It is at this step that uncertainty becomes more intense, particularly if laboratory or engineering development is involved. Development always takes longer and costs more than estimated. The project champion must clearly state at this point what is and is not predictable in order to control expectations and minimize disappointments.

Here's an example, discussed briefly in the preceding chapter, that illustrates this "one step at a time" approach. In the late 1970s, many supermarkets were opening in-store bakeries. Although these operations were universally unprofitable, they were considered essential to attract traffic. An innovator in a company that sold bakery machinery and prepared mixes had an idea for a system that might solve the profitability problem. Stores would be supplied with frozen baked products, which they would convert to a warm, fresh state in minutes with a machine that would use an infrared- and microwave-based heating process. The first proposal called for a concept study to determine the system's acceptability among supermarket chains and learn the economic (investment/return, margins, labor costs) and capacity requirements. This proposal was approved, and the study was conducted within the time limits and budget proposed for that step.

Based on the study's results, a second proposal was developed to put together a working model of the equipment. This step was needed to determine its feasibility, design specifications, and cost range. The proposal also included a first rough estimate of potential market size for machinery, mixes, and frozen baked products as well as a protocol for using an alpha site to verify the data upon which the market estimate was based. This step was also completed very close to time and budget commitments, with a great deal of resourcefulness exhibited by the product champion in the process. Each of the preceding steps was positioned as an effort to learn whether this idea could be transformed into a commercial reality and, if so, how. As a result of this testing, a number of changes to the concept were developed and openly presented. Up to this point, no major economic decision had been required.

Upon completion of this feasibility study, a business plan was prepared. It was quickly approved, both because of the project manager's credibility and because the information accumulated in the preceding steps provided the basis for writing a sensible and credible plan. As it turned out, the business was not successful, but no losses were incurred because the plan provided for recovery of all costs in that eventuality.

Step 3: Build a business plan.　　Because of the enormous uncertainty associated with the development of any new business, the preparation of a reasonably reliable business plan must be deferred until enough is known about the idea to give the plan a fair shot at credibility. The business plan is presented *after* the concept has been proved and enough facts have been obtained through feasibility analysis and product development to provide the basis for making reasonable assumptions upon which the plan can be based. The preceding steps must therefore be completed before acquiring the bulk of the resources needed for startup, which is triggered by approval of the plan.

In constructing the business plan (which, from a physical standpoint, should be modular and in loose-leaf form), the venture team must keep the following things in mind: (1) the plan will be based principally on assumptions; (2) many of those assumptions will turn out to be wrong; (3) the plan will require changes; and (4) venture managers will tend to be evaluated based on their ability to meet planned objectives.

In an organization with an innovative culture, senior managers who understand the inherent unpredictability of new ventures will continually ask, "How are things going?" In organizations without such a culture, the venture champion can help change the culture as well as advance the project by being consistently realistic, open, and direct with authorizing management. Since an anti-innovative culture tends to demand plan fulfillment, seek stability, and resist change, it is important for the champion to openly and realistically clarify expectations so that, in a sense, there is "planned" surprise (i.e., learning new things) and there are planned changes to the plan, by means of adjustments made at key milestones, as described in Chapter 7. Growing acceptance of this dynamic process is in fact a cultural change of some significance. The venture manager accumulates credibility by committing to what can be done and then doing it better and faster than promised. However, in addition to building a technically sound business plan, provisions must be made at this time for managing the expectations of senior management.

To accomplish this, the planner should define success criteria for each stage in the plan and make the process for achieving these criteria as predictable as possible. (Venture managers frequently mention lack of a definition of success as a significant obstacle to venturing.) The two criteria most useful at any point are: (1) meeting the learning objectives and (2) applying what is learned to future actions.

Because many of these actions are likely to be quite different than originally planned, explanation or defense will be required, which leads to our next principle.

Find and Use Allies, Especially an Executive Champion

In conducting the step-by-step exploratory process of developing a new venture, it is critically important for the venture manager to find allies within the organization. Such allies should include people with knowledge and skills who can contribute to the program; people with influence who will support the program; and an executive champion who can act as a buffer, an adviser, and a guide through the corporate bureaucracy. At Du Pont, for example, innovators are encouraged to get assistance from people outside their immediate area of activity, who will actually perform technical work on a voluntary basis. At 3M, innovators are encouraged to seek sponsorship anywhere in the firm that they can find it.

Having an executive sponsor or champion is an important success factor in venturing. For major projects or businesses, the executive champions should be the CEO and the top management group. Only such sponsorship and support by then CEO Regan made Merrill Lynch's "Cash Management Account" venture possible and successful. Without the sponsorship and drive of Al Neuharth, Gannett CEO, *USA Today* would never have gotten off the ground and would have been abandoned long ago. Even he, as CEO, needed to find allies on the board in order to keep the venture alive. (Note: As of January 1992, *USA Today* was reported to have lost $18 million in 1991 but is expected to turn a profit in 1992.)

Be Your Own First and Most Rigorous Critic as You Change Your Plan

Venture management's ability to remain both enthusiastic and realistic will reinforce its credibility with senior management. The venture manager should critically examine every aspect of the venture, not only at milestones but throughout the venture creation process. He or she must relentlessly probe for hidden assumptions and expose these assumptions to the hard light of reality. If the project should be discontinued, venture management should be the first to recommend it, in the best interests of both the corporation and the venture team.

Recognize Your Own Weaknesses and Act Decisively to Compensate for Them

As important as it is for venture managers to realistically assess the venture's progress, it is just as important for them to turn this critical eye toward themselves. Greiner, in his classic article "Evolution and Revolution as Organizations Grow" (1972), describes five phases of development, which involve growth through (1) creativity, (2) direction, (3) delegation, (4) coordination, and (5) collaboration. And as we saw in the preceding chapter, each of the several stages or phases in a venture's life cycle requires a unique set of leadership skills from the venture manager. The firm can obtain the required skills either by replacing existing personnel or by training existing personnel and helping them to make the necessary changes in their approach to leadership.

During the second phase, growth through direction, there is usually a functional organization, job assignments are more specialized, and communication is more formal. The focus is on efficiency; the style is directive; and control is exercised through standards and cost centers. Upper-level people usually provide direction and require lower-level managers or supervisors to act simply as functional specialists. Thus, crises develop if the people who understand more about the nitty-gritty details of the business have less to say about what direction it should take. Such crises can be avoided by delegating more, by moving decision making closer to the action site. Unless this is done, the people who know the most about the business are likely to leave. A move toward empowering others is particularly difficult for highly directive managers to make, but without such a move, growth stagnates and the firm will experience an increasingly urgent need to replace management—sparking another crisis.

The third phase, growth through delegation, focuses on expanding the market. As the name of this phase implies, the style is delegative, and control is exercised through reports and profit centers. This approach results in faster response to customers and accelerated new-product development. A consequence of decentralized operations at this stage of business development is perceived, and often actual, loss of control by the firm's top executives, who become concerned about duplication, the need for coordination of planning, and controlling the allocation of resources, particularly money. Sometimes, the result is a return to centralization—a solution that negates the benefits of the powerful market orientation of decentralized business units and may doom the firm if its products and markets are even moderately diversified. Such organizations must respond swiftly to customers, guided by direct and intimate knowledge of their wants and needs. If growth is to occur, it must happen through coordination methods that do not sacrifice previous gains.

But the coordination mechanisms found in almost all large and medium-sized multidivisional enterprises include the establishment of product groups, formal planning procedures and reviews, and a corporate staff for control and review. Proposals for capital expenditures are examined carefully; ROI becomes a measure of performance for product groups; stock options and companywide profit incentives are instituted; and growth is expected to be achieved through more efficient use of the company's resources. Although these coordination mechanisms have been essential to the growth of such enterprises, in them can be found the seeds of the next crisis—the crisis of red tape that results from the lack of confidence between line and staff and between headquarters and field. As Greiner (1972) describes it:

> Line managers . . . increasingly resent heavy staff direction from those who are not familiar with local conditions. Staff people . . . complain about the uncooperative and uninformed line managers. Together both groups complain about the bureaucratic paper system that has evolved. Procedures take precedence over problem solving, and innovation is dampened. (43)

A wide array of approaches have been used to solve this crisis of red tape: empowering the organization's people, restructuring (i.e., slashing overhead, consolidating, disposing of operations), and becoming more aware of the need to stay close to the customer.

Understanding business life cycles and their implications is indispensable for the corporate entrepreneur. Unless the venture manager acts to supply the management skills needed at each stage, new management will be required. This does not mean that all the skills have to reside in one person, but the leader of the business must be aware of his or her strengths and weaknesses and must take the initiative in building a team with the necessary combination of talent and skills. Self-knowledge is a critical prerequisite for achieving that combination.

Avoid Premature Publicity, Both Internal and External

In the enthusiasm and excitement of actually launching some innovative activity, senior management may be strongly tempted to sound the trumpets before anything has really been accomplished. Resist this temptation! All the evidence indicates that such premature publicity only causes damage. The first thing that happens is that those involved in the new venture become crown princes or princesses and objects of jealousy on the part of their poor, benighted colleagues who are forced to work in the firm's dull, old businesses. Second, expectations rise. Since those expectations are rarely met, the initial highs of recognition and praise are followed by the lows of cynicism and demoralization, which, in turn, are followed by the departure or discharge of those who have been lionized.

Premature publicity also aids competitors, both by giving them more time to counterattack and by providing them with information that would be useful for recruiting promising entrepreneurs. Granted, there are exceptions, particularly in high-tech ventures, when early publicity can be used deliberately to induce potential customers to postpone buying a competitor's product. Although this type of early-stage publicity may be a strategic necessity, failure to fulfill such promises can have a high reputation cost.

Celebration should be postponed until there is real accomplishment in the marketplace, in application, or in proprietary protection. Although in-house recognition of innovative initiatives encourages effort, it must be done with sensitivity and on a scale appropriate to the situation. One financial services company has found it effective to hold an internal ceremony with rewards for the innovators, without any external or print publicity. Finally, whenever publicity does occur, it is vital to ensure that recognition is given to the team and individual team members, not just to one lone hero.

Do Not Automatically Decide to Sacrifice Profit and Cash Flow for Market Share

A few studies, particularly Biggadyke's (1979; discussed in Appendix A), have shown that new entries that sacrifice early profit and cash flow for market share do better in the long run. This conclusion has been reinforced by reports on the Japanese practice of sacrificing early profit for market share. But this strategy is not applicable to all ventures, and the dangers of using it as a universal guideline are as follows: many companies can't afford this strategy, and if they try it, they will run out of money before breaking even; with strong enough proprietary protection, this strategy is unnecessary and wasteful; if the firm experiences a change at the top, the new CEO may refuse to tolerate continued losses or demands for cash; and most likely, the firm's ongoing businesses will come under pressure for cash and profit, with help from the stock analysts baying at management's heels. All these pressures could lead to the abandonment of a new business.

Share and profit are not related by a simple equation. Competition, market status, affordability, and competitive insulation must also be considered. It cannot automatically be assumed that the venture will gain share only by *losing* money!

NYNEX learned that market share was less important than profits in managing its retailing unit, which was running profitably when NYNEX decided to go for share. After acquiring IBM's retailing operation, NYNEX went after market share, just as the gurus say one should, and incurred large losses. Top management then decided that the market share strategy was too costly and unnecessary, with no light at the end of the tunnel, and switched to a money-making strategy. This latter strategy succeeded, and the business has continued to grow. Another firm started by achieving a new venture's profitability and share objectives in a single region. Then it went about establishing share in other regions but carefully separated the costs of enlarging share from the costs, profit, and cash flow associated with the core venture in the already profitable region.

To summarize, the most important factors that contraindicate a universal strategy of long-deferred positive cash flow and profit are frequent changes in chief executives, the threat of takeovers, and a volatile economy. Thus, when planning the business, management must define the terms of success

276

and then select the strategy that is precisely designed to achieve the success of the specific venture in the specific firm.

Recognize and Adapt to the Venture's Life-Cycle Stage

Starting a new business is so different from running an established one that the use of the parent company's standard policies, procedures, and management practices often jeopardizes the venture's existence. Even the methods that worked successfully in starting the venture can become dangerously outdated as the venture matures. Management can kill the venture by failing to adapt to its changing needs.

Professionalization calls for changes. Making these changes requires the ability to:

- Recognize *when* change is needed
- Recognize and act upon the limitations and capabilities of the venture team, especially those of the venture manager

Earlier in the chapter, we mentioned the phases of development described by Greiner (1972): growth through creativity, growth through direction, growth through delegation, growth through coordination, and growth through collaboration. He argues that a company's transition through these phases occurs either in an evolutionary manner or through a revolutionary and disruptive change process, depending on management actions.

After startup, the first phase of growth is achieved through creativity. Management focuses on "make and sell," the organizational structure is informal and characterized by an entrepreneurial style, and progress is measured in terms of market results. Up until this point, the venture champion has needed such skills as technical expertise and the ability to get resources to the startup point, but he or she may very well lack the "making and selling" skills required at this stage. For example, the venture manager may be a marketing person who is weak in the "make" area. During this phase, the venture manager must also do a great deal of hands-on work, leading, and inspiring, and key people must be able to perform multifunctional tasks.

As the business grows, so does the need for administration. If this need is not anticipated and met, problems appear: substandard quality, billing and shipping errors, late deliveries, slow collections, human resource tensions, and excessive and obsolete inventory. The situation is further complicated by the usual growing requirement for capital, which places additional pressure on the already overworked entrepreneur.

Thus, a crisis of leadership develops, and there is a need for a good directive manager to run the business. This need can be anticipated and provided for by the founding venture manager; if not, it will be provided for by the corporate parent—either in anticipation of a crisis or in response to one. For example, David Ben Daniel (1983) described such a situation, which occurred when he was a group vice president of Exxon Enterprises: "We found that we needed one venture manager to carry us to $2 million [in] sales, another to $10 million [in] sales, and still another to build a big business." A CEO responding to a survey on venture compensation (Block and Ornati 1987) wrote that there was one incentive plan for the business starter and then another plan for "the one who comes in to straighten it out." An anecdote about a venture capitalists' meeting has one venture capitalist asking the other, "How are you doing?" The response: "Fine, we just got rid of our entrepreneurs." Although venture team members may handle "doing" and perhaps "managing" very well, they can fall apart when it comes to "managing managers."

In addition to the Greiner model, another simple model of the stages of a new venture is based on the number of people employed. The person responsible for leading the venture will initially have to do more and manage less. A rule of thumb is that this leadership mode can work effectively until the number of employees reaches about 20. Around that point, there is a greater need for managing and less time for doing; hence, management rather than hands-on work becomes the primary task of the entrepreneur.

This same model then proposes a second rule of thumb —that when the number of employees reaches about 75, the venture's leader must manage managers. This evolution follows the pattern that Michael Roberts (1986) describes as movement from management by direct coordination to management by indirect coordination—an absolute necessity if a business is to grow significantly.

This transition is particularly urgent in new ventures that are either experiencing very rapid growth or must achieve such growth (for example, ventures in the cellular telephone business, in which giants are battling for market share and one of the more successful firms identifies its most significant problem as finding managers).

Although the challenge to entrepreneurs is especially intense as a business moves beyond its first stage, the founders who survive that first stage continue to face new challenges as the venture moves into its later stages. It is to those surviving founders that this principle and the following one are addressed.

Convince Senior Management That New Ventures Need Different Policies and Procedures Than the More Mature Parent Organization

Just as ventures pass through stages in their life cycles, so also is the parent firm passing through stages in its own life cycle. Sykes and Block (1989), in their article "Corporate Venturing Obstacles: Sources and Solutions," observe that every new venture is in a *different* life-cycle stage than its parent. It is those differences that are the source of the internal obstacles to success facing a new venture.

The culture, policies, and procedures of the parent firm—which often appear to be irrelevant, arbitrary, and a bunch of bureaucratic nonsense to those trying to get a venture off the ground—are nothing more than the adaptive mechanisms that the parent found effective as the base business developed. Part of the venture manager's job is to understand the life-cycle stage of the sponsoring business unit and, with the help of the executive champion, use that information to convince senior management that normal control practices are not applicable to an early-stage new venture and that there is a need for policies and procedures appropriate for the venture's life-cycle stage. It will be easier to convince senior management if the argument is presented in terms of differences in life-cycle stage rather than as an attack on bureaucracy and bureaucrats.

Provide Leadership as Well as Management

Building a new business demands both leadership and management. Venture managers must provide both. They must address themselves to the five key tasks shown in the following list if they hope to achieve growth and survive as leaders of the developing business. (Long-term survival in the venture leadership position may not be an objective for the venture's founder, however, since in terms of desire and talents, that individual may be best suited for the role of founding other ventures for the firm.)

1. Provide leadership that produces a can-do, opportunity-seeking, egalitarian venture culture—leadership that is involved, not distant; that creates clarity and focus, and most important, offers a vision of what the venture can become.
2. Concentrate on people—their selection, training, empowerment, and as necessary, replacement.
3. Delegate whole tasks (e.g., "create a new product," "develop a new market," "prepare a plan," "build a plant," "create a salesforce"), not individual actions. That's managing managers.
4. Make sure evaluation is based on performance, not on behavior, unless the behavior is destructive to the culture being sought.

5. Use objective outside resources, especially people who know the industry and market. Include corporate staff people if they are objective and knowledgeable.

CONCLUSION

Venture managers have a difficult and challenging mission. First, the company has to be convinced to support an effort that begins with an uncertain outcome. This calls for persistence and powerful selling skills, and creates every conceivable pressure to downplay the hazards and exaggerate the rewards. Once resources are obtained, the task changes to one of creating an enterprise and thereafter to building a growing, successful business. Throughout the process, the parent company's support must be maintained through a combination of performance *and* managed expectations. In the midst of all this, the new venture's leaders must grow and adapt to the changing character of the job. Following the ten survival principles presented in this chapter will help them succeed in their challenging mission.

Guidelines

1. Undercommit and overperform.
2. Act as if it's your own money at stake.
3. Find and use allies, especially an executive champion.
4. Avoid advance publicity unless it will help sell your product.
5. Be the first to recognize when the venture should be redirected or stopped.

REFERENCES

Ben Daniel, Dr. David. 1983. Presentation to an Internal Corporate Venturing class at the Graduate School of Business Administration, New York University.

Biggadyke, R. 1979. "The Risky Business of Corporate Diversification." *Harvard Business Review* (May–June): 103–111.

Block, Z., and Ornati, O. 1987. "Compensating Corporate Venture Managers." *Journal of Business Venturing* 2: 41–51. (One of the individual responses to the survey conducted).

Cohen, Laurie P. 1991. "Low Balling: How Some Companies Send Stocks Aloft." *The Wall Street Journal* (May 6): 1.

Gibson, Richard. 1990. "McDonald's Net Rises But Lags Expectations." *The Wall Street Journal* (July 23): A7.

Greiner, L. 1972. "Evolution and Revolution as Organizations Grow." *Harvard Business Review* (July–August): 37–46.

Kupfer, Andrew. 1990. "America's Fastest Growing Companies." *Fortune* (August 13): 48–54.

Roberts, M. J. 1986. "The Transition from Entrepreneurial to Professional Management: An Exploratory Study." Ph.D. diss., Harvard Business School.

Sykes, H. B., and Block, Z. 1989. "Corporate Venturing Obstacles: Sources and Solutions." *Journal of Business Venturing* 4, no. 3: 159–166.

11

The Internal Politics of Venturing*

Rational managers often find the idea of having to "play politics" disturbing; novice venturers, fired up by what they regard as the enormous potential of their enterprise, can find the idea downright distasteful. But however unpopular organizational politics might be, its crucial role cannot be ignored, since it can make or break a new venture.

Ignoring politics is tantamount to passively accepting its results. Many venture managers who have formulated venture strategies and plans that are *technically* sound still have trouble implementing them because they fail to understand and anticipate the new business's political requirements. Given the small size of the venture relative to the parent and

*The ideas in this chapter draw heavily off: Starr, J. A., and MacMillan, I. C. "Resource co-optation via social contracting: Resource acquisition strategies for new ventures," *Strategic Management Journal* 11 (Summer 1990): pp. 79–92.

its absolute dependence on the firm's resources, venture plans must be "politically correct" as well as technically correct.

The harsh reality is that all organizations are inherently political, made up of individuals acting in their own interests. To implement a venture plan, the venture manager must often attempt to influence other people, particularly the key stakeholders on whom the venture depends. Failure to identify those stakeholders and to anticipate and manage their behavior can drastically slow the venture's progress, if not halt it entirely.

There are three types of startup problems in particular that appear to require political solutions. First, venture managers often have to overcome problems of legitimacy, both inside and outside the firm (Stinchcombe 1965)—they must convince needed supporters of their viability. Second, venture managers are often desperately short of resources, yet they must compete for them internally against powerful, established departments that resent the venture's intrusion onto their resource turf. Third, as the harbingers of change and innovation, venture managers frequently find themselves facing organizational indifference or resistance, if not outright enmity, on the part of those inside and outside the firm who have a vested interest in the existing order or simply cannot be bothered to provide needed support. To overcome these problems, venture managers often have to resort to political strategies—that is to say, strategies designed to get people to behave in ways they might not initially choose.

The power of good organizational politics can be seen in the case of a Swedish manager who deliberately nurtures and uses influence networks as a means of assisting his ventures. In one very successful venture, he capitalized on a major opportunity to start a robot-controlled foundry equipment business by identifying and confirming this need in Europe via a network of consultants that he maintains to help him identify just such venture opportunities. He then used another network of carefully nurtured engineering professors to confirm that the technology was in place to produce such equipment. Next, he mobilized every member of his consultant network to help him persuade each of their foundry clients to put up a piece of the $200,000 funding he needed to develop the prototype, persuading the consultants to vouch for his capability and integrity. This amount was easily raised, and without the manager's having to give up a single percentage of the action. Finally, he persuaded the foundry clients to aggressively help him debug the prototype as it was being developed. The clients willingly tolerated the disruption to their production systems during the process of debugging the prototype because they identified with it—as "their" product.

This chapter is designed to help venture managers understand and use political strategies such as those so skillfully employed by the Swedish manager, both to overcome the barriers facing the new business and to promote its progress. We start by examining the aforementioned key political problems—lack of legitimacy, resource starvation, and organizational resistance and inertia—after which, we describe some of the approaches venture managers can use to build influence, a necessary prerequisite for addressing these problems. Finally, we consider how creative political strategies can be employed to overcome these problems.

SOURCES OF POLITICAL PROBLEMS

This section examines the three major venturing problems that must be dealt with in the political arena: lack of legitimacy, resource starvation, and organizational resistance and inertia—i.e., the struggle to establish credibility, obtain an adequate share of what the organization has to offer, and overcome both active and passive failure to cooperate with the venturing effort.

Lack of Legitimacy

Any venture faces a number of problems that stem directly from the simple fact that it is new (Stinchcombe 1965). Because the business has no track record, customers, distributors, and suppliers (justifiably) lack confidence in its ability to survive, which gives them little reason to provide support. The newer and more different the market being entered, the more serious this issue of legitimacy. Given the propensity of corporations to terminate internal ventures, even some insiders will question the new business's legitimacy.

Thus, the venture faces a credibility crisis at the outset and must somehow create an impression of viability and legitimacy before it will receive support. Building legitimacy by trying to systematically increase a reluctant customer and distributor base can be an extremely slow, painstaking, and therefore costly process.

Resource Starvation

To get under way, any new corporate enterprise requires an adequate supply of resources, including funds, people, materials, and often access to capacity in the organization's production and service systems. Yet as indicated earlier in the chapter, the manager in charge of the startup generally faces severe constraints in the amount of resources available for the venture. More often than not, the venture manager is seen as an internal competitor attempting to invade the resource allocation turf of the firm's established powerful and turf-conscious departments. This means that even if the venture manager succeeds in securing the needed resources, those resources may end up being conceded with reluctance and lingering resentment.

Resistance and Inertia

The most serious political problems facing the new venture arise from resistance and/or inertia from inside as well as outside the organization. The sources of this resistance and inertia are manifold:

- *Indifference:* Often, the venture's small size renders key parts of the organization indifferent to providing the cooperation the venture requires in order to get off the ground. Although the venture manager may need support from engineering or production departments, marketing, or the salesforce, he or she may receive very little attention simply because the venture is considered insignificant compared to the ongoing business. This can also happen in external relations, with suppliers, customers, and distributors simply ignoring the venture's needs because it is so small. And even if they do pay some attention to the venture, they are likely to neglect it when they receive requests from larger and more powerful departments.

- *Distraction:* The people responsible for conducting the company's major ongoing businesses may simply be too distracted by the pressures of serving those businesses to assist the venture. If the venture manager happens to need, say, the support of the manufacturing facility to do short runs, this activity becomes, at best, a distraction from the principal business and, at worst, a disruptive irritation.

- *Competition:* Outright enmity on the part of external competitors can lead them to mobilize their clout with distributors and suppliers to deny support to the fledgling venture.

- *Disaffection:* Direct resistance to the venture's progress and even attempts to subvert it can be initiated by people in the organization who either do not believe in the venture, are envious of the venture or its manager, or feel that the venture is disturbing their comfortable routines. In particular, staff functions whose mission is to ensure homogeneity in the organization may attempt to smother the venture under procedures, rules, and policies. Anything that is new and requires different treatment disrupts and threatens their systems. This attitude can extend beyond the boundaries of the firm—to agencies, unions, or any other entity that has a vested interest in preserving the status quo.

- *Direct threat:* The final category consists of determined opponents of the venture who see it as an affront to their position or a direct threat to their part of the organization. Once again, this source of resistance can extend beyond the organization's boundaries, or affected parties within the firm can mobilize external resistance to hamper the venture.

The preceding major problems share a common element—namely, they represent situations in which, to get a new business's needs met, the venture manager must attempt to induce someone or some unit to change current behavior patterns from what the person or unit might otherwise prefer to do to what the venture manager needs done. Therefore, it is important for the venture manager to develop an understanding of the tools that can be used to gain influence and shape behavior, which are discussed in the following section.

BUILDING INFLUENCE

Because venture managers generally have limited formal access to sources of power, influence, or authority, they must rely on their ingenuity and persistence to build influence and use what little they have effectively.

To build an influence base, venture managers, in essence, create "social capital"—an inventory of liking, trust, gratitude, and/or obligations that can later be implicitly "traded" when favors are extracted or obligations are called (Homans 1958 and 1961; Blau 1964). Although the mental records may be ambiguous, each party knows that at some time in the future, on a completely different and totally unspecified transaction, the influence builder may ask a favor, thus "cashing in" the obligation.

Here are four major approaches for building an influence base suggested by Walton and McKersie (1969):

1. Solving and receiving help with problems, together with the related approach of giving and receiving favors

2. Sharing information
3. Creating opportunities for people to demonstrate their skills and competence
4. Building and using influence networks

These approaches are summarized in the following subsections.

Solving and Receiving Help with Problems

Although solving problems for someone is an obvious way to develop social assets such as liking, gratitude, or obligation that can be used to create influence, surprisingly, *asking* for help can generate influence just as effectively. People often develop an intense affinity or a high sense of responsibility for those whom they assist. Venture managers who seek and follow advice are frequently able to elicit other types of support as well. Senior managers who have proffered advice become champions of the corporate venture they have advised, and individuals who have given advice may also provide endorsements, recommendations, or even funding.

For example, a venture manager charged with developing a margarine business appealed to the contract manager of the engineering equipment supplier for assistance with the design of a particularly difficult and expensive piece of the facility. Soon the contract manager was aggressively helping the venture manager drive down the total price of his own contract. This included a recommendation to use some secondhand equipment that was being freed up in another job that the contract manager's firm was handling. The contract manager eventually took great pride in the fact that he had helped cut 40% off the cost of his firm's contract!

As they seek to build social capital and elicit support, venture managers should also keep in mind the related strategy of giving and receiving favors, which operates similarly to the strategy of solving and getting help with problems.

Sharing Information

Information is valuable currency in business. By sharing information that is important to others, the venture manager may be able to build up a credit of social obligations or affinities that can be "spent" at a future date.

For example, a venture manager starting a new pump business for an engineering supply company was at a distinct disadvantage competing with several established manufacturers for a fairly large contract from a refinery. Fortunately, the venture manager discovered that the refinery's plant manager was having a problem with a newly installed cooling tower system and suggested that the plant manager call one of his other customers who had solved a similar problem the week before. The plant manager followed the advice and got a solution in minutes. As a result, he was quite willing to award the contract to the venture manager. By exploiting his network and providing sorely needed information, this venture manager created feelings of gratitude that secured a valuable sale.

Creating Opportunities for People to Demonstrate Their Skills and Competence

People enjoy a chance to show their skills, flex their muscles, and display their talents. Creating or seeking opportunities for others to shine and look competent in public can engender considerable social goodwill. The Swedish venture manager mentioned earlier in the chapter consistently provided such opportunities to his consultant network and, as a result, reaped the benefits of their skills. This approach works extremely well inside organizations, as demonstrated by a management information venture manager we interviewed who had increased the profits of his business fiftyfold in ten years via new ventures. He ascribed much of his success to a policy of "Always accept the blame yourself; always give the credit to others."

By devoting time and attention to the preceding three strategies, it is possible for the venture manager to rather quickly develop an influence base, which can then be further leveraged by networking.

Building and Using Influence Networks

Managers who have spent time building an influence base are in a good position to start organizing networks of people inside and outside the firm. These individuals, with whom the managers have developed influence, provide a strong reservoir of ideas and support (Schon 1967; Quinn 1979; Burgelman and Sayles 1986), which will prove invaluable when the new business encounters its inevitable obstacles. As needed, venture managers can draw on this network of contacts to help them induce, persuade, obligate, or coerce the venture's opponents. They can even magnify their influence by asking members of the network to use *their* network contacts, if necessary (Granovetter 1973; Aldrich and Zimmer 1986; Aldrich 1988). For instance, the Swedish venture manager mentioned in the earlier example consciously and systematically nurtured several networks, two of which (consultants and engineering professors) played a crucial role in his foundry equipment venture.

The astute use of influence networks by new-venture managers yields a number of significant benefits (in addition to the obvious benefit of saving resources):

- Members of the network tend to exercise their influence to generate more pervasive, positive sentiments toward the venture.
- As a result of these favorable sentiments, early setbacks will be more easily tolerated and forgiven, both inside and outside the firm.
- This spirit of tolerance also means that "networked" stakeholders, both inside and outside the firm, will be more willing to help with problems.

291

USING POLITICAL APPROACHES TO SOLVE POLITICAL PROBLEMS

In this section, we will examine strategies for dealing with the three political obstacles most often faced by new ventures—lack of legitimacy, resource starvation, and organizational resistance and inertia.

Overcoming Lack of Legitimacy

If the venture does not have legitimacy, it may be unable to start at all, or it may be able to start only after incurring a debilitating delay while building credibility. How can a new business establish legitimacy quickly and thereby avoid such crippling costs?

The basic strategy for gaining legitimacy is to use personal influence or influence networks to somehow secure endorsements that will convince the necessary supporters of the venture's viability and credibility. The Swedish venture manager mentioned in an earlier example was able to solve the problem of legitimacy by securing endorsements from his network of consultants, thus piggybacking on the consultants' credibility with their clients. Without such endorsements, it is unlikely that any sane foundry manager would have allocated funds to develop the "paper" prototype that the venture manager was proposing.

In another example, a young venture manager was charged with creating a synthetic filter cloth business in a very conservative customer industry, which had always used natural cloth. To establish legitimacy, he employed his persuasive skills to convince the purchasing agent of the leading firm in the industry to provide him with an order for a trial batch. He then used this information to influence other companies in the industry to do the same. In the eyes of the lesser competitors, the order from the industry leader was viewed as a sufficient endorsement of the product to warrant a trial.

Securing endorsements is particularly important for ventures that are entering new market areas. In such cases, if the venture manager can rapidly acquire legitimacy via political gambits, the new business can gain the significant additional benefits of:

- Earlier customer acceptance
- Earlier distributor acceptance
- Earlier revenue streams

Overcoming Resource Starvation

When it comes to securing resources, accounts of entrepreneurial activity in established corporations are replete with tales of resourceful politicking. Venture managers hijack materials and equipment, appropriate production capacity and personnel time, conceal development activities, and cash in personal favors to secure the resources needed for their new business (Quinn 1979; Kanter 1983 and 1988).

The basic mechanism that venture managers can employ to do this is to co-opt resources that are currently being underutilized. This is one of the most flexible and easiest ways to gain access to resources (Selznick 1948 and 1949; Thompson 1967; Pfeffer and Salancik 1978; Burt 1980 and 1983). However, the key question is, why should any owner of an underutilized resource willingly give it up?

The answer lies in the extent to which venture managers can draw on the social capital they have generated through the influence-building processes described in the preceding section: sharing information, solving problems, doing favors, creating opportunities for others to demonstrate their good qualities, and tapping their network of contacts. These activities create an inventory of goodwill, liking, trust, gratitude, or obligations that is often just as valuable as currency to the small business. Sometimes, it can prove even more valuable.

Other research (Kanter 1983 and 1988; Burgelman and Sayles 1986), along with many case examples, suggests that there are three major classes of co-optation strategies for taking advantage of underutilized resources: borrowing, begging, and scavenging. Each of these strategies has distinct characteristics related to permanence of ownership of the resource and the resource's perceived value in the eyes of the original owner.

- *Borrowing:* Borrowing strategies are employed to temporarily or periodically secure the use of assets or other resources, on the premise that they will eventually be returned. One corporate venture manager who grew his business tenfold in a decade is very aggressive about "borrowing." On occasion, when his own funds run low, he has charged expenses for new projects to the accounts of other divisions of his firm. He has found that it takes at least a year before the corporate auditors spot these charges, and by then, the projects have usually generated enough revenues to repay the accounts. By the time this manager's activities are discovered, he has done so well that his sins are forgiven. (Note: We do not recommend this particular form of "borrowing"!)
- *Begging:* Begging strategies are employed to secure resources by appealing to the owner's goodwill. In this way, venture managers gain the use of the resources without needing to return them, despite the fact that the owner recognizes the value of the assets. In her research, Kanter (1983) identifies many cases of "tincupping," in which venture managers begged or scrounged resources from the rest of the firm.
- *Scavenging:* Scavenging strategies extract usage from goods that others do not intend to use or that they might actually welcome an appropriate opportunity to divest themselves of. This approach involves learning about unused or underused resources (e.g., obsolete inventory, idle equipment, or underutilized personnel) and killing two birds with one stone by putting such a resource to use while at the same time relieving the original owner of the burden of carrying it.

294

These three co-opting strategies allow internal corporate entrepreneurs to secure resources that would otherwise have to be obtained at much greater cost. This lowball approach to acquiring resources has several implications: by appropriating underutilized resources, venture managers lower the *cost* of startup; they dramatically reduce the initial investment, which lowers the *risk* of startup; and they increase the venture's return on assets (by reducing the denominator of ROA).

As a result of resource co-optation, venture managers will:

- Engage in fewer resource allocation battles, thus reducing both internal enmity and the expenditure of energy.
- Suffer fewer resource setbacks and disappointments.
- Suffer fewer resource shortages.
- Have ventures with lower asset intensity.
- Have ventures with lower fixed cost/revenue ratios.
- Achieve cash and profit break-even in less time.
- Have higher survival rates.
- Have a greater return on assets than venture managers who act like the typical trustee manager (Stevenson and Gumpert 1985) and "pay full fare" for their resources. (These managers tend to have the same painfully slow growth in profits as those discussed by Weiss [1981] in his comparison of corporate ventures with much more profitable independent ones.)

Overcoming Resistance and Inertia

Of the three major types of political problems cited at the start of this chapter—legitimacy, resource starvation, and resistance/inertia—the latter problem is the most intractable, and it comes from both inside and outside the organization. Therefore, the balance of this chapter is devoted to a discussion of the political strategy needed to attack this prime source of venturing obstacles.

We have identified six major steps that are essential to a political strategy for overcoming the organizational resistance and inertia that so often hamper the progress of new ventures. These steps, which are discussed in the following subsections, are:

1. Clarify the venture's crucial immediate and long-term objectives.
2. Identify potential political obstacles to progress.
3. Identify potential opponents and allies.
4. Anticipate responses by key targets.
5. Formulate a political strategy.
6. Monitor the progress of the political strategy.

Clarify the Venture's Crucial Immediate and Long-Term Objectives. The first step in attacking resistance and inertia is to clarify the venture's current crucial objectives. This clarification process serves two purposes: First, it enables the venture manager to identify who, inside and outside the firm, will be affected if the venture accomplishes the stated objectives. These people will almost certainly want to either support the venture or obstruct its progress. Second, it enables the venture manager to identify who will need to help if the venture is to succeed, and establish whether those parties are prepared to give their support.

The venture manager has to consider two sets of objectives: immediate and long-term. Immediate objectives are those that must be accomplished for the venture to reach the next major milestone. Knowing these objectives tells the manager who is likely to be immediately affected or needed, and provides the basis for urgent political action. Long-term objectives are concerned with the venture's revised ultimate objective. Whatever the venture's original objectives were, there is a need to periodically review where the venture should be going now. This new direction is often shaped by the expected moves and countermoves of those who have a vested interest in the outcome.

Identify Potential Political Obstacles to Progress. The next step is to systematically identify all the people, groups, or organizations on which the venture's outcome depends. These parties include:

- The major internal units that would be affected by the venture's success (for example, departments competing for the resources needed by the venture).
- External competitors for the venture's prospective customers and distributors.
- Such groups as shareholders, employees, unions, and suppliers. (Their possible interest in the venture should be considered, but these parties should be retained in the analysis only if they seem relevant to the outcome.)

Once again, it is important for venture managers to devote attention to the groups that will be affected when the new business achieves its next major milestone, but they should not ignore groups that will have a long-term impact.

(Note: This step and the next several steps in the process of overcoming resistance and inertia may initially appear very cumbersome—and can in fact become so if the venture manager goes overboard [e.g., by attempting to identify every conceivable obstacle to the venture's progress]—but remember that the analysis should constantly be simplified and refined to focus on the three or four most crucial items. The logic is that if these crucial items are not handled properly, nothing else will work anyway.)

This process of identifying the key parties on which the venture's outcome depends provides the backdrop for systematically thinking through the major obstacles the venture will face from groups that are vested, or need to be vested, in its outcome. To do this, the venture manager should review the various interest groups and consider the following issues:

- *Identify sources of support:* What groups presently support the venture? Are there potential allies that are either indifferent or too distracted to provide support and that therefore need to be mobilized in order for the venture's next major stage to succeed? Who will be making the decision to provide support?

- *Identify opponents:* Which internal and external parties are likely to be disaffected or threatened by the venture? What damage can they inflict and how? Can they block the venture's progress and, if so, how? How effective are their attempts likely to be? Who will be making the decision to take such action?
- *Anticipate opponents' actions:* What actions can opponents take at this stage to subvert the venture's progress and via whom? Can they threaten suppliers? Customers? Distribution? Can they seek management or government intervention?

This analysis will identify the principal movers and shakers—the individuals or groups that can make or break the new venture. Once this *limited number* of key parties has been identified, they can be targeted for the next round of political attention.

Identify Potential Opponents and Allies. The preceding analysis will enable the venture manager to identify the venture's opponents—those who will be or think they will be adversely affected if the new business succeeds. In particular, the analysis should turn up two or three key internal parties who are likely to obstruct the venture's progress, and help the manager pinpoint their strengths and weaknesses. It should also identify two or three key external parties that have a vested interest in the venture's failure. These internal and external opponents are the new business's political debits.

On the credit side, the venture manager should be able to spot several key allies inside and outside the firm. All other parties that would benefit from the venture's success should also be identified, for even if they have not yet become allies, they are potential allies. These are the players whose support is most critically needed to promote the venture's progress.

Particular attention should be paid to those who can help the venture meet its immediate objectives in order to reach the next milestone. It is pointless for the venture manager to waste scarce resources striving toward venture objectives on his or her own if such allies are available and are willing and able to provide assistance (or can be convinced to do so).

Thus, the venture manager should end up with two lists—one showing the three or four key people or groups that will be needed to support the venture and a second showing the three or four key people or groups that are likely to oppose the venture.

Besides identifying the key allies and opponents, the manager should identify any currently indifferent or distracted parties whose support is nonetheless needed if the venture is to succeed. Any political strategy should include plans for mobilizing the support of these currently uncommitted individuals or groups. Once the friends, foes, and important neutral parties have been identified, the venture manager can develop a political strategy designed to maximize the assistance they provide, or minimize the damage they cause, to the venture. This means that both potential allies and potential opponents are targets of the strategy, and similar political tools can be used to affect their behavior. So we will call a key potential player, whether it be an ally or an opponent, a "target."

After identifying whether the target will support, oppose, or be indifferent to the venture, the manager needs to ask the following questions about each target:

- Can we use our existing influence to shift the target's support?
- Can we build influence with the target?
- Can we use our network to do so?

Once these questions have been answered, the venture manager can proceed to examine the context in which these targets make their decisions. Understanding this context is essential in securing the support of key allies, who can then help to convert the indifferent, reprioritize the distracted, and win over or neutralize the opponents.

Anticipate Responses by Key Targets.   Even with all this background work in analyzing the environment and key targets, the impact of actions designed to change the targets' behavior is far from predictable. Politics is not an exact science. Human interactions are inevitably complex, so it is important for the venture manager to consider and be prepared to deal with a range of possible responses from each target. A strategy that works effectively with one target may fail completely with another. Understanding the context in which the target operates allows the venture manager to be flexible and readjust his or her strategy in light of the target's anticipated response.

Allison (1971) has identified three models—the rational actor model, the bureaucratic process model, and the organization politics model—that can enable venture managers to understand the context in which a target functions and thus help them predict how the target is likely to behave in response to any political move they might make.

The rational actor model.   In this model, the target is seen as an objective decision maker with a well-defined set of goals who perceives options clearly, examines the available alternatives carefully, and selects an alternative on a rational basis. To anticipate responses under this model, the venture manager must understand the target's objectives, goals, and relative priorities and how the venture will affect him or her. The venture manager needs to know the major resource commitments of the target's organization, where most of the target's discretionary resources are being focused, and his or her key values, since all these factors establish a direction and a momentum from which it is tough for the target to deviate. By considering the same factors that the target uses in making decisions, the venture manager can generate a list of the rational decisions the target could make with respect to the venture.

The bureaucratic process model. Although identifying the rational decisions the target *could* make provides a useful starting point, the venture manager must realize that these are not necessarily the decisions the target *will* make. Anyone who has spent more than five minutes in an organization knows that organizations are not run by independent managers making strictly rational decisions. Target managers perforce operate in the context of their organization, and these organizational factors limit the courses of action available to them.

The bureaucratic process model therefore considers the target to be someone embedded in a web of rules, procedures, policies, and programs. The target's decisions will be determined by the particular perspectives of the department and organization in which he or she operates, with each department having its own narrow perspective on the problem, its own set of goals, and its own desired choices. This means that it may be very difficult for the venture manager to elicit the particular response he or she is seeking for a number of bureaucratic reasons:

- It conflicts with coordination procedures, rules, and so forth.
- It conflicts with control procedures.
- Critical delays may be involved before information reaches the decision-making level.
- The target's performance evaluation procedures may influence how action regarding the venture will get to the decision-making level.
- The differing perspectives of various departments may cause internal arguments and delay.

So to evaluate the target's potential responses, the venture manager should answer the following questions:

- What are the major policies that drive decision making in the target's operation?

301

- What rules, procedures, and so forth must the target follow?
- What are the target's major monitoring and control systems?

The answers will help the venture manager delete from the list of rational responses those that the target will probably avoid selecting because they conflict with the bureaucratic structure of his or her organization. In addition, the more bureaucratic the target, the less likely he or she is to stray from the bureaucratic path.

The organization politics model. Although the bureaucratic model may be a convenient simplification, actual organizations are far more complex than this model would imply. Internal politics affect how the rules are applied, and therefore, the organization politics model regards the target as being embedded in a series of coalitions in the organization, each with a leader who must represent the interests of the coalition. Decision making is thus characterized by political perspectives, as each coalition leader views the possible alternative actions in terms of how they will affect the interests of his or her coalition; how they will affect the power and influence structure of the organization; and how they will affect the leader as a member of the coalition, as a member of the organization, and as a person.

So in order to anticipate how the target will respond, the venture manager must answer the following questions:

- What are the dominant coalitions? What are the major countercoalitions? To which coalition does the target belong?
- To which commitments are coalition leaders currently paying attention?
- Who can exercise what discretion at what level? How do these individuals behave when the person with the authority to make a counteracting decision is on vaca-

tion? What are the consequences of exercising discretion unsuccessfully?

- What are the consequences of failed decision making for those who fail?

The answers will allow the venture manager to eliminate the responses that the target will find politically unacceptable, however rational and however much in keeping with the organization's bureaucratic structure those responses might be. In addition, the more political the target's orientation, the more likely he or she is to respond in a politically expedient manner.

Performing the preceding three analyses will enable the venture manager to more accurately anticipate the target's responses and then shape actions that will be most effective in changing the target's behavior.

Formulate a Political Strategy.   All of this planning and analysis has been leading up to action. Once the key allies have been identified and their possible reactions assessed, the next step is to approach each of them. Since goals of the venture manager and his or her allies will not be perfectly congruent, the venture manager should identify any major conflicts that are likely to arise between the parties if a particular alliance is formed. If those conflicts appear insurmountable, the manager should forego any attempt to form an alliance with that target.

Since the venture manager wants to reach an agreement that his or her allies will be enthusiastic about implementing, the manager should attempt to structure "win-win" agreements—i.e., agreements that will benefit both parties.

Here are the questions the venture manager must ask in designing his or her approach to a particular ally:

- What do I need this ally for?
  —To mobilize an internal or external party who is currently indifferent?

—To help change the priorities of someone who is currently distracted?

—To help win over someone who is currently disaffected?

—To help win over, obstruct, block, or neutralize someone who is currently an opponent?

- What can I offer that will persuade, induce, or oblige this ally to support me?

    —Can I demonstrate that we will both benefit?

    —Can I offer something in exchange for the ally's help? (If you do A for me, I will do B for you, such as help you get needed resources or support your efforts to advance a particular project.)

- Can I use my influence base and draw on whatever social capital I may have with the ally that could cause him or her to feel a sense of liking, trust, gratitude, or obligation toward me?

- Do I have time to build influence by solving problems, sharing information, and so forth?

- Can I use members of my current influence network to accomplish any of the preceding objectives?

If none of these approaches is feasible, then the target will simply not become an ally and provide support. Recognize, too, that the only support that will be forthcoming will be provided in the context of each target's rational, bureaucratic, and political constraints, as described in the preceding subsection.

Having engaged the ally, it is now important for the venture manager to reach an explicit agreement on the actions that both parties will take to move the project forward. It is especially important to agree on what each party will do to ensure that the next milestone is achieved. The particular issues that the venture manager and his or her ally must address include the following:

- Who will take what specific actions against which opponents? What is their response likely to be? What will we do if they fail to respond that way?

- What key implementation steps must be taken, and how should those steps be timed?
- How can we tell if things are not going as planned, and how will we let each other know?
- When and how will we review progress?
- What major contingency plans are needed, and what events will trigger those plans?

This careful examination of critical execution issues helps ensure that when political action is launched against opponents, either it will flow rapidly and smoothly or necessary regrouping and replanning will automatically be triggered.

Once again, it is important for the venture manager to keep the process as simple as possible by concentrating on a finite number of key allies and opponents. When agreement has been reached with these allies, there remains little to be done but launch the strategy, *focusing the most effort on those activities that will move the venture to the next major milestone.*

Monitor the Progress of the Political Strategy. No political strategy works flawlessly, so the venture manager must monitor progress and adapt his or her strategy in response to unfolding challenges and opportunities. As the venture achieves each milestone, the manager should use that as a chance to re-examine key political alliances and phase out those that are no longer needed. The manager should also seek to forge new political alliances that will be critical both to achieving the next milestone and to ensuring the venture's longer-term success.

CONCLUSION

It is easy to assume that developing a political strategy is not worth the energy, time, and effort it takes or that the task is just too difficult to accomplish. Other issues in the venture startup may seem more urgent and more concrete.

305

But it would be shortsighted for venture managers to focus exclusively on the new business without considering the context in which it operates. That would be like a crew of astronauts focusing exclusively on the mechanics of building a space station without first ensuring that their pressure suits provide an adequate flow of oxygen to sustain them while they're performing the work. The fact is that politics can quickly kill a new venture—even one that is well positioned from a technical standpoint—or it can ensure its success.

Venture failures are as often associated with problems of legitimacy, resource starvation, and resistance or inertia as they are with poor execution of the technical, marketing, or financial effort. Therefore, it is worth devoting at least some effort to thinking through the politics of the venture.

The danger, however, lies in overcomplicating things— in spending inordinate amounts of time and energy weaving convoluted webs of intrigue that simply collapse under the weight of their own complexity. Although, in this chapter, we have provided a very detailed analysis of the politics of venturing, we would remind venture managers that this analysis is meant to clarify the process of examining the venture's political connections, not to create a new bureaucratic hurdle for the venture to overcome. Venture managers should use these guidelines to exercise due caution in moving forward, but without losing sight of the most important objective—to ensure that the venture does in fact continue moving forward. The essence of venture politics, then, is to keep things simple—identify the few key problems, know who the venture's key friends and enemies are, understand what makes them tick, and plan actions that will solve the venture's key problems through these key players.

Guidelines

1. Politics exists. Either manage it or be managed by it.
2. Identify the venture's key objectives and needs.

3. Identify the venture's key allies and opponents.
4. Analyze their needs and find ways to co-opt, influence, or neutralize these parties, as appropriate.
5. Continually monitor the progress of the political strategy and adjust it as necessary.
6. Involve the executive champion.

REFERENCES

Aldrich, H. 1988. "I Heard It through the Grapevine: Networking among Women Entrepreneurs." Paper presented at the National Symposium on Women Entrepreneurs, April 7–9, at Baldwin-Wallace College, Berea, OH.

Aldrich, H., and Zimmer, C. 1986. "Entrepreneurship through Social Networks." In *The Art and Science of Entrepreneurship*, edited by D. Sexton and R. Smilor, 3–24. Cambridge, MA: Ballinger Publishing Company.

Allison, G. 1971. *Essence of Decision*. Boston: Little, Brown.

Blau, P. 1964. *Exchange and Power in Social Life*. New York: John Wiley & Sons.

Burgelman, R., and Sayles, L. 1986. *Inside Corporate Innovation*. New York: Free Press.

Burt, R. 1980. *Toward a Structural Theory of Action: Network Models of Social Structure, Perception and Action*. New York: Academic Press.

———. 1983. *Corporate Profits and Cooptation*. New York: Academic Press.

Granovetter, M. 1973. "The Strength of Weak Ties." *American Journal of Sociology* 78: 1360–1380.

Homans, G. 1958. "Social Behavior as Exchange." *American Journal of Sociology* 62: 606–627.

———. 1961. *Social Behavior: Its Elementary Forms*. New York: Harcourt Brace & World.

Kanter, R. 1983. *The Change Masters*. New York: Simon & Schuster.

———. 1988. "When a Thousand Flowers Bloom: Structural, Collective and Social Conditions for Innovation in Organizations." In *Research in Organizational Behavior*, edited by B. Staw and L. Cummings, 169–211. Greenwich, CT: JAI Press.

MacMillan, I., and Jones, P. E. 1986. *Strategy Formulation—Power and Politics*. St. Paul: West Publishing Company.

Pfeffer, J., and Salancik, G. 1978. *The External Control of Organizations: A Resource Dependence Perspective*. New York: Harper & Row.

Quinn, J. B. 1979. "Technological Innovation, Entrepreneurship and Strategy." *Sloan Management Review* 20: 19–30.

Schon, D. 1967. *Technology and Change*. New York: Delacorte Press.

Selznick, P. 1948. "Foundations of the Theory of Organizations." *American Sociological Review* 13: 25–35.

———. 1949. *TVA and the Grass Roots*. Berkeley: University of California Press.

Stevenson, H., and Gumpert, D. 1985. "The Heart of Entrepreneurship." *Harvard Business Review* (March–April): 85–94.

Stinchcombe, A. 1965. "Social Structure and Organizations." In *Handbook of Organizations*, edited by J. March. Chicago: Rand McNally.

Thompson, J. 1967. *Organizations in Action*. New York: McGraw-Hill.

Walton, R., and McKersie, R. 1969. *A Behavioral Theory of Labor Negotiations*. New York: McGraw-Hill.

Weiss, L. 1981. "Start-Up Businesses: A Comparison of Performance." *Sloan Management Review* (Fall): 37–53.

12

Learning from Experience

Those who do not study the past are doomed to repeat it.

—Santayana

Rats are different than people. They learn from experience.

—Anonymous

In recent years, a great deal of interest has developed in creating the learning organization—one that "continually expands its capacity to create its future" (Meen and Keough 1992). Information acquisition in itself is not learning or knowledge. Learning is "a continual process of discovering insights, inventing new possibilities for action, producing the actions, and observing the consequences leading to insights" (Meen and Keough 1992).

It is not within the scope of this book to discuss a total

corporate program for building a learning organization. For that, we recommend Senge's *The Fifth Discipline: The Art and Practice of the Learning Organization* (1990).

The underlying principle of organizational learning is the Plan, Do, Check, and Act cycle for quality management, which originated with Shrewhart at Bell Laboratories in the 1930s and was used later by Deming in his systematic approach. That approach is inherent in the planning and control processes we describe in Chapters 7 and 9.

A new venture is a microcosm in which the need to "expand its capacity to create its future" is greatly magnified. Learning, in the broadest sense, is not a postponable option, but a necessity for survival and success.

While most of what we present in this chapter refers to essential information gathering, it is important to keep in mind that this information is converted into knowledge, which creates a learning organization.

In no other area of human activity is the difference between rats and humans more pronounced than in corporate venturing! As important as it is to learn from experience, we were surprised to discover in our contacts with venturing firms that very few systematically study their successes and failures to achieve a better understanding of the process of managing new ventures. They find it difficult even to capture a simple, factual, chronological record and history of each venture.

There are many reasons for such shortsightedness: The key people involved with the venture may have left the firm; the executive responsible for the venture may have been reassigned to a distant location; a number of individuals may have participated in the venture, with each having been involved with a different aspect of the experience at a different time; or as so often happens, few records may have been kept other than accounting figures, and those records that do exist may be squirreled away somewhere but are not always consolidated and readily accessible. Furthermore, most venturing experiences will not have been positive, and there may be a certain reluctance to unearth these skeletons. For all these reasons and more, each new venture tends to start off as a blank slate.

To avoid this, any venture must be set up right from the very start in a way that enables the parent company to study the business's success or failure and extract maximum learning from the experience. This chapter explains how to collect the information that must be studied and then apply this knowledge to future ventures. We have described several levels of learning effort, ranging from preparing a simple report to conducting a highly detailed, intensive information-gathering project. Although few companies are likely to undertake this latter type of in-depth learning effort, which is best suited for very major ventures of great importance for the firm, we have described it fully here, not just in the interests of thoroughness but because the description can serve as a source of ideas for whatever level of effort the organization does choose to undertake.

THE IMPORTANCE OF LEARNING FROM VENTURING EXPERIENCE

Experience is the best teacher—provided one makes the effort to sign up for the course! Throughout this book, we have referred to the learning requirement associated with new-venture management and the need to continually adjust plans and actions to what is learned. Each venture is an experiment—a live, expensive business experiment. Learning is critical not only to enable venture management to redirect the individual venture more effectively but also to enable senior management to gather cumulative information on the firm's venturing experiences that will help it manage the venturing function as a whole more effectively in the future.

Conducting a venture without systematically studying the experience and learning from it is analogous to performing a scientific experiment without documenting the procedure that was followed, collecting and recording the data, and drawing conclusions. A new venture is no less an experiment than one that is conducted in a laboratory, although the variables are far less subject to the control of the organizational "scientist."

If a firm is to learn from its venturing experiences and use what is learned to improve future performance, it must make an organized effort to get the facts, study them objectively, and draw conclusions about what to do (and what to avoid) in the future—i.e., it must accumulate venturing know-how.

It is ironic that managers are often very curious about what *other* companies have done and how their ventures have performed, but overlook the most relevant learning of all— the learning that can be extracted from their own venturing experience. Such experience has been achieved at great expense to the organization, and to ignore or discard it is to squander an irreplaceable asset.

FAILURE: THE RICHEST SOURCE OF LEARNING

Although failure is a tough experience, far more can be learned from venturing disappointments than from venturing successes, but it takes a strong stomach, great determination, significant effort, and extraordinary objectivity to do so. This section examines what various studies can tell us about the causes of venturing failures.

Back in 1977, Hill and Hlavacek analyzed 21 venturing failures in 12 large multidivisional firms. Not surprisingly, venture managers had quite different explanations for the failures than senior managers, but of 17 failure causes identified, venture managers and senior managers agreed on only two— "inadequate distribution channels" and "conflicts with other divisions"! Top management most frequently cited "inability to meet budget guidelines" as a failure cause, whereas venture management pointed to "large overhead to absorb," "insufficient top management support," and "budget too small." The value of identifying these contrasting perspectives lies primarily in learning that they do in fact differ and in what respects. The authors supplemented their observations with their own analysis of failure causes, the leading ones being "weak planning by the venture team," "a weak or nonexistent venture charter," and "absence of critical top management reviews."

In another study, von Hippel (1977) reached very different conclusions than Hill and Hlavacek. The primary findings of von Hippel's study of 21 ventures in 20 large firms were that failure was highly correlated with ventures directed at customers new to the firm and, conversely, that success was highly correlated with ventures directed at existing customers.

Block (1989)—in an analysis of major venture failures by Federal Express, Time-Life, and Polaroid—argued that the magnitude of those failures can be explained by the parent companies' having continued to operate the ventures based on early assumptions that turned out to be wrong, rather than redirecting the ventures in a timely or adequate manner or discontinuing them entirely.

Yet the fact is that successes and failures have occurred under every combination of circumstances—with good as well as poor planning, with ventures directed at existing customers as well as new ones, with and without venture charters, with and without either support or impatience on the part of top management. Hence, the findings of previous research in this field are useful only as general guidelines (albeit they are rarely followed). Each firm is unique in terms of its peculiarities, people, history, needs, goals, and leadership and must examine its own experiences in order to discover the specific reasons for its venturing successes or failures.

MAXIMIZING LEARNING

In attempting to determine the best way to learn from its venturing experience, the firm should consider three levels of learning effort:

- *Level 1:* The venture manager is asked to write a report about the venturing experience, including a statement of the most important things learned and recommendations for the future designed to help the firm's overall venturing effort. A useful question for the manager to address is, "If you could do this project over again, what would you do differently?" This first level of learning effort represents the simplest and easiest approach. It will yield information that is useful but far from complete.

- *Level 2:* Key venture and senior management people hold one or more meetings to discuss selected topics from the debriefing protocol presented later in this chapter. Minutes should be kept and reports written presenting conclusions and recommendations for future actions, with the views of both venture and senior management included. One firm held regular meetings of all its venture managers and other key venture team members to share experiences and identify internal obstacles that should be removed by senior management.

  The company can hold separate meetings dedicated to assessing the venturing experience, or it can perform this assessment as part of the agenda of other meetings held in connection with the venturing activity. If it decides to hold separate meetings, they can be conducted either periodically or at the time a venture changes its status in some way (e.g., by being terminated, combined with an existing unit, or established as an ongoing business unit).

- *Level 3:* The company conducts a full-fledged, in-depth study of the venturing experience, which will probably require the participation of people from outside the firm to obtain objectivity as well as expertise. This third level involves a really significant research project—one that is time-consuming and may be quite difficult to accomplish. An undertaking of this magnitude should probably be reserved for very major projects involving amounts of money that are highly significant to the firm.

314

The balance of this chapter explains the steps that should be taken and the issues that should be addressed in conducting this latter type of learning effort—i.e., a detailed, intensive study of a venture. Again, we would remind you that few organizations will want or need to take every one of these steps and address every one of these issues, but you will find it helpful to study this information, identify the elements of it that are most relevant to your particular firm and venture, and then incorporate those elements into the design of your firm's learning effort.

CONDUCTING AN IN-DEPTH STUDY OF A VENTURE

The process of conducting a full-fledged assessment of a venture involves recording information on an ongoing basis throughout the course of the venture; debriefing involved parties; consolidating the factual material into a narrative history; and finally, performing analyses, drawing conclusions, and taking action based on those conclusions. The approach described here is stimulated and triggered by the longitudinal research methodology used by Andrew Van de Ven et al. (1989) at the University of Minnesota in its innovation research program. We suggest that you study this process and use those parts of it that seem worth the effort for your firm and venture.

Step 1: Arrange to Record Information and Events

Information and events related to a new business can be recorded by keeping a venture log, in very much the same way as a captain documents pertinent data about a voyage by keeping a ship's log. Another method is to appoint a venture "historian," who collects, records, and files information and key documents. Both content and process should be recorded—including minutes of meetings, cross-functional activities, critical events, major decisions, and individual and team actions.

Step 2: Using a Debriefing Protocol, Debrief the Key Players and Some Observers

Although collecting basic documents is a good starting point, the most important aspects of the venture's story are likely to fall outside the written record. So the second step consists of searching for information that is not likely to have been recorded. This information can be collected by interviewing key players from both venture management and corporate management, as well as corporate people who were involved with the venture and others who were not involved. The actual interviews should be conducted by individuals who had no stake in the venture or its outcome. University students and faculty with case research and case writing experience may be used.

We suggest that a debriefing protocol be used to structure and provide guidelines for these interviews. The sample protocol presented in the following subsections illustrates the types of debriefing questions that can be asked. (Although all questions relevant to a particular firm and venture should be answered, many of the answers will be contained in the venture log or venture file, thereby eliminating the need to raise these issues during the interviews.)

Origin of the Venture.   The answers to the following questions should provide a clear picture of how the venture idea first came into being and why it was pursued. (Note: In recording the answers, be sure to include the dates and elapsed time for each event.)

- Where did the venture idea originate?
- When was the idea first presented? To whom? By whom? (Indicate the individual's title and responsibili-

ties.) In what manner (e.g., written, verbally, at a formal meeting, informally)?

- What were the initial reactions? By whom?
- How did the idea's proposer respond?
- Was any money requested? How much? For what?
- Was money provided? How much? From what budget or source?
- Was there any evidence of political issues or conflict during this activity? If so, describe.
- What was the essence of the proposition at the time it was first presented? (Specify the venture's intended function, market fit, and purpose for the firm.)
- Did the venture idea require significant product or technology development and/or entry into a new market (i.e., one unfamiliar to the firm)?
- Did the discussion of the proposition result in any changes in the basic idea? If so, describe.
- What follow-up actions were planned as a consequence of the presentation and subsequent discussion?

Concept Testing. Was a concept test conducted? By whom? When? How was the test designed? Did the test results confirm the desirability of pursuing the concept in its original form? If not, what changes were made? (Indicate changes to the concept, the market segments to be targeted, the product design requirements, and the technology requirements.) If no concept test was conducted, why not?

Market Research. What target markets were defined? How was the market potential determined? What was done to verify actual want or need for the product and what it would take to cause the market to buy? Was there any disagreement about the market potential? What arguments were offered in support of the opposing viewpoint(s)? How was the disagreement resolved or otherwise handled?

How were the market research results reviewed? By

whom? In what format? Did the review result in any changes in the venture concept? If so, what were those changes?

What was defined as the new venture's present and potential competition? What conclusions were reached about the characteristics of the market? (Indicate the anticipated size, growth rate, nature of the competition, want or need for the proposed product, and other market characteristics relevant to the venture.)

Product Development.   What predictions were made about how much it would cost and how long it would take to develop the product to the commercialization stage? Was the technology base for product development already present, or was further work needed?

How much did product development actually cost, and how long did it actually take? How were the differences between estimated and actual cost and time handled? By allocating additional funds? Through budgeting or control mechanisms? By management?

Were any changes made in the composition of the product development team? Why? When? Did any key people leave the firm or get transferred to another assignment within the firm?

Development of the Business Plan.   At what stage was a business plan prepared for the venture? Who prepared it? What was the rationale for choosing that person (or those persons) to prepare the plan? Who else was co-opted or participated in putting the plan together? How long did plan preparation take? (Include elapsed time as well as working time.)

Who reviewed the business plan? What was the reviewer's response? Was the plan changed as a result? If so, specify the primary changes. Why were those changes made? How many revisions of the plan were required before approval? Were formal or informal criteria for acceptance known to those who prepared the plan?

Were business plans for other ventures also being reviewed in the same general time period? In comparing the plan for this venture with plans that were rejected, what factors seem to account for this plan's approval?

Authorization of the Venture.   Describe the process used to authorize the venture. What body or individual authorized it? When?

Organization of the Venture.   What process was used to select venture management and members of the venture team? What factors were considered in choosing the venture manager? What was his or her previous experience?

Was the venture team given any training? Did the team use outside consultants? What kind? Why were those consultants used? What compensation or incentive arrangement was made with the venture manager and team? Did the arrangement include any financial penalties for venture management? Was any safety net provided?

To whom did the venture report? What factors were considered in making that decision? Was there an executive champion who acted to protect and support the venture team and to facilitate the acquisition of resources? Who was that individual? What were his or her position and standing in the firm?

What arrangements were made regarding the availability of funds and financial controls? Was a time-related budgeting system used, or was the release of funds triggered by the achievement of milestones?

What control mechanisms were used? Written reports? If so, how often were they produced? Meetings? If so, how often were they held?

How much leeway did venture management have in changing the budget, spending money, and increasing or decreasing head count?

How was performance evaluated? By whom?

How was corporate or divisional staff used in connection with the venture? To ensure adherence to policies? To provide assistance when requested? Was venture management required to use staff personnel—for example, for recruiting people, for designing or constructing plants, or for implementing internal financial control systems?

What organizational form was used for the venture itself—such as a joint venture, a new subsidiary, a new division, or a project team? Why was this form chosen? Did the form change? If so, why? Who made the decision to change?

Major Underlying Assumptions.   Since any new business is based largely on assumptions, identify the important assumptions underlying this venture and the process by which those assumptions were made. (Refer to Chapter 7 for a detailed discussion of how to identify and test key assumptions.) In searching for major assumptions, consider the following areas:

- The market
- The environment (especially the economy)
- The competition
- Organizational support and collaboration
- Product costs and selling prices
- Technology
- The break-even point
- Economic return related to time
- Governmental regulations
- Distribution method

Were those assumptions articulated, either in a document or in some other manner? Were any tests designed to validate the assumptions?

The point here is to reconstruct the assumptions that provided the basis for starting the business. The test for identifying a critical assumption is to determine whether it was a go/no-go assumption: "If we had known that this assumption was false, we would not have started the venture or we would have regarded the venture as being fatally flawed."

Up to this point in the learning process, all effort has been directed toward assembling essential information and constructing a history of the venture prior to startup, establishing what the expectations were, and examining the major assumptions.

Step 3: Prepare a Chronological History of Venture Performance

Now that a wealth of raw data has been collected, it is time to synthesize that information into a chronological history of the venture's performance and major activities. Interviews, reports, revised budgets, minutes of meetings, and memos can serve as source material for this step, and the venture log can be particularly useful as well. It is especially important to highlight critical decisions and events, including changes in personnel, processes, and procedures.

When constructing this history, search for changes in assumptions, the performance results that prompted those changes, and the action plans that were modified as a consequence.

Up to this point in the learning process, the effort has been focused on assembling and synthesizing information. Although the extent to which this data collection effort should be pursued depends on the significance and complexity of the venture itself, it is essential that the report be as brief as the facts will permit.

Step 4: Draw Conclusions

Gathering all the information and answering all the questions suggested in the preceding steps will not, in itself, produce learning. For learning to occur, you must assimilate this material and draw conclusions from it. In doing so, you should be seeking two levels of learning.

The first level is "technical" learning—the answers to such questions as: What did we do "wrong"? What did we

321

do "right"? Knowing what we now know, what would we do differently in terms of our assumptions, decisions, and actions? These questions should be asked with respect to both content and process.

The second level of learning, to complete what Argyris (1977) calls "double loop learning," is probably more important. Here the objective is to discover *why* errors, now seen in retrospect, were made and why they were not recognized and corrected early enough. In this learning step, the answers to questions concerning the policies, values, practices, and use of authority and power that may have affected the ongoing learning process must be assessed.

To achieve both these levels of learning, the following key questions need to be considered:

- Where (i.e., in what areas of the business's development) were the most significant differences between what was expected and what actually happened? Were the expectations unreasonable at the time? If so, why?
- Was the response to emerging realities quick enough and correct? If not, why not? What can we do differently in the future to prevent a repetition of this type of error? (Or conversely, if the venturing experience was successful, what can we continue doing in the future to ensure that this level of performance is maintained?)

The target areas for inquiry should include:

- *Market factors:* need, size, growth rate, target segments, competitive insulation, competitive response, pricing, selling cycle time (elapsed time from first approach to first order), marketing and selling costs, and so forth.
- *Production factors:* capacity, costs, delivery time, quality levels, and so forth.
- *Product factors:* performance characteristics and

322

function, service requirements, switching costs, life, maintenance requirements and costs, quality control requirements, customization needs, economic value, and so forth.

- *Development factors:* technology status, costs and time, level of continuing R&D requirements, and so forth.
- *Economic factors:* break-even point, margins, capital investment requirements, startup costs and time, staffing levels, investment recapture time, potential upside gain, potential downside risk, and so forth.
- *Human factors:* choice of the venture management team, training requirements, performance evaluation, and so forth.
- *Resource factors:* timing and process for allocating the funds; availability of support from functional specialists, staff people, and other organizational units; availability of physical resources; and so forth.

Step 5: Apply What Has Been Learned

How will whatever has been learned be reflected in training activities and in the modification of policies and procedures? After all, there is not much point in carrying out the preceding steps in the learning process unless the firm reaches some conclusions regarding what action should be taken and then implements that action. In planning remedial action, a special effort should be made to correct the underlying causes for errors and misjudgments and for lack of necessary flexibility and support.

CONCLUSION

At the time the firm decides to venture, it should also select the method it will use to capture and record what is learned from that experience. Then, in organizing the venture, the firm should make it a point to ensure that the documentation that will be required to implement the selected approach is systematically maintained.

More can be learned from failures than from successes. Therefore, in assessing its venturing experiences, the firm should concentrate on its disappointments and study the differences between the successes and failures.

Venturing experience and the learning that can be derived from it are precious and must be captured in a timely manner, while key participants are still available to provide their input. If the company fails to keep a record of what was learned, the benefits of that experience and learning will be lost forever.

And finally, the venturing experience is likely to have no learning value whatsoever unless the firm applies what has been learned to make appropriate changes in future venturing efforts.

Guidelines

1. Organize the venturing process to ensure that the organization learns from experience.
2. At some point and in some way, keep a record of the venturing experience.
3. Be sure to get input from venture management and members of the venture team, senior managers, and staff personnel.
4. Try to record the experience as close to real time as possible, keeping in mind that the passage of time distorts memories; failure and success color recollections; and people move, die, or are fired.
5. Analyze the venturing experience to learn what should be avoided and what should be repeated in the future.

REFERENCES

Argyris, C. 1977. "Double Loop Learning in Organizations." *Harvard Business Review* (September–October): 115–125.

Block, Z. 1989. "Damage Control for New Corporate Ventures." *Journal of Business Strategy* (March–April): 22–28.

Hill, R. M., and Hlavacek, J. D. 1977. "Learning from Failure." *California Management Review* 29, no. 4: 5ff.

Meen, D. E., and Keough, M. 1992. "Creating the Learning Organization." An interview with Peter M. Senge. *The McKinsey Quarterly*, 1:58–67.

Van de Ven, A. H.; Venkataraman, S.; Polly, D.; and Garud, R. 1989. "Processes of New Business Creation in Different Organizational Settings." In *Research on the Management of Innovation,* edited by A. H. Van de Ven, H. L. Angle, and M. S. Poole. New York: Harper & Row.

von Hippel, E. 1977. "Successful and Failing Corporate Ventures: An Empirical Analysis." *Industrial Marketing Management* 6: 163–174.

Appendix A

Abstracts of Some Investigations of Corporate Venturing

Biggadyke (1979)

Subject of Research. A total of 68 ventures started by 35 *Fortune* 200 companies, all in existing markets.

Results. Of the ventures studied, 18% achieved profitability in two years, 38% in four years. Median performance was 7% ROI in years seven and eight.

Conclusions

- Ventures that pursued market share rather than immediate profit performed better than those that did not.
- "It appears that new ventures need, on the average, eight years before they reach profitability" (106).

- "Entry on a large scale is the best strategy . . . but not for every opportunity in sight" (110).
- Companies should start fewer ventures with more resources rather than many with less.
- Venturing is very risky (when starting big).
- The time it takes to reach profitability can be reduced by spending more earlier to obtain market share.
- Overall: Companies should think big, enter big, go for share, and not be impatient.

Biggadyke's research has often been quoted as evidence of how long it typically takes for ventures to become profitable, which has led to the widespread impression that the norm is eight years. His data clearly show, however, that nearly 50% of ventures become profitable within four years.

Fast (1981)

Subject of Research.   A total of 11 startups funded by venture capitalists.

Results.   Of the startups studied, an 18% ROI was achieved by year three and a 230% ROI by year eight, contrasted with the results reported by Biggadyke for corporate ventures.

Conclusions.   Fast notes that venture capitalists differ from corporate venture groups in the following respects:

- Venture capital investment is staggered, usually in installments, over one to four years.
- Use of the limited partnership format locks in the pool of capital, in contrast with corporations, which withdraw support after a few years.
- Venture capital groups keep their overhead lean and low, unlike corporations, in which the group oversee-

ing multiple ventures often develops a big internal staff and a cumbersome bureaucracy.
- Venture capitalists use board membership as a means of persuasion but have little or no involvement in day-to-day decisions; however, they do assist in formulating strategy, recruiting key personnel, and dealing with the financial community.
- Go/no-go decision points are used to trigger "rounds" of financing.

Fast suggests that corporations invest in venture capital pools as a means of learning how to handle new ventures more effectively.

von Hippel (1977)

Subject of Research.   A total of 18 ventures.

Results.   Of the ventures studied, 60% were successful; 40% were failures. (Von Hippel's criteria for success were a 10% pretax profit and rapid sales growth within three to five years.)

Conclusions
- Success is related to prior experience with customers.
- Ventures directed to new customers "invariably fail."
- Successes break even in one to eight years. Failures never do.
- The best ideas come from customers.

Porter (1987)

Subject of Research.   Diversified acquisitions, joint ventures, and startups of 33 large corporations from 1950 to 1986.

Results.   On the average, 56% of startups were successful versus 46.6% of acquisitions. ("Success" was defined as entities still in existence. More specific data were unavailable.)

The variation from one company to another was enormous, as indicated in Table A-1, which shows data from Porter that have been rearranged to compare startups with acquisitions.

Conclusions Based on Porter's Study.   Since Porter's own conclusions relate to diversification as a strategy, we have not presented them here. Instead, what follows are a number of additional conclusions that we have drawn based on Porter's data.

- Venturing into new fields and new industries can be and has been at least as successful as acquisitions as a diversification strategy for many corporations and has been highly successful for some.
- Because the range of performance is so wide, information about the average performance of many companies is of no value in helping an individual company make a strategic decision.
- In contrast, information about the performance of individual companies can give valuable insight into the reasons for their success or failure.

Sykes (1986)

Subject of Research.   Exxon's new-ventures program from 1970 to 1981, managed by Sykes. The program involved 19 internal ventures and 18 venture capital investments.

Results.   Venture capital investments of $12 million yielded a return of $218 million. No internal ventures became profitable. (The amount spent was not reported.)

Conclusions.   Sykes' conclusions are based on an analysis of the relative performance of the ventures and are stated in

Table A-1: Disposition Percentages for Acquisitions and Startups

Company	Acquisitions			Startups	
		Percentage Disposed of			Percentage Disposed of
	Number	(NI)	(NI/NF)	Number	
Johnson & Johnson	69	17	33	25	14
Procter & Gamble	25	17	17	11	0
3M	91	26	24	75	2
TRW	81	26	42	17	63
IBM	10	33	33	37	20
Du Pont	20	38	60	40	61
ITT	205	52	61	20	38
Exxon	24	62	80	45	27
Scovill	46	64	64	2	100
RCA	23	80	86	39	99
CBS	72	87	88	18	86
Gulf + Western	169	79	75	13	100
Xerox	42	71	100	21	50
GE	65	65	100	46	33
Average of 33 companies	—	53.4	60	—	44

Source: Adapted from an exhibit in Michael Porter, "From Competitive Advantage to Corporate Strategy," *Harvard Business Review* (May–June 1987): 43–59.

Notes: NI = new industry; NF = new field. An industry is said to be in a particular field. (The insurance industry, for example, would be in the financial services field.) A manufacturing company like Xerox that entered the insurance industry as its first step into the financial services field would be entering a new industry in a new field.

terms of what he would do differently if he could do it over again.

- If the organization is entering a new area of business, it should acquire an established company.
- Venture capital should be used as a primary probe strategy.
- Venturing must be an important mainstream operation—i.e., it must fit the parent organization strategically and get a long-term commitment of resources.
- A completely entrepreneurial environment is impossible to maintain in a large multiproduct corporate setting because of compensation, product compatibility, and liability issues.
- Venture management's experience in the relevant industry is a significant determinant of venture success.
- A venturing environment that encourages resourcefulness is more important than ample financing.

Block and Ornati (1987)

Subject of Research. Compensation practices and venture performance of 207 ventures in 42 *Fortune* 1,000 companies.

Results. Of the ventures studied, 50% were reported to be successful; 20%, failures; and 30%, too early to tell. (No definition of "success" was supplied to the survey's respondents.) No relationship was found between percentage of successful ventures and compensation method used.

Conclusions

- The incentives used were not sufficient (all respondents reported a salary percentage limitation).
- Financial incentives may not affect venture performance results but may affect the retention of key people.

Block and Subbanarasimha (1989)

Subject of Research.   Venturing performance and management practices of 43 U.S. and 149 Japanese companies, mostly large and public, involving 1,077 ventures. (See Table A-2.)

Results.   (See Tables A-3 and A-4.)

- Of the U.S. companies surveyed, 59% reported that their overall venturing operations were profitable, as opposed to 31% of Japanese companies.
- Some 13% of the U.S. companies and 16% of the Japanese companies reported an ROI from venturing equal to or better than from the company's core business.

Table A-2: Sample Composition

	United States	Japan
Number of respondents	43	149
Number venturing	39	126
Annual Corporate Sales[a]		
Under $500 million	26%	48%
Over $500 million	72%	52%
Corporate Sector		
Manufacturing	66%	74%
Nonmanufacturing	34%	26%
Ownership		
Public	96%	82%
Private	4%	18%

Source: Adapted from Z. Block and P. N. Subbanarasimha, "Corporate Venturing: Practices and Performance in the U.S. and Japan," working paper (Center for Entrepreneurial Studies, Stern School of Business, New York University, 1989).

Note: Percentages were calculated for venturing companies only.

[a]$1 = ¥155.

Table A-3: Venturing Performance

	United States	Japan
Number of ventures reported	328	749
Average number of ventures per company	8.4	5.9
Ventures started since 1984	65%	71%
Individual Venture Performance as of the End of 1986		
Ventures That Were:		
Profitable	41%	26%[a]
Unprofitable	43%	54%[a]
Discontinued	9%	5%[a]
Meeting expectations	44%	not available
Impact of Overall Venturing Performance on the Company		
Companies That Reported:		
An addition to their net profit	59%	31%[a]
An ROI from venturing equal to or greater than from the base business	13%	16%
Positive cash flow to the company	44%	26%[a]
A contribution to current sales:		
greater than 5%	56%	68%
less than 5%	42%	30%

Source: Adapted from Z. Block and P. N. Subbanarasimha, "Corporate Venturing: Practices and Performance in the U.S. and Japan," working paper (Center for Entrepreneurial Studies, Stern School of Business, New York University, 1989).

[a]Indicates a statistically significant difference between the figures for U.S. and Japanese companies.

Conclusions

- Overall firm performance in venturing is most likely determined by the size of the losses in the losers, rather than the percentage of ventures that are profitable.
- Time-to-profitability expectations must be based on the specifics of market development, competitive strength, and resources which will be applied, not on any general formula.

Table A-4: Comparison of Venture Age versus Corporate Venturing Performance

Corporate Venturing Performance	Age (Years)	
	U.S. Ventures	Japanese Ventures
ROI greater than from the base business	2.3	3.1
ROI less than from the base business	3.1	2.5
Profit for corporation	2.7	2.9
No profit for corporation	3.0	2.4
More than 70% of ventures profitable	2.8	2.0
Less than 30% of ventures profitable	2.6	2.8

Source: Adapted from Z. Block and P. N. Subbanarasimha, "Corporate Venturing: Practices and Performance in the U.S. and Japan," working paper (Center for Entrepreneurial Studies, Stern School of Business, New York University, 1989).

- Financial incentives, to help control losses, need to be developed.
- Ventures should not be initiated solely because of the presence of a venture champion.
- Venturing programs initiated to challenge or develop management are likely to fail.
- A separate venturing organization appears to be less desirable than organically integrated venturing activity.
- No difference found between performance of organizations that stayed close to present markets and technology and those that did not.
- The management practices of the better performing U.S. firms and Japanese firms were more alike than the practices within each country sample.
- More detailed studies of individual firm practices and performance are needed, rather than using statistical data to determine individual action by any one firm.
- Some 41% of individual U.S. ventures and 26% of

individual Japanese ventures were reported to be profitable.

- The mean time required for ventures to achieve profitability was 2.7 to 3.0 years for both U.S. and Japanese companies.

Du Pont Review (1988)

Subject. Internal review of innovation and ventures at Du Pont between 1967 and 1986.

Results. Du Pont initiated 85 new-direction businesses, which produced sales of $2.8 billion and earnings of $318 million in 1988. No data were included for discontinued ventures, nor did the review compare the total cost of these ventures with the return from them.

Conclusions. Proprietary technology, patient development, heavy investment, conservative financial management, and outstanding people were found to be success factors. The following lessons were learned:

- Market-test early and respond to the test results.
- Build a first commercial plant that is small and flexible.
- Put together a lean, dedicated entrepreneurial team with a single clear leader.
- Keep the venture separate from the established business.
- Be sponsors of a venture, not judges.
- Manage uncertainty with flexible planning.
- Train entrepreneurial leaders.
- Keep visibility low.
- Recognize and reward intrapreneurs.
- Tolerate failure, not stupidity.
- Provide one-stop shopping for "yes."

REFERENCES

Biggadyke, R. 1979. "The Risky Business of Corporate Diversification." *Harvard Business Review* (May–June): 103–111.

Block, Z., and Ornati, O. 1987. "Compensating Corporate Venture Managers." *Journal of Business Venturing* 2: 41–51.

Block, Z., and Subbanarasimha, P. N. 1989. "Corporate Venturing: Practices and Performance in the U.S. and Japan." Working paper. Center for Entrepreneurial Studies, Stern School of Business, New York University.

Du Pont internal review. 1988. Presented to a New York University class in corporate venturing.

Fast, N. 1981. "Pitfalls of Corporate Venturing." *Research Management* (March): 21–24.

Porter, M. 1987. "From Competitive Advantage to Corporate Strategy." *Harvard Business Review* (May–June): 43–59.

Sykes, H. B. 1986. "Lessons from a New Ventures Program." *Harvard Business Review* (May–June): 69–74.

von Hippel, E. 1977. "Successful and Failing Corporate Ventures." *Industrial Marketing Management* 6: 163–174.

Appendix B

Venturing with Corporate Venture Capital

Venture capital investment is a form of venturing engaged in by many corporations. This appendix identifies the success factors associated with the venture capital business, examines the results of early corporate venture capital experience, discusses the obstacles encountered by corporate venture capital units as they attempt to provide the essential success factors, and suggests some methods for overcoming those obstacles.

THE VENTURE CAPITAL BUSINESS

The venture capital business is a unique enterprise unrelated to normal corporate activity. It is a high-risk investment business in which ultimate success is achieved by cashing out through the sale of equity interest. Venture capitalists who finance relatively new firms deal and work with entrepreneurs and must have a keen understanding of and empathy with them. Although investment decisions are based on careful analysis and evaluation, such decisions are, in the end, made "between the belly and the backbone."

Although venture capitalists never deliberately enter into an investment with the knowledge that it will be a failure, they do have a clear understanding, rooted in experience, that only a small minority of investments will yield rewards commensurate with the risk. The median rates of return to venture capital pools reported by *Venture Economics* in the decade from 1980 to 1989 ranged from a low of -2% to a high of 35%. Only two to three investments out of every ten are truly successful—i.e., return 5 to 10 or more times the investment.

The following factors appear to be necessary for success in the venture capital business. (The italicized items on this list are success factors that can be particularly difficult for corporate venture capitalists to provide.)

- High integrity (needed to attract entrepreneurs with proposals)
- Contacts with investors and potential sources of deals
- *Ability to generate a flow of deals*
- Ability to attract investors
- Relationships with other venture capital firms that could lead to syndicated deals and referrals
- *Ability to analyze business plans and entrepreneurs*
- Negotiating ability
- Ability to exercise due diligence
- *Ability to monitor and guide investments*
- *Experience in venture investment*
- Knowledge of the field chosen for investment
- Operating experience in the chosen field
- *Focus on specific industries*
- Adequate capital
- *Ability to build a portfolio of investments at different stages*

The preceding broad overview of the venture capital business provides a background for the following section, which examines how corporations have fared in their attempts at venture capital investing.

THE CORPORATE VENTURE CAPITAL EXPERIENCE

In the past two decades, American business has had an on-again, off-again romance with corporate venture capital programs, in which the company participates in some way in venture capital investments. More than 100 major U.S. firms have at one time or another tried using such programs to aid in new-business development (Sykes 1990). Although a few corporate venture funds have thrived, many others have sputtered and finally discontinued operations.

The very term *corporate venture capital* implies a contradiction. Large corporations are usually nonentrepreneurial in the way they make decisions and operate, whereas venture capitalists by definition and desire function in a highly entrepreneurial environment. This raises questions as to whether—and if so, how—these two disparate cultures can be reconciled. Thus far, attempts at reconciliation have produced uneven results.

To date, there have been few comprehensive studies of corporate venture capital activity, and the studies that have been done tend to focus more on individual cases than on the corporate venture capital community as a whole. One study, for instance, concentrated on the effectiveness of corporate venture capital investments in three major corporations (Hardymon, De Nino, and Salter 1983). In 1986, Sykes presented a detailed examination of Exxon's corporate venture activity, which included a number of comparisons between Exxon's internal and venture capital investments and demonstrated the importance of management experience for achieving success with corporate venture capital investments.

Much of this appendix draws on two comprehensive studies of corporate venture capital—one by Siegel, Siegel, and MacMillan (1988) and the other by Sykes (1990)—both of which were based on responses to extensive questionnaires completed by corporate venture capitalists. The Siegel, Siegel, and MacMillan questionnaire was mailed to 142 corporate venture capitalists and generated 52 responses, 29 of which came from corporate venture capitalists in *Fortune* 100 companies. The Sykes questionnaire was mailed to 86 firms with corporate venture capital programs and generated 31 responses.

This appendix addresses the question of which approaches to corporate venture capital activities are most likely to produce successful results. In order to do this, we start with an in-depth discussion of the major obstacles facing corporate venture capitalists, which provides background for the subsequent discussion of the key decisions that senior management must make regarding the corporate venture capital function.

OBSTACLES CONFRONTING CORPORATE VENTURE CAPITALISTS

The major obstacles to effective corporate venture capital programs tend to fall into two classes. The first class consists of obstacles stemming from the relations between the parent corporation and the corporate venture capital activity, and the second consists of obstacles related to the corporate venture capital activity itself. This section examines both types of obstacles and then closes with a discussion of how the corporate venture capitalist's growing experience with this type of investing can help to lessen the impact of these obstacles.

Obstacles Stemming from the Relations between the Parent Corporation and the Corporate Venture Capital Activity

This subsection provides an overview of several major obstacles to corporate venture capital activity that stem from the relations between that activity and the parent corporation within which the activity must be carried out. These obstacles include:

- Failure to clarify the mission of the corporate venture capital activity
- Short time horizons
- Inadequate financial commitment
- Underestimating risk
- Inflexibility
- Incompatibility between corporate and entrepreneurial cultures

Failure to Clarify the Mission of the Corporate Venture Capital Activity. Research indicates that without doubt the most serious obstacle to venturing with corporate venture capital is lack of clarity regarding the mission of this endeavor. Unless senior management spends the time and makes the effort to define the roles of the firm's venture capital arm, there will be increasing confusion as the activity gets under way and investments start to be made. Corporate venture capitalists will inevitably make inappropriate investments, which may subsequently have to be divested with enormous loss of purpose on the part of corporate venture capital management as well as significant damage to the firm's credibility with the venture capital and entrepreneurial communities. As we shall see later in the appendix, lack of credibility is a significant problem in its own right and needs no aggravation.

Short Time Horizons. The next most serious obstacle facing corporate venture capitalists is that corporate management appears to lose patience too easily, failing to understand that new ventures require considerably more time to achieve success than established businesses do. This problem becomes particularly acute when the organization is under short-term cash flow pressure for whatever reason. In order to make the highly unpredictable investments demanded by very uncertain ventures, a venture capital program needs a pool of funds whose availability is assured on a long-term basis. This problem is therefore related to the next one.

Inadequate Financial Commitment. The third most difficult obstacle facing the corporate venture capital function is the parent company's unwillingness to make the financial commitment required for a successful investment program. Remember that venture capitalists assemble large pools of funds to invest in portfolios of ventures rather than in individual ventures. This portfolio approach reduces the exposure to loss from investing in individual ventures, but considerable funds are needed in order to make enough investments to benefit from the portfolio effect.

Underestimating Risk. Corporate management tends to be unable to comprehend the risks associated with venture investing. Because it is simply not equipped to handle these risks, it becomes extremely nervous when any ventures start to fail.

Inflexibility. Corporate management also tends to be unable to cope with the significant variations from plan and budget that typically occur when investing in new ventures. This inflexibility leads it to apply rigid, inappropriate controls that only damage the ventures' potential.

Incompatibility between Corporate and Entrepreneurial Cultures. Beyond the more direct obstacles described in the preceding subsections, there are significant cultural differences between the corporation and a venture capital activity. Venture capitalists have fundamentally different decision processes, time horizons, planning and control mechanisms, and even business values, in that they thrive on informality, inductive thinking, and flashes of insight rather than formal analysis and deductive reasoning. Unless such differences are recognized and managed, they can lead to serious misunderstandings and severely disrupt relations.

Obstacles Related to the Corporate Venture Capital Activity Itself

The major obstacles to corporate venture capital activity related directly to the activity itself include the following:

- Lack of authority
- Staffing difficulties
- Entrepreneurial distrust
- Inadequate flow of deals and lack of opportunity to participate in syndications

These obstacles are discussed in the following subsections.

Lack of Authority.   The most serious obstacle directly related to corporate venture capital activity is that in order to operate such a program successfully, corporate venture capitalists must have the authority to make significant investment decisions relatively quickly. Since time is often of the essence, the parent company can seriously handicap the venture capital function by requiring that detailed plans be submitted for a review that drags on over a period of weeks. There is a real need for the corporation to understand the unique demands of the venture capital business and find ways to allow autonomous, independent decision making without compromising the corporation as a whole. This is one of the most serious obstacles cited by corporate venture capitalists in their questionnaire responses.

Staffing Difficulties.   The next most serious obstacle is the inability to attract qualified venture capital managers. As we explain later in the appendix, the compensation offered and the restrictive nature of the corporate environment combine to render the closely controlled corporate venture capital operation a less than desirable place of employment for effective venture capital managers. This problem is compounded by high turnover rates in the pool of corporate venture capital managers, who tend to leave the firm for more exciting and much more remunerative jobs in independent venture capital partnerships.

Entrepreneurial Distrust. The third most difficult obstacle involving the venture capital activity itself is the fact that entrepreneurs harbor a fundamental distrust of large corporations. This distrust has two components: The first is the entrepreneurs' suspicion that the corporations will steal their ideas. The second is their fear that even if the corporations don't steal their ideas, they will control their ventures to satisfy corporate objectives at the expense of the ventures' well-being. This distrust goes beyond the entrepreneurs, for a parallel distrust often prevails among independent venture capitalists, which leads to the next obstacle.

Inadequate Flow of Deals and Lack of Opportunity to Participate in Syndications. The aforementioned distrust of large corporations on the part of both entrepreneurs and independent venture capitalists results in a dearth of good deals. Entrepreneurs tend to shop their ideas to the independents first, and therefore, as one corporate venture capitalist put it, "By the time anything gets to us, it's sure to be something from the bottom of the barrel."

The Benefits of Experience

Fortunately, over time, the more experienced corporate venture capitalists find ways to lessen some of the impact of various obstacles that plague their less experienced counterparts. As they succeed in moving beyond the first few deals, corporate venture capitalists learn how to handle:

- The cultural incompatibility between the corporation and the venture capital activity
- Corporate management's lack of a clear mission for the venture capital function
- Corporate management's lack of patience with ven-

ture capital investments that do not rapidly produce a good ROI

- Corporate management's tendency to underestimate the riskiness of venture capital investing
- The corporate venture capitalists' lack of authority and need for autonomy from cumbersome corporate approval processes
- The entrepreneurs' fear of corporate control
- The inadequate flow of deals

A number of "learning curve" benefits accrue to these experienced corporate venture capitalists. It appears that after the first few successful deals, a mutual confidence starts to build between them and the parent company. In particular, over time, they learn how to ameliorate some of the major cultural conflicts and become more proficient both at handling relations with the corporation and at attracting deals from nervous entrepreneurs. They also learn to deliver ROI. So as these corporate venture capitalists gain experience, they are allowed to operate more like independent venture capitalists—the corporation gives them greater authority and a more certain financial commitment.

Senior managers must keep the obstacles discussed in this section in mind as they make the key decisions regarding the corporate venture capital activity, to which we now turn.

BASIC FRAMING DECISIONS FOR THE CORPORATE VENTURE CAPITAL FUNCTION

In setting up a corporate venture capital activity, senior management must make decisions regarding a number of critical issues. These issues, which are examined in the following subsections, include:

- The objectives of the corporate venture capital activity

- The mode of operation (i.e., whether the firm will invest via a venture capital fund pool or invest directly in specific ventures)
- The funding method and approval process
- Investment criteria (i.e., decision-making standards used to select the ventures in which the firm will invest)
- Compensation arrangements
- Sources of deals for corporate venture capital investments

Objectives of the Corporate Venture Capital Activity

Because the objectives of corporate venture capital activities are largely strategic rather than financial, they are somewhat different than for independent venture capital firms. The fundamental idea is for the parent company to get a "window" on potential new growth areas, which is appealing given the historical pattern that major new-business growth has generally originated with small, innovative firms.

As far as corporate venture capital objectives are concerned, the basic decision that must be made involves the scope of the strategic objective. This scope can range from very broad to very focused, as the following spectrum of possible opportunities demonstrates:

- To provide a window of opportunity by exposing the company to completely new technologies and/or markets (the most common objective)
- To seek opportunities to manufacture and/or market new products
- To identify companies that might be potentially profitable targets for acquisition
- To seek exposure to new manufacturing processes
- To create or enhance desirable business relationships (such as research contracts or marketing arrangements) via appropriate investment

- To learn how to conduct a venture capital investment program

From the discussion of obstacles in the preceding section, it should be clear that whatever scope is selected, it is very important for the firm to clearly specify that scope, because without a well-defined mission, corporate venture capitalists experience major difficulties. (Again, lack of a clear mission is the most frequently cited obstacle to corporate venture capital activities.) And in specifying the scope, the firm must give careful consideration to two important success factors: knowledge and experience in the specific industries in which it will be investing.

Although the underlying aspiration may be to achieve one or more of the strategic objectives indicated earlier in this section, particularly exposure to new technological and/or market opportunities, most firms also tend to emphasize profitability as a necessary criterion for making corporate venture capital investments. The inclusion of profitability objectives is important, since a single-minded focus on strategic benefits, without a hard-nosed assessment of profit potential, leads to investments that lack long-run viability. For instance, a corporate venture fund should only confine itself to investing in a few "strategic" industries if there are enough opportunities to make high-grade investments within those industries to ensure an adequate flow of deals. Investments that may appear exciting from a corporate perspective, for technological or marketing reasons, but are not financially attractive may well drain resources rather than produce opportunities.

On the other hand, there is a danger that the emphasis on profitability can also become single-minded. Crises in the parent corporation often force it to focus increasing attention on short-term returns, to the detriment of the "patient money" requirements of venture capital investing. Therefore, it is crucial to maintain a balance between the corporate venture capital function's strategic mission and its profitability requirements. When there is a corporate crisis, the actions of senior management can either prevent or create short-term pressures to gut or paralyze the venture capital operation. All in all, the research findings suggest that senior management should include profitability objectives for the corporate venture capital program but take care to ensure that those objectives do not result in the program's succumbing to short-term pressures.

As far as the objectives themselves are concerned, the evidence suggests that firms are better off when their objectives involve seeking windows of opportunity and building business relationships. Acquisition as an objective appears to be counterproductive: entrepreneurs are very wary of such objectives, and this wariness has an inhibiting effect on the flow of deals. Corporate venture capitalists whose primary objective was to learn how to conduct a program of venture capital investment also reported dissatisfaction with their results.

In summary, we suggest the following when it comes to setting objectives for the corporate venture capital activity:

- Senior management must be absolutely clear about the activity's mission. The scope of the effort should be well defined right from the start.
- Financial objectives as well as strategic ones should be established.
- Senior management must recognize its responsibility to protect the corporate venture capital function from short-term pressures.
- The firm should concentrate on using corporate venture capital activities to seek windows of opportunity and, in particular, to build business relationships. These types of objectives tend to be the most successful.
- The firm should avoid using corporate venture capital activities to seek acquisitions and learn about venture capital investing. These types of objectives tend to be the least successful.

Mode of Operation

The second major decision that needs to be made involves the mode of operation, which can take two forms: venture capital limited partnerships, in which the firm participates as a co-investor and limited partner in a venture capital fund pool, or direct venture capital investments, in which the firm invests directly in specific ventures. About half the corporate venture capitalists use direct venture capital investments, and half use venture capital limited partnerships. Furthermore, just over half use both methods.

Venture capital limited partnerships are attractive if the parent company is concerned with the legal implications of its access to proprietary technical and/or market information of the ventures in which it invests (Hardymon, De Nino, and Salter 1983). Venture capital limited partnerships are also useful when the corporate venture capitalist has little experience and few experienced venture capital managers, since this method enables the company to piggyback on the expertise of the other members of the partnership. The learning benefits are not great, however, because by its very nature, the limited partnership role seriously restricts the transfer of experience.

There is evidence (Sykes 1990) that both approaches have their merits. Venture capital limited partnerships were found to provide contacts with other venture firms as well as contacts that led to venture opportunities, thus increasing the flow of deals. Direct venture capital investments were found to be valuable for enhancing and leveraging existing business relationships. Therefore, there is real benefit in using both modes, and the prospective corporate venture capitalist should seriously consider using both.

Funding Method and Approval Process

The next major set of decisions involves how venture investments will be funded and the process by which the organization will approve proposed investments in particular ventures.

In establishing the arrangements by which funds will be released for investment in ventures, the firm has its choice of the following funding options:

- A relatively large, separate pool of funds specifically earmarked for venture capital investment can be created on a one-time basis.
- A separate pool of funds specifically earmarked for venture capital investment can be created on a periodic basis.
- Deals can be funded on an ad hoc basis.

Nearly half the corporate venture capitalists surveyed by Siegel, Siegel, and MacMillan (1988) had their deals funded only on an ad hoc basis.

In establishing a process for approving investment in particular ventures, a firm also has its choice of several options. Among the possibilities are that approval from corporate management is:

- Not required at all.
- Required but is typically a formality.
- Required for deals above a designated size and is based on corporate management's thorough evaluation.
- Required for all deals and is based on corporate management's thorough evaluation.

The majority of corporate venture capitalists among those surveyed by Siegel, Siegel, and MacMillan (1988) were given little authority to select which ventures should be funded without approval from corporate management. Fully half the corporate venture capitalists surveyed were required to seek in-depth evaluation and approval for all deals. Nearly two-thirds of those surveyed were required to seek formal approval for any projects of significant size.

These funding and approval rigidities add considerably both to the frustration of the corporate venture capitalists and to the distrust and frustration of the entrepreneurs involved in the investments. Compare their situation with that of an independent venture capital partnership, in which pools of capital are set aside for as long as ten years, to be drawn down whenever the ventures in the investment portfolio require it and in which approval decisions are made by venture partners fully conversant with the ventures.

Evidence of the value of greater autonomy of operation came from the Siegel, Siegel, and MacMillan study (1988), which identified two major groups of corporate venture capitalists. The smaller group was dubbed "pilots," because these individuals had a considerable degree of independence: they were given far greater authority to make investment decisions and were able to operate with a much longer-term and more dependable financial commitment from the parent corporation. The larger group was dubbed "co-pilots," because these individuals had significantly less independence: they had to share decision-making authority with corporate management and operate with a considerably less dependable financial commitment from the corporation, since capital was contributed only on a periodic or deal-by-deal basis.

Almost all the pilots regarded ROI as a major objective of venture investing. In their screening of ventures, this group placed relatively heavier emphasis on entrepreneurial talent and leadership and financial considerations than did the co-pilots. Criteria related to strategic benefits weighed less heavily in their investment decisions.

Co-pilots attached greater importance to strategic benefits. Almost all considered at least one strategic objective to be essential, and the majority regarded ROI as a less than essential objective. This group's investment criteria reflected corporate priorities. Criteria relating to strategic benefits were much more important than criteria relating to either the entrepreneur or financial performance.

With respect to the obstacles to corporate venture capital activities discussed earlier in the appendix, the co-pilots assessed eight of these obstacles as being more damaging than did the pilots. Four of the obstacles—senior management's lack of a clear mission for the corporate venture capital function, lack of flexibility, lack of patience with respect to venture capital activity, and inability to relinquish authority to the corporate venture capitalist—appeared to be a direct result of the company-mandated close organizational relationship between the firm and its co-pilot corporate venture capitalist. The imposed closeness of this relationship also seemed to magnify obstacles related to the attractiveness of the corporation as a source of funds: the entrepreneurs' fear of corporate control and of their ideas' being pirated, a general incompatibility between corporate and entrepreneurial cultures, and inadequate flow of deals were all viewed as more serious by the co-pilots than by the pilots.

The results of this study constitute rather convincing evidence that close control is a serious impediment to corporate venture capital activity.

Finally, this argument is further supported by the performance results of pilots and co-pilots. Pilots not only report higher satisfaction in achieving ROI generally, but they also do no worse than co-pilots in achieving strategic benefits. Thus, pilots achieve equal or higher levels of performance and are plagued by far fewer obstacles than their co-pilot counterparts, which, again, seems to constitute convincing evidence that a pilot approach to corporate venture capital activity is generally more effective than a co-pilot approach.

Autonomy of decision making and a long-term, reliable commitment of capital are necessary conditions to create an environment conducive to an effective corporate venture capital program. This means that in designing its program, the company should push autonomy of decision making and independence of funding sources as hard as it can. The corporate venture capital function should be established as an independent entity and should have access to a committed, separate pool of funds. This will enable corporate venture capitalists to respond aggressively to, and manage, investment opportunities with minimal corporate interference. Creating an independent entity in this manner will also tend to defuse entrepreneurs' justifiable concerns regarding such interference. The obvious exception to these recommendations is if the firm has no experience in this type of investing—in which case, the best approach is a high emphasis on venture capital limited partnerships, coupled with an aggressive, proactive program of training by the partners in venture capital decision making.

Investment Criteria

Once objectives, mode of operation, funding method, and approval process have been determined, the next major decision involves the criteria that will be used to select ventures in which to invest. When it comes to defining investment criteria, it is perhaps wisest to refer to the criteria already used by the independent venture capital community, since those investors have a track record in making such decisions.

Table B-1—from Siegel, Siegel, and MacMillan (1988) and MacMillan, Siegel, and Subbanarasimha (1985)—lists the criteria most generally used by venture capitalists. These data have been enhanced with criteria that were identified in interviews with corporate venture capitalists as ones that pertain specifically to corporate situations. These additional criteria appear in the final section of the table, headed "Corporate Fit Considerations."

As can be seen from the results of the surveys, corporate venture capitalists place considerable emphasis on the qualities of the entrepreneur and less emphasis on the characteristics of the product or market. This is consistent with past studies examining the investment criteria of independent venture capitalists (MacMillan, Siegel, and Subbanarasimha 1985).

However, corporate venture capitalists also weight corporate strategic considerations heavily, as can be seen from the nine criteria they most frequently rated as essential, listed

Table B-1: Investment Criteria

Criteria	Mean	Standard Deviation
The Entrepreneur's Personality		
He or she is capable of sustained effort.	3.65	0.52
He or she is able to evaluate and react well to risk.	3.47	0.58
He or she is articulate in discussing the venture.	2.96	0.63
He or she attends to detail.	2.80	0.76
He or she is able to take criticism.	2.58	0.86
He or she has a personality compatible with mine.	2.10	0.74
The Entrepreneur's Experience		
He or she is thoroughly familiar with the product.	3.42	0.61
He or she is thoroughly familiar with the market.	3.60	0.63
He or she has demonstrated leadership ability in the past.	3.12	0.70
He or she has a track record relevant to the venture.	2.85	0.67
He or she has assembled a functionally balanced management team.	2.77	0.83
Characteristics of the Product		
The product is proprietary or can otherwise be protected.	3.10	0.73
The product has been developed to the point of a functioning prototype.	2.67	0.79
The product enjoys demonstrated market acceptance.	2.29	0.72
Characteristics of the Market		
The target market enjoys a significant growth rate.	3.19	0.72
The venture will stimulate an existing market.	2.50	0.70
The venture will create a new market.	2.44	0.67
Competition in the market will be minimal during the first 3 years.	2.37	0.77
Financial Considerations		
The venture will generate a return equal to at least 10 times the investment within 5 to 10 years.	2.94	0.79
The investment can easily be made liquid.	2.15	0.92
Corporate Fit Considerations		
The product fits with the corporation's long-term strategy.	2.77	1.20
The venture is in a market or an industry that is attractive to my company.	2.81	1.19

Table B-1: (continued)

Criteria	Mean	Standard Deviation
My company will be the controlling investor in the venture.	2.12	1.13
The size of the specific investment should be no greater than 10% to 20% of the total funds available to the venture activity.	2.12	1.00
The venture's long-term sales potential will have a material impact on corporate performance.	1.96	0.97

Sources: Adapted from R. Siegel, E. Siegel, and I. C. MacMillan, "Corporate Venture Capitalists: Autonomy, Obstacles and Performance," *Journal of Business Venturing* 3, no. 3 (Summer 1988): 233–247; I. C. MacMillan, R. Siegel, and P. N. Subbanarasimha, "Criteria Used by Venture Capitalists to Evaluate New Venture Proposals," *Journal of Business Venturing* 1, no. 1 (Winter 1985): 119–128.

Note: In the Siegel, Siegel, and MacMillan study, corporate venture capitalists in the sample were asked to rate the criteria shown in this table on a 1 to 4 scale. The following meanings were assigned to the rating scale: **1** = The criterion is irrelevant. **2** = The criterion is desirable. **3** = The criterion is important (i.e., if a venture fails to satisfy this criterion, it would need to demonstrate significant redeeming qualities to justify investment). **4** = The criterion is essential (i.e., if a venture fails to satisfy this criterion, it is fundamentally flawed and would be rejected out of hand, no matter what other redeeming qualities it might have).

in Table B-2. Two of these criteria are that the venture's market/industry must be attractive to the firm and that the product must fit with the firm's long-term strategy. This causes a problem, because there are some interesting parallels between corporate-related selection criteria and the obstacles to corporate venture capital activities. In fact, it has been found that such criteria tend to worsen the impact of a number of the obstacles. The corporate venture capitalists who responded to the surveys indicated that three of the corporate fit criteria in particular correlated significantly with several of the obstacles. These problematic criteria are as follows:

Table B-2: Investment Criteria Most Frequently Rated as Essential by Corporate Venture Capitalists

Criteria	Percentage of Corporate Venture Capitalists Rating Each Criterion as Essential
The entrepreneur is capable of sustained effort.	67
The entrepreneur is thoroughly familiar with the market.	67
The entrepreneur is able to evaluate and react well to risk.	48
The venture is in a market or an industry that is attractive to the corporate venture capitalist's corporation.	39
The product fits with the corporation's long-term strategy.	37
The target market enjoys a significant growth rate.	35
The product is proprietary or can otherwise be protected.	31
The entrepreneur has demonstrated leadership ability in the past.	31
The venture will generate a return equal to at least 10 times the investment within 5 to 10 years.	28

Source: Adapted from I. C. MacMillan, R. Siegel, and P. N. Subbanarasimha, "Criteria Used by Venture Capitalists to Evaluate New Venture Proposals," *Journal of Business Venturing* 1, no. 1 (Winter 1985): 119–128.

- *An insistence on investing only in products that "fit" the parent firm:* This criterion appears to aggravate both corporate venture capitalists' frustrations over the inadequate flow of deals and entrepreneurs' fear of the corporation's taking control of their ventures. These aggravations then combine to enhance corporate venture capitalists' frustrations with their lack of autonomy in decision making and thus worsen the culture clash between the parent company and the corporate venture capital activity.

- *An insistence on investing only in markets or industries attractive to the parent firm:* This criterion also aggravates corporate venture capitalists' frustrations with the inadequate flow of deals and worsens both the culture clash and clashes over authority issues. It also aggravates the problem of the organization's lack of patience as the corporate venture capitalist vainly seeks the elusive opportunities that fit the market or industry sanctioned by the fastidious parent.

- *An insistence on the parent company's having a controlling interest in the venture:* This criterion disrupts the flow of deals, causing the corporate venture capitalist to accuse the firm of lack of flexibility, which, in turn, generates frustration with lack of authority and lack of financial commitment. The preceding problems combine to seriously aggravate culture clashes and increase confusion regarding the mission of the corporate venture capital activity.

Thus, it can be seen that excessive concern by the parent company with controlling the investment process and directing where venture investment should be made serves no constructive purpose. In fact, it increases the already formidable challenges of attempting to venture from within an established firm.

If the organization is in the corporate venture capital business purely to make money, as venture capital firms do, then it must remove the imposed limitations. If, however, the organization intends the corporate venture capital activity to function as an entry strategy into new businesses that are to become part of the company, then it must maintain the imposed limitations.

The ideal is for the corporate venture capitalist to seek deals that not only meet the criteria used by independent venture capital firms (i.e., the criteria associated with successful investments) insofar as possible but also fit the parent firm's strategy, do not stray into products or markets that compromise the parent's values, and can potentially be controlled by the parent. Although this approach may reduce the number of deal options, it makes sense in the long run.

Compensation Arrangements

Another decision facing the parent firm as it sets up a venture capital activity is how to compensate the corporate venture capitalists who will be managing the fund. The following are the most commonly used compensation arrangements:

- Base salary only
- Base salary plus a bonus based on the venture capital activity's performance over the short term
- Base salary plus a bonus based on the venture capital activity's performance over the long term (more than five years)
- Base salary plus direct participation in the venture capital fund

Ideally, the corporate venture capital fund should be managed by experienced venture capital professionals, who should be sought out from the independent venture capital community or the small but growing pool of experienced corporate venture capitalists. Seasoned corporate executives may comprise part of the management team (Sykes' results reinforce the importance of having a staff with managerial experience, 1986). But if senior management hopes to attract the type of top-quality managers we are talking about, it must be prepared to offer compensation and authority commensurate with their level of skill and experience. In practice, though, this seldom happens.

The majority of corporate venture capitalists are compensated in a manner that has little or nothing to do with the performance of their company's investment portfolio. It typically takes several years or longer for ventures to mature into successful businesses, yet nearly three-quarters of the corporate venture capitalists who responded to the surveys reported that they were compensated by a base salary only or by a base salary plus a bonus based on the investment portfolio's short-term performance. Thus, it is not surprising that those firms that do manage to attract or nurture capable venture capital managers eventually start to face problems of attrition, as those managers defect to the independent venture capital firms, which offer much more realistic compensation.

The basic recommendation is for the parent company to develop a compensation system that recognizes, and thus enables the firm to retain, the rare talent needed to select and monitor venture capital investments—i.e., a truly competitive compensation system that reflects the reality of the uncertain corporate venture capital environment and rewards corporate venture capitalists accordingly. In short, corporate venture capitalists should be treated like independent venture capitalists. (Although this of course implies compensation levels higher than those of the parent corporation, establishing the venture capital fund as a separate organizational entity tends to minimize the political problems that could arise from this discrepancy.)

Sources of Deals

The final major decision the company must make regarding its corporate venture capital activity is where it will find deals. As shown in Table B-3, corporate venture capitalists report three major sources of deals. The most important source is other venture funds, followed by direct contact by entrepreneurs (this latter despite the problems of distrust described earlier in the appendix as one of the obstacles confronting corporate venture capitalists). Finally, other depart-

Table B-3: Sources of Corporate Venture Capital Deals

Sources	*Percentage of Corporate Venture Capitalists Who Reported Using Each Source*
Venture funds	35
Direct contact by entrepreneurs	30
Departments within the parent company	25
Financial intermediaries	8
Lawyers and accountants	0
Other	2

Source: Adapted from H. B. Sykes, "Corporate Venture Capital Success," *Journal of Business Venturing* 5 (January–February 1990): 37–47.

ments in the firm are often able to identify opportunities, particularly opportunities that leverage business relationships.

The lesson from these data is that to maximize the flow of deals, the corporate venture capitalist should aggressively interact both with other departments within the company and with other venture capital firms. In the long run, these strategies will generate deals whose momentum will attract the entrepreneurs.

CONCLUSION

For a corporation, venture capital investing is, in effect, a type of new venture. All the guidelines and recommendations we've given throughout the book regarding new ventures—particularly those pertaining to the relationship between the corporation and venture management—also apply to venture capital activities.

In attempting to successfully manage a venture capital fund, corporate venture capitalists face a number of obstacles, some of which stem from the relationship between the parent firm and the corporate venture capital activity and some of which are directly related to the corporate venture capital activity itself. As corporate venture capitalists gain experience, they tend to learn how to overcome a number of these obstacles or at least lessen their impact.

In setting up a corporate venture capital function, senior management must make several decisions that will critically affect the outcome of this effort. In particular, top managers must define the objective of the corporate venture capital function (just to make money, just to support the company's strategy, or both) and ensure that the fund is managed consistently with that objective. And since focus is vital for a venture capital activity, top management must select certain key industries on which to concentrate its effort. It must also recognize that experienced and successful venture capital managers are rare and entrepreneurial. Finding them and keeping them require incentives and a level of autonomy that are competitive with those offered by independent venture capital firms. One final word of warning: the firm must know the success factors required in the venture capital business and either make sure it can supply them or stay out of the business.

REFERENCES

Hardymon, G.; De Nino, J.; and Salter, M. S. 1983. "When Corporate Venture Capital Doesn't Work." *Harvard Business Review* (May–June): 114–120.

MacMillan, I. C.; Siegel, R.; and Subbanarasimha, P. N. 1985. "Criteria Used by Venture Capitalists to Evaluate New Venture Proposals." *Journal of Business Venturing* 1, no. 1 (Winter): 119–128.

MacMillan, I. C.; Zemann, L.; and Subbanarasimha, P. N. 1986. "Criteria Distinguishing Successful from Unsuccessful Ventures in the Venture Screening Process." *Journal of Business Venturing* 2, no. 2 (Spring): 123–138.

Rind, K. W. 1981. "The Role of Venture Capital in Corporate Development."
Strategic Management Journal 2: 169–180.

Siegel, R.; Siegel, E.; and MacMillan, I. C. 1988. "Corporate Venture Capitalists: Autonomy, Obstacles and Performance." *Journal of Business Venturing* 3, no. 3 (Summer): 233–247.

Sykes, H. B. 1986. "Anatomy of a Corporate Venturing Program: Factors Influencing Success." *Journal of Business Venturing* 1, no. 3 (Fall): 275–294.

———. 1990. "Corporate Venture Capital Success." *Journal of Business Venturing* 5 (January–February): 37–47.

Tyebjee, T. T., and Bruno, A. V. 1984. "A Model of Venture Capital Investment Activity." *Management Science* 30, no. 9: 1,051–1,066.

Index

365

About the Authors

Zenas Block is Clinical Professor of Management at the Stern School of Business, New York University, and an Adjunct Professor at Rensselaer Polytechnic Institute. During his career, he has been involved in establishing 27 new businesses, most of them corporate ventures. Starting as a lead technical resource, then later as a venture manager, corporate parent representative, corporate senior manager, and independent entrepreneur, he has experienced and studied corporate venturing from a variety of perspectives. He developed the Stern School course "Entrepreneurship in Corporations," was the lead founder of the Center for Entrepreneurial Studies at NYU, and has been teaching, consulting, conducting research, and publishing in this field since 1978. He is a graduate of City College (CCNY) with a B.S. in chemistry.

Ian C. MacMillan is the Executive Director of the Sol C. Snider Entrepreneurial Center and George W. Taylor Professor of Entrepreneurial Studies at Wharton. MacMillan joined the center in June 1986, after having served as Director of the Center for Entrepreneurial Studies at New York University. He also taught at Columbia University and Northwestern University. He received his BSc. from the University of Witwatersrand, and his M.B.A. and D.B.A. from the University of South Africa.

Prior to entering the academic world, MacMillan was a chemical engineer, and gained experience in gold and uranium mines, chemical and explosives factories, oil refineries, soap and food manufacturers, and on the South African Atomic Energy Board. He has been a director of several companies in the travel and import/export business in South Africa, Canada, Hong Kong, and Japan. MacMillan has extensive consulting experience, having worked with such companies as General Electric, IBM, Du Pont, GTE, Citibank, and Metropolitan Life.

MacMillan has published numerous articles and books on organizational politics, new ventures, and strategy formulation. He is editor of the *Journal of Business Venturing*. His articles have appeared in the *Harvard Business Review, The Sloan Management Review,* and *The California Management Review.*